LOOKING FOR LOVE

LOOKING FOR LOVE

The Shocking Story of a Desperate Child and the Woman Who Listened

Sugar Jones

with Rosemary Kingsland

Published by Virgin Books 2008

2 4 6 8 10 9 7 5 3 1

First published in Great Britain in 2008 by
Virgin Books
Random House, 20 Vauxhall Bridge Road,
London SW1V 2SA

www.virginbooks.com
www.rbooks.co.uk

Addresses for companies within The Random House Group Limited
can be found at: www.randomhouse.co.uk/offices.htm

The Random House Group Limited Reg. No. 954009

A CIP catalogue record for this book is available from the British Library

ISBN 9780753513200

The Random House Group Limited supports The Forest Stewardship
Council [FSC], the leading international forest certification
organisation. All our titles that are printed on Greenpeace
approved FSC certified paper carry the FSC logo.
Our paper procurement policy can be found at
www.rbooks.co.uk/environment

Mixed Sources
Product group from well-managed
forests and other controlled sources
www.fsc.org Cert no. TT-COC-2139
© 1996 Forest Stewardship Council

Printed and bound in Great Britain by CPI Bookmarque, Croydon CR0 4TD

Typeset by Palimpsest Book Production Limited, Grangemouth, Stirlingshire

To Motherhood

CONTENTS

Foreword

> It matters not how strait the gate,
> How charged with punishments the scroll,
> I am the master of my fate:
> I am the captain of my soul.
> from 'Invictus' by William Ernest Henley

Sugar Jones is just one of the thousands of lost and damaged youngsters who we support at Kids Company. Many of these children – a significant proportion of whom are in their teens and even early twenties – have been virtually abandoned by their equally damaged parents, or, for a variety of reasons, have fallen through the cracks in the services provided by the Government.

When a young person comes to us, no matter what their background, we never turn them away. We provide a safe haven for them. According to their needs, we will do whatever it takes to nurture and restore their physical and mental health. We will house them and feed them, provide support teams and offer therapy. We will educate them, so they can grow into young adults who are able to help themselves and to contribute to society. Through Kids Company, they find safety, solace, friends, peace of mind, and, above all, somewhere they can be themselves.

Every child needs someone in their life who cherishes them and welcomes their company. Kids Company staff become compassionate companions to these children, reducing loneliness and inspiring hope.

We are not an orphanage or a state institution – although we fully co-operate with the official bodies put in place by the Government to care for all of the country's vulnerable and precious children and young people. Kids choose to come to Kids Company – they find us through word of mouth on the street – and they are free to come and go as they wish. Each child is matched with a key-worker who cares about their needs and works with them to address every aspect of their wellbeing, always on the youngster's terms. We encourage quality and advice, but we are non-judgmental. At Kids Company, for the first time, children feel that they are in control of their lives and destinies. We then help them to build on this.

As a nation, we are struggling with a legacy of damaged children who grow up unable to parent, and who, as a result of their own fractured childhoods, create offspring who have to survive like they did. Over the years, I have learned how much courage and dignity these young people have. Sugar, through her sense of strong morality and determination, is seeking to escape the cycle of abuse. For her own children, she aspires to create safety and a different life. She wanted to share her story with you, to make people understand that every child wishes for good things. Some get help, others don't.

All proceeds of this book are going directly into the care of Sugar and her children. Her mother needed help and did not receive it, but Sugar hopes to be able to help her one day too. The love between them is profound, but pain has damaged them both. It is not for us to judge, but to learn from their story.

Camila Batmanghelidjh

Prologue

Sugar, Aged thirteen

London, 1999

'You'll be OK,' Tawni says. 'Go to the corner and do what I told you. Remember, bring them back here.'

I nod and take a deep breath as I saunter down the street. I feel kinda wobbly, my stomach hurts. Keep walking – you can do it, I tell myself to hide my panic. I glance over my shoulder, and Tawni nods encouragingly, then fades into the shadows of the alley. I'm just a scrawny thirteen-year-old – and I'm on my own. Deep breath, fight that feeling of wanting to spew or run away. My mum's words when I was just a kid come back, 'No guts – no glory. No daughter of mine is a coward. Get out there and fight.'

I twirl my little bag by the strap, stick out my bum and padded tits and wobble along in Mum's high heels. They're too big and I've stuffed toilet paper in the toes. They make me walk like a duck with a wiggle that I think adds a few years, gives me a screw-you attitude.

'Come on, guys, I'm available,' my sexy wiggle says. I lick the unfamiliar red lipstick on my lips and try to quell the butterflies in my stomach. *Go get that money, Sugar!* You need money! My mum disappeared one night without a word. One by one the gas and electric has clicked off, there's no food, except for what we shoplift. We're hiding from the landlord and I have to feed my little brothers. I need dinner money for school, and bus fares.

Overhead, trains rumble into London Bridge station, but down here, it's quiet and dark, like being under the floorboards where only rats scurry about their business. I arrive at the corner and position myself, one hand on hip, casually swinging my bag, my eyes watchfully darting from side to side. Who will be the first? Some commuter who's veered off the straight and narrow on his way home, a stockbroker from across the river in the City, or a down-and-out smelly old drunk who thinks he can have it for free? Maybe a cool black dude from that recording studio by the river, a rap star. *Mm-mmm!* Come and get me, brother.

Cars drive by. One or two slow, stare. I close my face and glance away. They drive on. I have to get him out of the car and back to the alley, where Tawni waits. She's fourteen, a year older than me, and experienced at this game. She's told me, 'Don't go for kerb crawlers. They'll want to do it in the car, away from the safety zone.'

I don't hear him come along the street until he speaks softly, right behind me. He's got a posh voice, but tries to give it the common touch. 'Hello, love. You waiting for someone?'

I flick my gaze over him. He's an old geezer, probably can't get it up. But old means he won't fight back. Nice suit. I bet he's got a big fat wallet. My first time. I didn't think it would be with a white man.

I smile. 'D'you wan' a nice time, mistah?' I say, keeping my voice low and enticing.

'Do you have somewhere –?'

'Sure thing. It's not far, OK?'

'How much?'

Tawni said only the idiots asked how much – the reg'lars all knew. I'm in luck, regular punters know all the tricks. 'Man, it depends on what you want. Fifteen for a taste of honey. You wanna go all the way to Paradise, it'll cost you more – a lot more.' Tawni had told me what to say. 'Make it flow'ry,' she'd said. 'Tell him you're a virgin. They all want virgins. If you had a pimp, he'd get more for you.'

'Nah, I don't want to go professional,' I said, and we looked at each other and giggled.

I stroke his arm and smile. 'But darlin', I'm worth it. I'm a virgin, but I can do it real good.'

'How much do you want?'

I don't want to frighten him off. 'Forty quid.'

'OK.' He falls in beside me as I totter towards the alley. Close to, I can smell his aftershave and realise he's a lot bigger than me. I bet he's one of those fit old geezers who works out and plays tennis at the weekend. I'm just a kid, but I'm agile, I can get away quick as

Jack Flash. 'Sugar, yo don't think like that, girl,' I scold myself. We reach the alley and I jerk my head towards its black mouth.

'Down there?' He says it nervously, though now he wants it so bad he doesn't see the stinking bins and squalor, just me, a sexy black girl in a short short skirt.

Tawni is hiding out of sight in a doorway. This first time, she will watch over me, make sure it goes like clockwork – but after, I'm on my own. Her presence lends me courage. I lead the way into the shadows and fumble at his clothes, loosen his belt, he's excited, breath quickening. I stop. 'You gotta pay me first,' I say, as if I've just remembered. I hold out my hand.

Agitated by the interruption, he reaches into his jacket pocket and pulls out his wallet. 'It's too dark to see,' he complains. 'I'll pay after.' He starts to put his wallet back.

It all happens too fast, before I'm ready. I fumble for the brick I put within reach on the bin lid, and drop it. *Oh, Jesus.* Then Tawni's there, leaping out of the doorway like a demon. She whacks him with the iron bar, I grab the wallet, he falls against the bins, groaning. I hear each sound separately, sharply, like percussion, like blood pounding in my head. We've killed him. He's dead. Tawni flies out of the alley like a bat out of hell.

The harsh rattle of the bins, the rumble of the trains overhead, a tug calling on the river. He moans, pulls himself up. Too dark to see how bad he is. While he's stumbling around in the darkness, groaning and cursing,

Tawni turns back. 'Come on!' she shouts, 'Come *on*! You ain't no Mother Teresa. Leave him.'

I come to my senses and run. We clatter down the street in our teetering heels, dive into another alley, out the other end, fly across the road, dodging cars, through the welcoming haze of the pub, past commuters swilling drinks and missing their trains, out the back door, out of our heads, out of this world, laughing wildly. Exhilarated, adrenaline flowing.

I can do this. We'll survive until Mum comes home.

Chapter 1

Jamaica, 1986

I was born in Kingston Jubilee Memorial Hospital on the island of Jamaica in 1986. They called it the island in the sun. Cruise ships called there every day, and plane-loads of tourists, who came looking for the sun, sea, sand and scenery. They also wanted to see the legendary places where pirates, slaves and planters lived a long time ago. They loved our idyllic island, with its waterfalls, hazy Blue Mountains, sugar and coffee plantations and lux- urious hotels. When they wanted to slum it, they wandered through the colourful street markets that were filled with tropical fruits and vegetables and alive with the beat of our music. They never saw the grinding poverty or realised it was the law of the jungle in the shanty towns.

My mum's childhood ended when she was eight years old, when her dad ran off with a woman with eight kids. She had to work at whatever she could to bring in money and when she wasn't working, she was looking after her baby brother while her mum worked. Her mother died two years later and my mum – Lulu – and her little brother, Nathan, went into an orphanage. Mum said it was an awful place for any kid to be raised in. The showers were thick with black mould and there were rats, fleas and cockroaches. It was so bad, she grabbed hold of Nathan and they escaped hidden in the back of a rubbish truck. They lived hand to mouth for a while, stealing and sleeping rough.

But for a girl, being out on your own in the world was worse. Girls from shanty towns need a man to protect them, and Mum took up with Leroy when she was just fourteen. He was a minor gangster, low down in the pecking order of his gang, but he became her boyfriend and official protector. He put her to work in strip clubs as a dancer and she was working right up to the time I was born. Mum named me Sugar, after a beautiful plantation near Kingston. She used to say that some day I would be rich and would have a place like that of my own. She had a lot of hope, considering few people escaped the grinding poverty and danger of the ghetto – as the crime-ridden slums of Jamaica are known.

By the time I was born Mum was twenty-three years old, and Leroy was ten years older. I was his first child, but nothing convinced him that he was my father. He said he'd never had a child before, so how come he suddenly did? Certain that Mum had been two-timing him, he beat her up and dumped her. She was without protection for eighteen months, which was tough on a woman in her line of business. Men hit on her, bosses wouldn't pay her, she was abused and insulted and considered easy meat. She had to work hard to provide for me and her brother on her own.

Leroy didn't help her, although she used to take me to his workplace so he could see me. Perhaps she went only in the hope of getting a bit of money when he was paid.

When I was about eighteen months old, Mum got together with a gangster I called Dadda B. He became my dad. I didn't know about it until later, but my birth dad and Dadda B fought it out over me and my mum. It must have been quite a fight, because after Dadda B won, in fear of his life, my dad fled to the US. I wasn't to see him again.

Things got better for us now that Mum had a boyfriend, though she continued to work as a dancer. He got us a concrete block house in a ghetto district known as Havendale – but Mum said it wasn't no haven. It was a noisy, dangerous, stinking cesspit, full of flies, mosquitoes and rabid dogs, at the bottom of some hills in the northern suburbs of Kingston. Many of these suburbs were pleasant, with golf courses and green spaces – but squeezed in between them were war zones like our ghetto. At night, the loud bangs we heard were as likely to be the sound of guns as thunder.

Mum and Dadda's relationship was very hot and violent most of the time. Mum liked to fight – I think it turned her on – and she would goad him until he threw a punch. One thing led to another, and they'd end up rolling on the ground like a pair of pit bulls. She gave as good as she got, but he was heavier and stronger and he always overcame her. She was so crazy, she'd scrap even when she was heavily pregnant with twins. I was three years old, and loved touching her swollen belly and feeling the babies move. It was like ripples. If I laid my hands out flat, the palms would get little kicks. I would raise my hands, and watch the stretched skin of her belly peak in little lumps as a foot or a baby's head pushed against it from the inside. I'd squirm in delight. 'Look, they walking! When they gonna pop out, Mamma?' I'd ask.

'When they ready,' she'd say, rubbing her aching back and frowning. 'Goddamn, they taking their time. They'll be tap dancin' 'fore they born.'

One day, after a particularly brutal skirmish, her belly was stiff and flat and she went into premature labour. Dadda had gone off on his usual circuit and there was nobody there to help her, except me. I was frightened and hiccuped tearfully, sure Mum was dying. Between yells of pain, she told me what to do. 'Go next door, get Iris,' she ordered. 'For God's sake, get going.'

I ran off and fetched Iris, who called a couple of other women neighbours and they soon had things under control. The first baby – a boy – was born dead. Two days later, Mum was still groaning and panting and Iris and the other women were bathing her face and giving her some herbal medicine. They used spells and rituals to help, but the second little boy was also born dead. Mum's hugely swollen breasts were so painful and full of milk, she'd cry. I learned to comb them out, using a wide toothed comb. I dipped the comb in warm water and started at the top with slight pressure down towards the nipple. I'd comb each heavy, dark-veined melon in turn with long, smooth strokes, watching the milk squirt out and run down her golden skin, while Mum sat in a big copper pan filled with hot water, moaning, waiting for the pain to go.

By the time Dadda B returned a few days later, it was all over and Mum was up and about again and as angry as a hellcat – but they made up and Mum got pregnant with my brother, Paul. When she was some months gone, Dadda B was sent to prison. Visitors weren't allowed, but Mum did her best to see him. She sold bottles she found in the gutter to raise money to catch the bus there and buy clothes and food for us. I was only three years old at the time, but I remember going with her and walking down the dirt road to the back of the jail, where we stood in a kind of trench, our feet in stinking, dirty water, while Mum shouted out for Dadda B.

Someone would get the message to him, and his head would appear over the top of the high brick wall. He'd peer through the wire mesh fence that topped the wall and he and my mum bawled at each other until his arms grew tired from hanging on, or a warden would drag him down and he'd suddenly disappear. It was hard for us because Mum was heavily pregnant and couldn't work as a dancer. In the end she got a job in a street café that paid very little, so it was always a toss-up between rent and food.

We were evicted from our home, so she went to see her aunties, Georgia and Gemma, who lived in Gully Bank, another ghetto half a mile from Havendale. It's a shanty town of tar-paper shacks scrambling up the side of a hill known as Constant Spring, after the perpetual spring that supplied a plantation at the base of the hill. Over the years, Kingston had spread outwards and the plantation was buried under expensive houses and a golf course. Shanty towns crept around the edges and filled up all the available spaces, using long-established squatters' rights to stake a claim.

Georgia and Gemma had a plot on Constant Spring where they built a haphazardly shabby one-storey dwelling. It had a framework of cheap pine timbers that was erected in an hour or so. The walls and roof were covered with waterproof black tar-paper from a big roll that was stretched over the spaces between the timbers. You could poke your fingers straight through the paper and see daylight – it felt like you could push the entire construction over with one hand. The floor was beaten earth. When it rained, water rushed in and everything got wet – not that there was very much furniture to get wet. There were two rooms divided by a flimsy screen. The aunties lived in one room, which contained a bed and a sofa. They slept on the bed and my great-uncle, – Uncle Clem, who was blind – slept on the sofa because they gave us his room. Mum and I shared a lumpy double bed and my Uncle Nathan's little camp bed was tucked alongside. Mum was so tired when she fell into bed after working in the street café for long hours that she flailed all over in her sleep and was always rolling on top of me. I'd wake up, yelling and pushing, and Nathan would drag me out from under her dead weight and take me into his tiny bed with him. In the end, I always slept with him.

We didn't have electricity and only a single, outside cold tap. We used kerosene lanterns and cooked with kerosene and charcoal. A window opened from our room onto a kind of lean-to indoor-outdoor kitchen. Our radio and tiny television ran on a car battery. Sometimes, people set up a big communal television down Haunted Lane with electricity stolen from a pole. The yard was shaded by big trees filled with fruit for most of the year. This fruit played an essential part in our diet. Even when we ran out of money for meat or corn, there was always fruit. We had East India mangoes, papayas, Jew plum, tamarind, coconut palms, ackee, avocado, breadfruit and we could eat the pulp from the pods of the 'stinky-toe tree'. Many of the fruits made good drinks – though some were strangely poisonous. Ackee, for example, had to open naturally and couldn't be eaten when too raw or too ripe. When ripe or raw, it caused Jamaican vomiting sickness and even death in extreme cases. When the stinky-toe tree – or tinky-toe, as we called it – flowered, its small creamy blossoms attracted sandflies and big red flying ants, as well as night-flying bats. Its fruit stank to high heaven, but tasted delicious if you could bear to eat it, holding your nose. It was a special tree because it was used in voodoo, for love spells and weddings, as well as having medicinal uses.

Constant Spring sounded lovely and it might have been once, but now the pure water was fed directly into a big reservoir and all that remained of the famous spring was a deep, mucky gully where the overflow rushed down when it rained. A wide, leafy boulevard at the bottom of the hill divided 'us' from 'them' – 'them' being wealthy, middle-class people in their rambling, detached houses with tidy gardens and watered lawns. They were the ones with good government jobs, servants and fancy cars. They didn't know what it was to be hungry or to live under the control of gangs, like us. Every district had its gang and there were killings if anyone strayed into another gang's territory. A girl from a shanty town had to find a man to protect her when she was about fourteen or she'd turn into a slag to be passed around and raped, while boys had to join a gang or leave Jamaica. It was dog eat dog and the law of the jungle.

I started school when I was four, during the time when Dadda B was still in prison, and around the time when Paul was born. Mum went back to dancing, and had to work extra hard to make the money for my fees and uniform. She took me to school to start with because the route from the ghetto was dangerous. We lived on one side of Gully Bank and had to walk up the hill and across the concrete bridge over the gully – sometimes it would be filled with rushing flash-flood water and Mum was terrified I might fall in and be swept away. There were no pavements, and we had to walk in single file along a narrow concrete ledge that was the only thing between the gully and the heavy lorries that roared up and down the dirt road. I saw one kid get knocked off the ledge by a load of kids racing past him. He was run over.

The school was surrounded by a heavy mesh fence. Within its perimeter the grounds were filled with tall shade trees. Whitewashed rubber tyres and pots filled with flowers separated paths from lawns and playing fields. A church with a huge cross dominated the top of the hill. I was in my element and right from the start I wanted to learn, even though I was bullied by bigger girls, who called me ugly.

I used to pour out my troubles to Uncle Clem. He'd say, 'Never mind, kid, you smarter than them,' and he'd tell me a story. I loved Uncle Clem. He used to work as an electrician, but when he went blind, he found work as a cut-rate barber. I guess he used the scissors and clippers by feel. Every day he'd come home with popcorn and I'd run to meet him and we'd walk back hand in hand while I told him about my day. We had a water pipe with an outside tap, but it was jammed into a narrow gap where there wasn't much space, so Mum used to go over to a neighbour's with our clothes and dishes in a big bowl and wash them there. One day, she was at the neighbour's with me, washing the dishes, when another neighbour, who'd been visiting the aunties, strolled by.

'Hello, Lulu, how you doin'?' she said, almost casually.

'I'm fine,' Mum said, clattering the dishes.

Still casually, the neighbour said, 'Oh, Clem's gone.'

Mum said, 'Gone? Gone where? How could you let him go – he's blind.'

The friend said, 'No, he's gone. You know – gone.' She pointed heavenward.

Mum screamed and grabbed me and we ran home. When we got in, the aunties were sobbing in a corner, and Clem was lying on his usual sofa, seeming asleep. Mum shook him, and his head just lolled like his neck was broken. 'God Almighty, he's dead,' she said, her mouth hanging open.

She walked down to the phone and called the morgue, but they couldn't take him until the next morning. The aunties covered him up, so the flies wouldn't get him. I was scared out of my wits and refused to go inside – I said I would sleep in the yard, but Mum said, 'Don't be so silly, he can't hurt you.'

But, taking no chances, my mum and the aunties performed a few purification rituals, with herbs and roots and Katanga limewater before we would go back in. The aunties sat up all night and rocked back and forth, crooning, but I still felt spooked, sleeping with a dead man in the next room. He didn't seem like my old Uncle Clem. He'd changed into a haunt. I was sad about Clem, because he was a kind old man, who used to tell me stories in his soft, deep voice – but I was numb, unable to understand that he wasn't ever coming back. I didn't cry until his funeral, and only then because everyone else was weeping and wailing. I couldn't feel a thing. I didn't really understand what being dead meant and maybe I thought he'd come back when he was better.

Mum paid for the funeral on tick and had to work hard to pay it back – and yet she didn't really seem upset that Clem was dead. Very little moved her – she was a strangely cold, unemotional woman and, deep down, I was scared of her coldness. Yet she had a strong sense of responsibility and keeping face, which often cost her a lot. Paying for a lavish funeral seemed a duty, something you had to do if you didn't want the evil spirits to get you, and since she was the only one working, that duty fell to her.

Two weeks after we buried Clem, Mum heard her dad had died. She didn't spill a single tear. It was the first time I realised I'd even had a granddad. He was mixed race, descended from wealthy English landowners, which Mum said explained why she was so pale-skinned. I was darker, she said, because my dad was more African-looking. It was my burden in life, she said, and she wished she'd given me a light-skinned father, so I'd be prettier and more like her. She was always saying unkind things like that and I learned to hate myself. Her dad left his house to be sold, the money split between all his children. Two of his brothers had been living with him, so we took one of them in. Our shack was now very full, with everyone sharing beds or sofas.

It was also falling down. Mum was always scared that the inflammable tar-paper and wood it was made of would burn down, especially when we were asleep at night. She used to leave a kerosene lamp burning and while at work, she'd visualise that it had fallen over and the place was in flames, so she'd run all the way home between every set of five dances to check on us. 'One day, that tar-paper will go up like a candle,' she said.

Just as soon as there was a hit of money, Mum and her younger brother – my Uncle Nathan – used some of their inheritance to start building a concrete house at the back of the aunties' plot, right next to the gully. They erected two rooms and half a bathroom, so we wouldn't have to wash under the cold tap in the yard or in a tin tub outside any more. Before the work was done, they ran out of money, so we had no kitchen.

In Jamaica, everyone was closely intertwined, going back to the days of slavery, and often the relationships were so mixed up, it was impossible to work out a family tree. Everyone was called 'uncle' or 'auntie' or 'cuz' – we even had brothers and sisters who weren't in the immediate family. Sometimes the relationship was very distant, but if anyone made money, they were honour bound to share it, or maybe they just did it to brag, to show how well they'd done. Not long after we ran out of money, one of these distant 'uncles' turned up from New York, loaded with dollar bills and clothes for us all. Mum was able to finish the build, with a full bathroom, a kitchen and another bedroom.

Stoned and silly on weed, all the uncles who lived with us at the time chopped down most of the fruit trees that supplied us with food and shade. When Mum saw what they'd done, she raved at them, saying they'd destroyed our home and made it look like a desert. She said the rains would come and wash the earth away off the side of the hill, and ghosts would roam around the barren earth. She was wild with rage, and grabbed a broken branch and beat them with it, while they fended her off, giggling foolishly, saying we had tons of firewood now – 'Hey, mon, could have a bonfire!'

It had been lush and green and the night wind blowing through the leaves sang me to sleep and, in the day, brightly feathered birds flew into the branches and hummingbirds drank nectar from deep-throated flowers. Now, our yard looked horribly bare. It even seemed like the soil had become poisonous. Nothing would grow on the dead soil, and even butterflies abandoned us. Once the trees were gone, they were gone. The uncles always regretted it, especially when they sobered up. When someone fancied some fruit to eat, a cold tamarind drink, or the sun beat down mercilessly and the inside of our house became as hot as a sauna, we were reminded again of what we had lost.

The previous year, Mum had used some of the money she'd inherited to set up a stall by the side of the road, to sell sweets, cigarettes and biscuits by day – and she had also sold our own fruit until the trees were murdered. Whatever money she made went towards the purchase of a big freezer so she could sell ice-lollies and bags of ice. She said she wouldn't always be able to work the clubs so she was looking for opportunities to take care of the future. Her enterprise and ambition seemed boundless. She put in a chicken coop and started raising hens to sell, as well as fresh eggs, but without shade, the chickens got too hot and sat in the dust and stopped laying. Nathan, who was heavily into music, was about to leave for New York, but just before he left, he made hutches to keep rabbits for sale and meat – but the rabbits were too hot without shade. They panted hard, their sides rose and fell with the effort, and they died. Mum said it was like the struggles of her life – however hard she worked, something came along to screw it up.

Chapter 2

Jamaica, 1990

About six months after Paul was born, when I was still four, Dadda B was let out of prison. He didn't live with us, but would drop by to visit. Mum was only one of his baby-mothers, a custom heavily tilted in men's favour that demeaned women – but women in our Jamaican ghetto culture put up with it because that was the way it was. I grew to love him and felt he was my real dad because he was the one who would comb my hair, iron my school uniform, bath us, do the cooking and take me to school when Mum was tired after working all night. He was good to us, but he was a gangster. I didn't mind – it was what men did and we weren't told it was wrong.

By scrimping and working hard, within a year or so Mum had saved enough from the stall to open a bar down the road in another ghetto area, known as Court, or Area, 100. She rented a building and we cleaned it and fixed it nicely with tables and chairs. The gang boss of Court 100 came in and demanded dues and, when she didn't pay him, he smashed up her bar. Dadda B went out and shot the opposition and he became the don of Court 100 as well as his own Court 85.

Jamaica still had the death sentence and Mum was so terrified he would get himself killed or hanged protecting her against rivals that she closed the bar and went to work as a dancer again, but it was too late. The war had already started. News was always coming back that men we had known sitting around in our yard, telling stories, singing and playing guitar and drinking beer, were being gunned down, one after another.

Mum was so sure that it would be Dadda B's turn next that she decided she needed the insurance of her own business so she could support me and my brother on her own. She managed to lay her hands on a stall in an arcade that, as far as she knew, wasn't in any gang's area. She saved up enough money for round trips to Cancun and Panama, where she bought very cheap, bright Mexican and South American clothing. Her stall was lovely. Some Saturdays I went in and helped her sell. One day I was helping her when a police officer – who fancied her and wouldn't take no for an answer – slapped her on the bum in a familiar way. She cussed him out and turned around, ignoring him. He was insulted, and pulled out a knife.

I screamed, 'Mum! Watch out!' But he was already slashing her back. Blood poured and she fell to the ground. I was sure she was dead. I sat on the ground crying and held her head. She groaned and tried to sit up. I looked around for help – the policeman had run off – and people came running. Someone called an ambulance and she was patched up in hospital. She couldn't work for some weeks and lost money.

'He won't get away with it. You my woman!' Dadda B raved, when he heard about it. He sat at the table in our house, loading his guns. By the time he'd finished he looked like Rambo.

Mum said, 'Leave it, I'll take care of it.'

'Shuddup, bitch,' Dadda told her. 'This man's bus'ness.'

He thought she was just talking big, but she wasn't. Before Dadda could track down the cop, Mum found him and threw a bottle of acid in his face. She was so pleased that she'd got her revenge, she gloated about it when she got home – and we knew enough not to tell anyone else. Everyone in the family sat around laughing, while she relived the moment and I felt proud of her – no one could get the better of my mum! There were no witnesses, but it started another war, with people taking sides and everyone in the arcade shooting and stabbing each other.

The shootings spread, and the police moved in to control the area. They asked endless questions, but everyone clammed up. It was worth more than their lives to talk and, in the end, like most of the other police investigations, it just fizzled out. It was a joke in the ghetto that the police never made any arrests unless they caught someone with a smoking gun in their hand and a TV crew there to take pictures.

But Mum didn't really win. She was blacklisted from

the arcade and lost all her stock, the fancy clothes she'd bought in Mexico and South America.

One night when they were in bed talking, Mum moaned about how she had lost her stuff, and Dadda leaped out of bed. 'I'm goin' to shoot them niggas,' he yelled.

Scared he'd be killed, Mum also jumped out of bed and grabbed his shoes and threw them into a water drum outside the door. A don can't be a don with bare feet, so, sheepishly, he got back into bed.

When her back healed, Mum started dancing again, but Dadda B hated her work. 'Yo my woman and I wan' yo to myself,' he shouted, trying to lay down the law.

'I got to live,' Mum said.

'Don't I give yo enough?' he said. 'I give yo money and buy the kids things.'

'It's not enough,' she said, dressing in a tight, skimpy little skirt and low-cut blouse. She added red lipstick and draped herself in long gold chains.

'Jis tell me what yo wan' and I'll give it to yo,' he said, emptying his wallet and throwing the notes over the bed.

Mum picked up the cash and folded it in her bra. She didn't speak and carried on getting ready for work. She was independent and liked to take care of herself. 'I ain't gonna rely on no one,' she always said. Even if it caused a row, she wouldn't be entirely kept by a man.

He couldn't believe she was defying him. 'Yo still goin' go work?' he yelled.

'Sure. You a big man, you give me money now – but you got other women, and I can't depend on you.'

He started to yell that she dressed like a whore and ran around with other men who only wanted her for her ass. They got into it and he slashed her lip with a knife. I was six and Paul was about two. We were scared witless and cowered against the wall, screaming. A geyser of blood gushed out of her lip and poured down her chin onto her breasts. 'Mama! Mama!' I moaned, sure she was going to die.

Red hot with rage, she grabbed a cutlass she kept for security and slashed at him. She caught his trigger finger and almost chopped it off, then she chased him across the yard. Howling with pain, he jumped on his Harley, revved up and shot off in a spray of gravel. She didn't say anything – she didn't even wince. She washed her mouth under the cold pump until the bleeding stopped. Then she stomped back inside to gaze stone-faced in the mirror. She got a cut-throat razor from the shelf and cut off the flap of skin, not even wincing with the pain. Her lip was raw red underneath, like cut meat.

I shrieked when I saw her cut herself with the razor and tried to grab her around the legs. I thought she was going to slit her throat. She shook me off and stared at herself. 'Get away, brat,' she said, her voice sounding thick as she tried to move her mouth. Then she shrugged and picked up her purse.

'Mama, where you going?' I sobbed. Paul cowered against me, sucking his thumb.

'To work,' she said.

'Mama, go hospital, see a doctor,' I said, almost too scared to speak. The raw cut looked awful, a ruddy gash across her lips.

'Who's gonna pay? You got money?' she said, really nasty. I shut my mouth and said nothing more. 'The customers ain't lookin' at my lip,' she said. 'They looking at my ass and tits.'

Dadda lay low for a while, but their fights never seemed to mark the end of things between them. One day, he casually strolled in as if he hadn't been gone for weeks.

'Oh, it's you,' she said.

He patted me on the head and swung Paul into the air and gave him a kiss. 'I got some tings for the kids in the car,' he said.

Mum nodded at me and we ran out to see what he had bought us. By the time we ran back in, dragging in bags of toys and clothes, he and Mum were in bed. Man, they were always hot as chilli peppers for each other, couldn't keep their hands off the other's body. He was back in favour and Mum looked happy again, not like she'd eaten a mouthful of soursop.

It turned out he wanted to borrow some of Mum's clothes. We all treated it like a joke and helped him dress up in Mum's bra, stuffed with cloth, one of her wigs, high heels and a blue satin frock patterned with yellow hibiscus flowers. She helped him paint his face with her make-up.

He stared in the mirror and blew a kiss. 'Goddamit,

yo sure is hot shit, Winston! I'd fancy yo but you can't fuck yo'self.'

We laughed, and he camped it up, wiggling his bum. He couldn't have stood out more, but he said that was part of the disguise. Security guards would never think a man could look so good. He put a gun in the handbag Mum had lent him and left in a taxi. I didn't really think he would do a robbery dressed like that, but when the news mentioned someone of his description holding up a bank, we fell about laughing, not seeing the enormity of what he'd done, just the humour. Most people we knew were crooked in some way, but you had to be to survive in the ghetto, so it never seemed wrong.

Dadda B never blamed Mum for maiming his finger. He just learned to shoot with the other hand. He got me and Paul to clean and load his guns and let us shoot at targets stuck up on trees at the back of the yard near the gully. Kids like us played in the gully and it was a shortcut up the hill for people going to the school and church at the top, and the possibility that we might hurt somebody didn't seem to bother him.

Mum hated us playing with his guns. 'Guns are the devil's toys,' she warned us. Each day on my way to school I used to pass by a stall owned by Mr Chin, a friendly Chinese man. He'd call out a greeting and offer me some little treat, like candy or popcorn. One day, I saw Mr Chin in the morning and waved. He returned my wave with a little bow and said, 'Come by evening, I will have popcorn for missy.'

When I ran home from school, looking forward to

my popcorn, I was shocked to see Mr Chin lying on the road, in a big puddle of black blood that had soaked into the dirt all round. A bullet hole was drilled through his head. I imagined I could see right through from front to back. He'd been caught in crossfire during a gang shoot-by. Nobody seemed to want to take him away and bury him. He was gone the next morning, in the garbage truck.

'Look and learn,' Mum said grimly, when I walked in weeping. Mr Chin hadn't done a thing – he'd just been in the wrong place at the wrong time. 'People who live by the gun, die by the gun,' she said. This didn't apply to poor Mr Chin, who had nothing at all to do with guns – but Mum loved her sayings and I just listened and nodded.

In her life she had known many people who had died violently, so when she saw Dadda B give us shooting lessons, she tried to stop it. She ran out of the house, shouting, 'You trainin' them to be gangsters like you.'

He just laughed. 'Quiet woman. Yo like the money. Yo like it when I spend it on yo lazy ass.'

Mum wouldn't be spoken to like that and they started scrapping in the dust of the yard like dogs. When it was over, instead of making up and climbing into the sack like they always did, Dadda left with a face like thunder. Mum threw some clothes into a bag.

'Where you goin'?' I asked.

'I'm leavin' and I ain't comin' back,' she said.

She called a taxi from the neighbour's house and after the dust died down in the road from the taxi driving away, Paul and I stared at each other. 'Who's goin look after us?' he asked, blinking away tears.

'We'll look after each other,' I said.

The aunties were there for us, but they were getting on and couldn't be bothered with two children. I was very relieved when a few days later, Dadda turned up on his big Harley. When he saw we were on our own, he moved in and cared for us. We had the best time. We went to the beach, riding on the back of the bikes, had lots of treats, and in the evenings his friends came round. We cooked out in the yard, they drank beer in the dark around the fire, sang and played guitar. It was like a holiday. After some weeks, Mum came home. We'd had so much fun that we didn't even look at her.

We loved being with Dadda B. Just before Christmas once, when I was seven and a half and Paul was three and a half, he came by taxi to get us and took us shopping to choose our presents. 'Bring them back, I don't want them going to your dump, it's a bad neighbourhood,' Mum said, as she waved us off.

'Yeah, yeah, yeah, I'll bring them straight back,' Dadda said, winking at us. Perhaps he looked on it as a challenge, because after we'd had a great time in the street bazaar at Halfway Tree, watching the crowds, the musicians and the street entertainers, and bought loads of toys and new clothes, he said we weren't going home just yet. We ended up at his place, hanging out with his gang buddies around the barbecue, cooking out steaks and fish and chicken. There were piles of buttered corn and sweet potatoes, beer for the men and fresh lemonade for us kids. Days passed, with music and singing, and sleeping in hammocks under the trees. It was the best time ever. A couple of days later, Mum arrived in a taxi to get us. The first thing she heard was gunshots from round the back. She came rushing around the side of the house to the backyard and saw Paul holding a handgun and shooting at targets.

She steamed right in, her arms like windmills whacking everyone, and all these gangsters were laughing and holding her off, pretending she'd hurt them. She was so angry she could barely get the words out. 'I want you kids in that taxi now. Get goin'! Move.'

Paul had been drinking beer and was belligerent. He'd never had so much fun around our yard with Mum and the aunties. This was real man stuff. He argued with Mum and tried to hide behind Dadda. She dragged him out, clipped him around the head and propelled him to the taxi. She shoved him in and yelled at the driver, 'Drive, drive!'

I was upset at being taken away from so much fun, but could never argue with her – it always seemed disrespectful and I think I was scared of her as well. But I could see that she was frightened. She was always saying that while we should learn to fight and take care of ourselves, she didn't want us around guns.

Dadda came around a few days later and she got pregnant again, but, as usual, being pregnant didn't stop them having huge fights. When she was almost nine months gone, he stabbed her in the belly. Amniotic fluid squirted out like a geyser under pressure and she fell to the ground shrieking, 'Yo done kilt me! I dead, I dying!'

I ran out to get help from a neighbour and saw Dadda shoot off, gunning his Harley. He looked scared. The neighbour called a taxi and ran back with me into our yard. Mum was sitting on the ground, pale as a spook, the blood gone from her face. Blood and birth fluid pumped out of the deep wound. When her eyes rolled back in her head, the neighbour said, 'She gone.' She stuck her finger in the hole to stop the blood from spurting out, and told me to run and get towels at once.

Paul started to howl, 'Mama, Mama!'

We got towels and a big sheet and wrapped them tightly around her belly, the neighbour walked with her finger still stuck in the wound to the taxi. We all piled in and, somehow, we got Mum to hospital. Three doctors came running when we walked in yelling, but when they saw this gaping hole in her belly and all the amniotic fluid gone from the sac the baby was in, they turned her away. 'We can't help her. She won't live, take her home,' they said. They were nervous, wanting to get rid of us as quickly as possible. They didn't want her dying in their hospital. She came from the ghetto. She wasn't worth much.

We got another taxi and returned to Constant Spring, with Mum groaning over every bump and pothole in the road. I was in tears, unable to imagine a world without my mum. Who would look after us? More neighbour women came, they put in medicine into the wound and bandaged Mum tightly to keep her belly together. Everyone was sure she would die, because the baby was 'dry' in the womb and germs could get in. They sent for a witchdoctor and all night everyone chanted spells, spread ashes, burned roots and sprinkled holy water.

Mum survived, but she walked with a careful waddle because the wound gaped and wouldn't heal. The great size of her belly and the strain on her shiny skin had forced it open, like the slash of ruby lips. I could look into it, and see the layers of fat, all white and glistening. It was like looking inside a gutted fish.

Dadda returned, sheepishly bearing gifts, and Mum stared at him blankly as she lay back on the sofa, her face pale and sweaty. She wouldn't let him stay, but she agreed he could visit us and give us money and toys. 'Yo' a deadbeat loser,' she told him.

He hung his head and said he'd try to do better.

Wayan was born two weeks later. When she went into labour, she stood up, legs apart, holding her belly together with both hands. Each time a birth ripple passed over the taut skin, she groaned from her very depths, like she was going to split in half. While the witchdoctor closed her eyes and rocked back and forth with mysterious chants, the rest of the attendant midwives counted down the pains and encouraged her to push. *One-two-three – push!* Finally, after a long hour, a boy baby shot out like a cork from a bottle. He landed with a little thump on the ground and let out a piercing shriek. Georgia grabbed the cord that hung down from Mum and cut it in half and Gemma picked him up, all slimy and wet, covered with dirt from the floor.

'Oh my, sweet Lord, look at that – his earlobe's cut in half,' she said.

Everyone stared. 'It was that devil's knife, sliced clean through his ear in the womb,' Gemma said. They all started wailing, saying the baby was cursed. Gemma washed him in a bowl of warm water and wrapped him in a towel, as the witchdoctor went into a frenzy, shaking her rattle, tossing ashes and sprinkling magic water.

The painful birth split her wound open even wider, and Mum had to go to the hospital to get her belly stitched up. This time, the doctors treated her because it was obvious she was going to survive. For a long time, she was tender and couldn't return to dancing.

Despite his dodgy start in life, Mum insisted that Wayan was lucky because he had survived against all odds – though in many ways, he *was* cursed because the awkward fall from the womb broke his leg. The pain made him cry hour after hour, day and night, week after week. Paul ran around, blocking his ears with his hands and shouting, 'Take him back! Take him back to the yard with no gate.' He meant the hospital, which had a big ungated courtyard ambulances drove into.

Dadda B came to see his new son with a small sack full of money – the kind of cloth sacks used by banks, so we all knew where it had come from. He pulled out a wad of notes and threw them onto the bed. Mum didn't care that it was stolen from a bank raid that morning, which we'd heard about on the radio. She took the money. 'He got half an ear and a broke leg, thanks to you,' she said.

'Oh, c'mon woman – be nice to me,' Dadda pleaded. Mum pouted and turned her face away, but I saw she was smiling. I guess they really loved each other.

I will always remember the summer when I was eight – because it was the best summer of all. The long school holidays went on and on and all us Gully Bank kids could stay up almost as late as we wanted while the womenfolks fried chicken or grilled sweetcorn and sat around gossiping. People dropped by, bringing beer and more supplies, and the parties went on night after night. There seemed to be tons of kids in our ever-expanding gang. There was me (the only girl), my brother Paul, some kids Mum was looking after for a while and our usual playmates from around Gully Bank. We ran wild in the streets or played in the gully, swinging on a rope across it and giving each other piggybacks across rushing water when summer storms hit. It was dangerous, but we could hear the really big flash floods roaring down the hill on the way to the sea and leaped out of the way in time, yelling, 'Duppy's gonna get you! Duppy's gonna get you!'

One time, the flood came when Paul was swinging across on the rope, screaming, 'Yo! Superman! Watch me!'

He slipped and fell and the water grabbed his legs. Somehow he hung on and scrambled to safety, his pants ripped, lips split and teeth knocked out. We ran into a neighbour's house, where we tried to clean him up. 'I ain't goin' home,' he said. 'Mum sees this, she'll kill me. I'm moving in next door.'

We were in awe. 'You goin' live here?'

'Yep,' he bragged. His bravado lasted five minutes. Mum came and dragged him home and gave him huge beats. She said, 'Now you got a sore ass as well as a sore face.' Then she beat me for letting the kids play in the gully, because I was the oldest, and a girl. It was a bitch being a big sister. Next day, Mum stayed home to see what we were up to and made me clean the house from top to bottom while the boys in our gang swept the yard. We slapdashed the place and had to do it again. Mum said we were too turbo – she was right. We couldn't help it, egging each other on in a frenzy of unstoppable laughter.

The gully still called to us, with its mixture of fun and danger. Old Jack, a drunken old man, lived under a canvas awning across the gully, and we loved to torment him. He'd sit in a big tree, drinking rum. One day, he fell out and landed flat on his back in the gully. I shouted, 'Old Jack drop out of Rum Tree!' We all ran to look. He was not moving, lying flat on his back at the bottom. 'Yo think he dead?' one of the kids whispered.

'Yeah, he dead,' I said.

I mentioned it that night, to the grown-ups sitting out in the yard, but they ignored me. I said it louder, 'Man dead in gully.'

They got torches and ran. They saw him down there, not moved at all in hours. Mum poured a bucket of soapy water on him and he got up. His head was bust, flies stuck in blood. 'Woo, head made of iron,' Auntie Georgia said. Old Jack crawled up the sides of the gully, back into the Rum Tree where he'd stashed his flagon, and carried on drinking.

'He'll die up there,' Georgia said. 'Birds will peck out his eyes. Old scarecrow.'

But he didn't die – he was always up the Rum Tree, drinking that summer away. One night, the boys were throwing stones at Old Jack and I was spinning on the rope, twisting it so it spun in wilder and wilder circles, having too much fun. Way past curfew, Mum came looking for us. She stood there smirking, fondly it seemed, at us kids having fun. I smiled back and she suddenly grabbed my T-shirt, brought a belt out over her head and – *Thwack! Thwack!*

'Ow-ouch!' I hollered and wriggled free. Mum still had stitches in her belly, but she chased us down Haunted Lane – we fled through the ghost field, screaming so those ghosts wouldn't catch us. We cut through a bad-tempered neighbour's house – didn't realise his pit bulls were out – dogs barking, hot on our heels, mean eyes, barrel chests. Boys in our gang ran one way, I doubled back, through the ghost field, found safety in Auntie Georgia's house, hid out for two days in her bed, pretending to be asleep. She never liked to wake a sleeping child. But ooh, I was hungry, hungry! The boys stayed with friends. Mum padlocked the gate and put flour on the ground so she could see if we'd been there. Boys returned home. Mum followed their footprints to the tangle of morning glory and 'rice and pea' vines, as I called them – got a long bamboo stick, poked and poked.

'Ow-oww!' they yelled.

'Got you,' she said. I was watching from a distance, howling with laughter, hopping up and down with glee as Mum hauled them out of the bushes and chased them with the stick.

When you're eight years old, it seems like the fun will go on for ever. But it all came to an end one day, when Dadda's life caught up with him. He was ambushed in the street right outside our yard and went down in a hail of gunfire. Mum wasn't there – but I saw it all. After the thunder of the guns, the street was strangely quiet. I ran out shrieking, to where he lay in spreading tides of blood. He'd been shot in his legs, knees and head and the blood flowed out from every part of him, like a watering can with holes in it.

As he lay dying, he asked, 'Where's Lulu? I love her and the kids.'

I sat in the dirt, sticky with his dark blood, sobbing and moaning. 'Dadda, don't die, please don't die.' But he gave a funny little sigh, and was gone.

His death destroyed my mum. For all their violent fights, they were passionately in love. She loved him more than she loved us, I think. She stopped eating and grew thin and gaunt, and all the uptight Christian women in our neighbourhood – who hated her because she was so vibrant and lived a life they sneered at – gossiped and pointed their fingers, saying she had AIDS. She didn't hear, or care what these cold-hearted creatures said, because she was weepy and heartbroken for months. She stopped looking after herself. She didn't comb her hair and it stuck out, wild and straggled as a thorn bush, she didn't use make-up and her face got a grey and dusty look. She threw her clothes on, even if they were dirty and torn. Some days, if she didn't have to work – by now she was cooking food in a shop – she wouldn't have bothered to dress at all.

But first, she had to organise Dadda's funeral. She was determined to give him a big send-off, even though they weren't married and she wasn't responsible for him. The aunties nagged her, 'Don' be no fool! You don' have to do this, Lulu. What did he care? He left you nothin', no money, nothin'. Who's goin' hep you care for the children now?'

Gemma said, 'He brung his fight here – we could've all got ourselves kilt. Don' you remember how he stabbed you when you was pregnant? You jus' a baby-mother to him, not a wife. Let some other fool bury him.'

Stubbornly, Mum shook her head. 'He deserves respect. His sons got to feel I done the right thing for their dad. They look back when they is men – say, you show him no respect? What kind of creature you?'

She worked extra shifts, took loans and sold his guns to raise money. He loved silver, so she hired a silver car and an ornate silver casket. Twenty bikers from his gang rode ahead on big Harleys, with a massed roar that made me tingle all over. Cars made up the rear, all packed with people I didn't know. It was a huge funeral. The cortege drove a long way into the country to

Mandeville, some forty miles west of Kingston, where his family came from, and Mum buried him next to his father in the sprawl of Dovecot Memorial Park.

Dadda B's death changed many things for us. His enemies wanted to destroy us. They put a curse on us and strange things started happening. One night, Mum was nursing the baby outside in the yard, and she left Paul asleep on the bed. The windows and shutters right next to the bed were closed, yet when we went in, they were wide open and Paul had gone. In his sleep, he had somehow opened the window and shutters, dropped down about four feet into the yard and crossed to behind the aunties' house to the steep gully beyond. We searched in the dark, looking for him and found him down in the bottom, still asleep. When we shook him awake, he was confused and said his dad had told him to jump into the gully.

A couple of nights later, when Mum was out working, I woke alone in the bed and heard Paul calling out in his sleep from the crib he shared with baby Wayan, 'Leave me alone! Leave me alone!' like he could see haunts. I got goosebumps and went looking for help. Iris, our neighbour, said, 'Put a coconut under the bed. If there's haunts there, it will scare them away.'

I found a fallen coconut under the palm tree in the front yard and did as she said. Instantly everything in the room started moving and shaking violently. I grabbed the baby and Iris took Paul and we ran out of the house. Shit-scared, we stayed with the aunties, moaning and praying, until Mum came home.

'It's Dadda B, doin' this,' Iris said. 'It's his evil side fighting with his good side.' She told us she'd had a dream about him driving us in a hearse. She was running away from it, and he ran over a member of her family. 'Man, it's evil – I can feel it all around,' she whispered, her eyes rolling in every direction. 'You gotta get out.'

A few days later, she came to our house, hobbling on suddenly hugely swollen feet – it looked as if she had elephantiasis. 'Look what he done,' she wailed, barely able to walk. 'I'm going away – and I ain't coming back.' I had never seen anyone so scared. True to her word, she packed up that afternoon and left Jamaica for America.

We were scared, but had nowhere to go, as things grew worse. 'Someone's laid a curse,' Mum said. 'It's not your dad, he loved us too much.' Our yard seemed to be hexed. After the first death by poisoning when the big trees had been cut down, thanks to lucky charms things had recovered a bit. But now everything in it died. The grass dried up, the new chickens in their coop died, the rabbits, the goats, the kittens and puppies we played with – they all took sick and died almost before our eyes. Only the few big trees that hadn't been cut down along the gully continued to flourish. Uncle Nathan (who had recently returned with a load of money from New York, where he had a small studio and was making hip-hop CDs) started to build a house of his own in the yard, squeezed in beside ours. A builder was almost killed when a heavy plank fell on his head. Luckily he was wearing a helmet, so he wasn't badly hurt. But other things went wrong with the construction, and an old man told Nathan to put blood and rum on the foundations.

With so much bad stuff going on, Mum decided to call in the Obeah-man to cleanse the place. The Obeah-man was a secretive African witchdoctor whose rituals and curses were so powerful that the cult of Obeah was illegal in Jamaica. To call on it was very expensive and, with the cost of the funeral, Mum was already in debt. Also, Dadda's enemies knew we were unprotected and it was a matter of honour and vengeance for them to kill everyone connected with a fallen enemy. It was like when a new regime wipes out the previous dynasty to stop sons growing up who will seek revenge or want to take back their territory. So our lives were in real danger – and all the money Mum had spent on the Obeah-man had no effect because, a few nights after he'd been, Dadda's enemies came looking for us. Mum heard them entering the garden and she pushed us right under the big double bed that was up against the window. Quickly, while the rival crew roamed around outside, she stuffed pillows under the sheet to look like us sleeping and she rolled under the bed, next to us. I was terrified when I heard them talking in low voices right next to the window. Someone forced it, moving quietly, but I was holding my breath and could hear every sound.

I heard the crisp click of triggers, then *Blam! Blam! Blam!* I grabbed hold of my brothers and put my hand over the baby's mouth. *Blam-blam-blam!* The rattle of bullets echoed off the wall, slugs went into the pillows, cracked a mirror with a loud report, splintered furniture. I was so scared I could hardly breathe. Wayan was wriggling and squealing like a damp little piglet in my grasp and Paul bit my hand where I was digging it into him. We were close up against the wall under the window and the bullets fanned over us and went all over the room.

After it was silent, we lay on the ground under the fusty bed for a long time, and finally Mum pulled us all out. 'You OK?' she asked, her voice thin and high.

'Yes,' I said. But I wasn't. I was scared stiff.

'We're going,' Mum said. She started throwing clothes into bags, picked up the baby and we walked to the bus. It was late and we had to wait a long time. I fell asleep by the side of the road, with my head on my bag. It was a long journey of some forty miles first to Mandeville, where we would change buses. We were going to stay with Dadda's brother, Uncle DeJohn, on his small farm in the high tree country of the Mocha Mountains. It was another thirty miles beyond Mandeville, where Dadda was buried. Mum said they wouldn't come looking for us there.

We had often stayed with Uncle DeJohn during school holidays. The mountains seemed so clean and fresh – though the first time I'd gone as a little girl they seemed scary, away from the ghettos and crowded, tumbledown houses I'd grown used to. He wasn't expecting us, but when we arrived he made us welcome – although he was very strict. He ran things like an army camp. He had house rules we had to follow – such as not being allowed to drink until you'd finished eating and no talking at table. If we didn't follow his rules, he'd just give us a look that scared the shit out of us. Mum would give us a world of beats, but we were more terrified of Uncle's stern glare. I think he was so strict because he was in constant pain from when he and Dadda B had played Russian roulette as kids and he'd lost. The bullet went deep into his gut and doctors couldn't dig it out.

It seemed as if the voodoo curse had followed us there, though. At night, if we wanted to go to the bathroom, we had to walk from our bedroom, through the sitting room to the bathroom. One night, a ghost was there and he stuck out his foot, blocking the way. We were terrified and ran back to bed. But eventually, we were bursting and had to go – it would be worse for us if we wet the bed. My brothers started to whimper and I started to wet myself. We had no choice. Shaking with fright, we peered through the door to see if the ghostly leg and foot was still there, blocking us. When we saw it was, I grabbed their hands and we ran straight through it, shrieking loudly.

Uncle came running out of his bedroom, holding a gun. 'What up, what up?' he yelled. By then, we'd made the bathroom. Clutching each other in the doorway, we pointed, too scared to speak. Uncle's eyes popped wide when he saw the ghost.

'Get gone, get gone!' he yelled. He grabbed us and dragged us back into his room. Soon as we were in and he'd slammed the door, he grabbed a cross on a silver chain off the dresser, got down the Bible and started to read from it, while swinging the cross back and forth. He had us sleep in his room after that and he read to us all night from his Bible until the spook left. It was a terrifying time for all of us, and even after the spook went, we were constantly on the lookout, in case it sneaked back in and got us.

We didn't go to school in the mountains, but Uncle was like a stern schoolteacher, making sure that we split our day up between playing, working and being educated. He made me read the newspaper to him each day, like I was a newsreader. We made a little studio by turning the table upside down and I'd sit in it on a chair like I was on TV. First, I'd read the headlines and then the stories, slowly and clearly, while he listened, nodding. If I messed up, he'd rap on the floor with a stick. He wouldn't accept the word 'can't' – if you said that word, you had to do whatever the task was for even longer. We hoed his crops, tended the animals, milked the goats, and did what he told us. We also had to help Mum keep the place clean while she cooked.

There were no children living nearby, but we were happy playing with each other. We could play in the forest, and splashed in the cold mountain stream that ran behind the house. Our favourite place to play was a huge wild meadow where Uncle's goats roamed. It was overgrown with low bushes you could boil and make a kind of tea from. I used to call them the rice and pea bushes because they were covered with masses of tiny pink flowers. They were like 3-D hearts. Butter-flies loved them and the meadow would be awash with brightly coloured butterflies, like a Disney film. At the far side was a clump of trees and we made this our fort, where we played exciting games all day long. There was plenty of fruit to eat on the farm, and chickens, eggs and goats – our uncle even grew coffee. We spent hours fishing with Uncle and ate the fish we caught – crayfish and a kind of crab. Mum would walk down the mountain to the shop or catch a bus to the small town for the little shopping we needed.

Each time Mum said, 'OK, kids, time to go home,' we saw another shooting on the television news. All my dad's soldiers in his old crew were being picked off, one at a time. His lieutenant was gunned down in front of his two children – exactly like Dadda was gunned down in front of us kids. We saw photographs of faces we recognised on the news and in the papers – men who had sat in our yard and jammed with Dadda during happier, lazy days. When we saw all this still happening, we ducked our heads and kept below the parapet in the safety of the mountains far away from the ghetto wars in Kingston.

Some six months later, news came that the fighting was over – it had run its course and everyone was dead or had fled. The gangster who'd killed Dadda went to live in America, and things quietened down. Mum came back from the local town and packed our things and we said goodbye to Uncle DeJohn. When I hugged him goodbye, I whispered in his ear that I would come back soon and be his little newscaster again. 'Good girl,' he said, coughing loudly, like he had dust in his throat. We climbed aboard the bus down at the bottom of the hill. I was sad to leave. I had become close to my uncle and grown to love reading to him. I liked the space, the fresh air and the peace, away from the ghetto. It was clean and the food was plain but plentiful. Mum didn't have to keep scrounging around to feed us and she stopped being stressed and bad-tempered. I wish we could have stayed – but Mum said she had to earn some money and it was safe at home now.

But the ghetto we were returning to wasn't really safe, and things weren't the same. New gangs had taken over, there were new, powerful dons, jostling for power. Mum didn't have anyone to protect her and, like all single women, seemed fair game to any man. Rape was a way of life and if you were a woman you had to have a powerful man to protect you.

Just a week after we returned from the country a bad man named DeMon tried to rape Mum when she was walking home from work off the bus. She came home in a terrible mess, her clothes all torn. She said she'd fought him off and he fled. Her power as Dadda B's woman had gone. She lost her spirit, cried a lot and for some weeks seemed utterly broken.

The kids at school seemed to know that we were weaker now and decided to pick on me. There was a bigger girl, tall and quite fat, who picked on me the most. Her name was Tia. She had wild, spiky hair and glaring eyes and she freaked me out. She was the ringleader. They'd steal my wooden pencil box, my pencils, my dictionaries that Mum bought me, and my dinner money, so I often went hungry. By the end of the day, my belly would be rumbling like a volcano. I never used to tell my mum, I knew she would be furious, but my sneaky brother Paul did, running home, bursting in, jostling to be first. 'Sugar's had a fight!' he'd crow.

'Yo chicken like yo' dad,' she'd yell when I came home bloody, my clothes torn. 'Who's gonna buy yo new clothes, who's gonna buy yo new books – not that no-good nigga who made yo.'

I made excuses, but she already knew all the details, thanks to those little snitches. 'Sugar's been fighting and got her ass whipped!' She almost exploded with rage as soon as she saw me, and picked up a belt. I raced around our little shack, shrieking as the blows landed, and then out into the yard, where my aunties stood, laughing, arms akimbo. 'Go, Sugar, run!' they called out. 'Yo gotta move faster'n that, Lulu, if yo goin' catch her!'

One day, suddenly Mum stopped chasing me. 'I ain't having a coward in my house, no way! You ain't my daughter, you chicken like yo' dad, with a big yellow streak.' She stood there like a crocodile, a long sneer on her face, teeth sharp, her eyes mean as ice, then turned and went back inside. I knew she was angry because she walked right in, not backwards, like we all did so the demons wouldn't follow us inside.

Eventually, I crept back in and curled up in bed. But in the morning I was shocked to see her packing a small suitcase with all my things.

I sat up. 'Mum? What you doin'?'

'I'm putting you out on the street. Yo' ain't my daughter – yo' a coward. No guts – no glory.' She dropped the case by the front door. 'Here – this is yours. Take it on yo' way out.'

I was so scared, I jumped up, snatched my school clothes and ran to my aunties' house at the front of our big yard. I washed quickly in cold water and grabbed a small piece of cold boiled corn and ate it while I ran to school. All day long, I shivered with fear. Where would I go? How would I live?

By the end of the day, I had switched from being soft to being a fighter. It was like I'd gone past fear into a level of courage I didn't know I had. Instead of sneaking out past Tia, head down, then running like hell and hoping to escape her two brawny arms, I made up my mind to fight back. Our way home led down a dangerous hill that lorries used to tear through at speed. There were no pavements and we had to walk single file along a narrow ledge. Tia always used to catch up with me and whack me on the head and sometimes I almost slipped into the path of a careering lorry. 'Yo! Cabbage-head!' Tia shouted as she ran by, giving my head a hard shove.

Despite my resolve, I tried to shrug her off, but a friend chanted, 'I'm goin' tell yo' mum, I'm goin' tell yo' mum!'

Suddenly I thought, 'No way will I let my mum chuck me out because of you.'

I chased Tia and when I caught up with her, I charged

at that big fat bully-girl and headbutted her in the centre of her big soft belly. My head sank into the rolls of fat with a squish and I heard the air go 'whoosh'. All the other kids were amazed. I heard their little gasps and excited comments as I turned and ran. I wanted her to follow me, which she did, thudding like an elephant. The other kids streamed along like a stampeding herd. They liked me – but they were sure I'd be squashed like a bug and they wanted to be there when I was.

Soon as we got to the gully, I turned and jumped on her and started fighting. I punched, I kicked, I bit. She was soft, like a jellyfish, with muscles as useless as bags of poop. I was thin and wiry, agile as a snake, my muscles hard as iron. When she whacked me, I didn't feel it. I didn't try to whack her – instead, I gouged at her face with my nails, tried to yank out handfuls of her hair.

'*Ow-eeaw!*' she yelled, tears spouting. Her mouth dribbled spit and blood where I'd mashed her lips against her teeth. We rolled down into the gully, over and over, still locked in a flailing ball. At the bottom, she crawled away, blubbering. I stood up, and grinned at the kids peering down from the top. My brother scrambled down to me. 'You OK, Sugar?' Paul asked. Wayan stood next to him, his mouth open with shock.

I was bloody, my green and white uniform was torn and muddy, clumps of hair were ripped from my head – but I had won. I was so upset, I cried all the way home.

Some little creep, full of self-importance, shouted out,

'I'm gonna tell yo' mum yo been fighting.' He raced off, almost bursting to get the news out.

I thought I'd be thrown out for sure, or get beats, but when I arrived at our gate, with a handful of kids still trailing behind, Mum was waiting, arms akimbo. She smiled, then she started to laugh. 'Well, girl, yo finally found yo' courage,' she hooted. 'Look at the state of yo – *woo-hoo!* Must've been some fight!'

She gave me a drink of carrot juice and told my brothers to fetch a towel. I went to the cold tap in the yard to wash off the mud and the blood. The cold water stung bad, but it cooled me down. I couldn't believe what I had done – but most of all, I couldn't believe my mum's reaction. She was happy! She'd really wanted me to fight. It was amazing. By the time I got indoors and put on the clean clothes she had laid out, she was chopping up some oxtail and vegetables to make my favourite dinner.

'Winners get a celebration feast,' she said with a big grin, as she rolled the oxtail bits in flour. She patted me on the head with a floury hand. 'Yo can unpack that case, darlin', put yo' things away.' Man oh man – *she was pleased with me*! I didn't know that she wanted me to be a fighter because she thought it was the only way I'd survive.

That was the watershed. Before, I was weak, always sentimental, always crying over anything. I became a different girl. I was glad I learned to fight, because no one could scare me no more. Kids respected me and Tia stayed out of my way. But the story wasn't done, because the next day, Tia's mum got a friend, who used to be a soldier, to attack my mum. He laid in wait with a knife. I don't know how, but my mum got that knife off him and beat the crap out of him. My courage seemed to have restored her ability to fight. She came home bloody and bruised, but smirking like a crocodile. 'That cow better emigrate, because if I see her, she's dead,' she said.

Just after Mum was attacked, when I was thinking we were coming out of the bad times, something really terrible happened to me. I was still eight years old and Yoland, one of Mum's friends, was baby-sitting us in her house on the edge of the ghetto, while Mum was at work. The gardener in the big house across the boulevard kept giving me sexy looks, and saying bad things to me. He gave me the creeps, but I ignored him. I couldn't tell Mum because she had too much to think about.

Yoland went out in the evening and left us on our own while Mum was at work. I got into the bed with my brothers and we all cuddled up. In the night, I felt the sheet being lifted away from me. In my half-sleep I thought it was our mum getting in with us and I scooted over to give her room. When I smelled the animal odour of drink and sweat and felt a heavy, un-familiar body, I was shit-scared. I felt I had to protect my brothers who were right next to me – but didn't know how. I froze. It was the gardener. He covered my mouth with his horny hand and rolled on top of me. Then I tried to scream and claw at him, but he was too strong and I was befuddled by sleep. I felt his knee forcing my legs apart, felt the piercing pain, and then I don't remember much.

When it was over and he'd gone, I looked to see if my brothers were all right – and they were still sleeping. I got out of bed, locked the door to keep them safe, and looked for Yoland – but she wasn't there. We were quite alone. I ran to the payphone down the road. I called Mum at the club where she was dancing – something I was never supposed to do. I had to wait while someone went to get her. When she came, she said, 'What's up? This better be good.'

I sobbed, 'Please come and get us. I'm not safe. He goin' kill me.'

'Who going kill you? What you talking about?'

'The gardener. He got into bed with me and hurt me –'

She swore. 'Where's Yoland?'

'I don't know.'

Instead of comforting me, or saying she was coming at once, she shouted at me for making trouble for her at work and told me to go back to my brothers, lock the door and stay put. I had to do as she told me, and as soon as I returned, the man came back, forced the door and raped me again and again. I lay under him like a rag doll, on the far side of pain, while my brothers just carried on sleeping.

The next day when I went home from Yoland's house, Mum was still steaming angry with me for interrupting her at work. She said she could be fired. She wasn't angry with Yoland for going out and not looking after us. I tried to tell her what had happened and when she heard about the gardener and how he'd got into bed with me and forced himself into me, she grabbed a belt and beat me within an inch of my life. 'Fuckin' slut,' she screamed. 'Yo axed for it, yo useless piece of shit. Why didn't yo fight back? Yo goin' be chicken all your life?'

I was a bloody pulp by the time she finished. Sobbing, I crawled to the tap in the garden to wash myself, her words ringing in my ears. *Fuckin' slut, fuckin' slut.*

From that moment I lost all my sense of self and worth. In the years to come, even though I could still laugh and play like any other girl, deep down I felt I was no good, worth less than nothing.

Chapter 3

Jamaica, 1995

L ife was an unending struggle until Mum met Milton a year later. I don't think she loved him – Dadda B was the love of her life and she never recovered from his death – but she had learned to use men to survive. Milton had recently returned from England, where he'd made a lot of money running some scams in London. This money was worth a lot more in Jamaica, so he was cock of the roost, bragging, chucking his cash around the neighbourhood and spending it on his large family, much of it on buying land and building a house for them.

Although he had a home near Kingston – where his mother and several members of his extended family lived – he wanted a love nest he could visit. The first time he came, he slept with Mum on her night off. We could hear everything, but we had to stay in our beds, and not be a nuisance. We knew another man in Mum's life meant security for us. He was gone by morning – but he'd only gone to collect his luggage. When we saw him unloading all his stuff, Paul and I looked at each other – *oh-oh* – this was new. As for many women in the ghetto, baby-fathers came and went. Mum had never had a man live with her before, but she seemed to welcome Milton moving in. She said she was tired of being on her own and DeMon had scared the hell out of her. She needed a protector, a man with status, who would give her cash.

But we didn't like him at first. He laid down the law, bossed us about and gave us orders – do this, pick that up, go to bed, wash the dishes, don't play in the street. We resented it because he wasn't our dad. He didn't even look like Dadda B, who we still missed. He was plump, with oiled curls and gold teeth. He wore bright Haitian shirts with hibiscus flowers and red and blue parrots on them and tucked his white trousers into red cowboy boots with white flashes. His shades were the biggest on the block, as big as saucers. Man, he was jazzy!

We paid him back for telling us what to do by playing pranks on him, like putting meat in his shoes so the dogs ran off with them and ate them. The dogs got beat, but they could usually get out of the way. The next thing, he brought his twins, Cassius and Smokey, to live with us, and their elder brother, Isaiah. Ruby, one of his baby-mothers, came to cuss him out, bringing Louis, their fourth child. He was just a toddler, maybe thirteen months, same age as my brother, little Wayan. She stood in the yard hurling abuse at Milton, while we ran and hid behind the trees, listening. Mum joined in – they were just like parrots shrieking in an aviary.

'And you can have this little bastard, as well,' Ruby yelled and stormed off, dumping Louis in the dirt. He sat there, bawling after her, but she kept going.

Mum wasn't bothered. She picked up the tot, stuck him a tin tub and washed him real good. She dressed him in one of Wayan's little T-shirts and fed him. She'd always taken in strays, kids whose parents were no good and beat them or starved them or just plain abandoned them. Kids popped out easily enough from baby-mothers, and the daddies weren't nowhere around. Most of the time, for black boys, making babies was the point – to show they could, that they were men. Looking after kids was women's work.

Jamaican mums loved their sons almost to the point of obsession – and part of that was making sure their sons had big dicks. At a certain age, mothers would take their sons and find a papaya tree – this is why most backyards had one – and they'd pick the boys up and sort of beat their penises against the tree and chant spells and stuff to make them grow. It was a voodoo ritual. Papaya trees possessed spirits that breathed growing power into dicks. A man with a short dick didn't get him a woman. I'd been taught since childhood that the cult of sex was very powerful. It was the reason we existed.

Like many women, Mum took in these abandoned kids. She'd give them baths, clothe them in our clothes, and each morning she'd make a huge pot of porridge and dole it out with a big spoon. She'd say that even if you were broke, you could always find enough for a sack of meal to cook a pot of porridge. The kids came and went – where to, I have no idea. One moment they were there, the next, they'd be gone. Mum also took people in who had nowhere else to stay, even though we had no room. A few weeks after Ruby had turned up and dumped her kids, Mum took Ruby herself in. Louis was happy, back with his mum. Milton was happy – he got two women waiting on him, keeping him warm in bed.

We'd got used to Milton and had fun with him, playing chasing games, asking him silly questions and sitting around on Sundays, eating jerk pork and listening to the grown-ups telling stories and gossiping. He still tried to boss us, but we knew it was all bark without the bite. He lived with us for about four months, then returned to England – he said to make more money, take care of his business. Just after he left there was a knock at the door and another woman stood there with her daughter, who was about my age. The mother's name was Ezola and her daughter was called Sierra. Sierra and I stared at each other and I had this feeling that she was going to be trouble. She had a sly, rather than mischievous, look about her. The first thing that happened was that me and my two brothers had to share Mum's bed, so these two interlopers could share the other bedroom with Ruby and her kids. Mattresses were put on the floor; there was no room to move.

The woman stayed for three weeks and left after a huge fight, leaving Sierra behind. She said she was going to tell the police that Mum was selling weed and Mum punched out her lights, knocking her clean across the yard. The next thing, Mum came home, slamming things and cussing, having been fired from her job. 'That witch told lies about me,' she ranted. 'I been given my marching order.' Sierra smiled slyly behind her hand, as if saying, 'Good.'

I could never say anything, because Mum would never have listened – hospitality was a big thing in Jamaica, because you never knew when you might need a place to stay – but Sierra took the clothes that Mum had put aside for me. We never wore all our clothes – we would keep some for best, and have some to grow into. Sierra just helped herself and I was jealous when I saw her waltzing around in 'my' stuff. It was funny, though, because I actually liked her. Perhaps I saw that her attitude was just a front and she was really unhappy deep down. We became like sisters. Suddenly, after six months, when I had got used to her, Sierra vanished. I missed her. Later, I found out that her mum had come and got her, and locked her up and starved her. She died of gastroenteritis caused by neglect.

At times like that I would think, 'Yes, my mum beats me, and sometimes she acts like she don't love me – but she'd never let me die from hunger and if I was real sick, she'd take me to hospital, even if she had no money.'

There came a time when Mum proved how much she really loved me. It completely changed my outlook on life and made me fiercely loyal to her, whatever she did. There was quite a network of news and gossip between

Jamaica and the rest of the world, to wherever Jamaicans had emigrated. My real dad, Leroy, must have heard on the grapevine that his enemy, Dadda B, was dead, and Mum was without a strong protector. True, she was with Milton – but he was just a casual boyfriend and he had a wife and family. In Leroy's eyes, she was now weak and vulnerable and, for some reason, he decided he wanted me with him in America – and he sent his new woman to Jamaica to get me. Only we didn't know this at the time, or what his real motive was when he sent a message asking me to go to the house where she was staying.

One morning, Mum said, 'Get dressed in your Sunday go-to-church outfit. You goin' see your father's girl-friend. That no-good skunk sent her over from New York with some clothes to give you.'

'My father?' I'd forgotten all about him. The only time I heard his name was when Mum was vexed with me, and said I was ugly, like him. Everything that was wrong with me was down to him and his bad genes, she'd say. I was used to it, but it still hurt.

'Yeah, him.'

As I ran to get ready, I asked, 'How long am I staying with her?'

'Just today – that's all. She'll give you all that stuff he sent, tell you what a genius arsehole your daddy is, and lie 'bout how much money he earnin' in the goddamn United States of America. I'm meeting you off the bus this evening, so don' be late.'

I walked with Mum to the bus stop. She made sure

I had the address pinned to my dress and the return fare in my pocket in case I got lost. It was quite an adventure, travelling across Kingston, and I looked out of the window eagerly, taking in all the sights. I loved the long rows of shops and stalls along the streets, the vibrant music, and people strolling about in the sun, shopping and just hanging out. When I was older, I decided, I would hang out down here and look cool, like I belonged. My Uncle Nathan was doing well with his music and had got his own place to live in Havendale. Riding in the bus, I saw posters of his CDs pinned up in some of the open-fronted stalls where music was sold, and nudged Mum. 'Look! It's Uncle Nathan!'

Mum looked proud. She loved her baby brother. She had stars in her eyes about how he would be discovered worldwide and become as big as Bob Marley and put our family on the map.

Arlette was waiting for the bus, like she promised. She and Mum barely spoke a word and Mum just handed me over. 'Don't be late,' she said to me, before crossing the road to catch the return bus. Arlette was a larger-than-life, dramatic-looking woman in a flamboyant kaftan and high-heeled sandals. Her nails were painted orange, like her lipstick. She looked like trouble, like the kind of woman who got men to start fights in bars over her. She was staying at a house belonging to a member of my father's family. It was a big, white building in a poor district, protected by iron grilles at the doors and windows. It looked a bit like a place where nuns lived and I was curious about going inside.

Arlette had laid out all these clothes for me in a small bedroom. I tried some of the dresses and shorts on, to see if they fitted.

'Your dad called your mum to ask the size, but she wouldn't say,' Arlette explained. It was news to me. Mum hadn't said a word. 'I asked for stuff for a girl your age, but girls your age are all different sizes, some tall, some short, some thin, some fat.'

The clothes were nice and they fitted OK. They were the first things my father had ever bought for me, even though Arlette had chosen them. He'd never sent any money towards my keep, nothing. I couldn't remember what he looked like – though Mum was always telling me that all I had to do was look into the mirror. I was a bit bored and, by the end of the day, looked forward to getting on that bus and going home, where everything was familiar.

'What time is it, are we going to the bus yet?' I kept asking.

'Soon, soon,' Arlette said. 'You wan' to watch some more TV?'

The TV was huge and in glorious colour – but I found it hard to concentrate. I felt things weren't right. When evening came around, while I was eating some ribs and corn on the patio, Arlette said casually, 'Your mum telephoned, she said she doesn't want you no more. She got too many mouths to feed. You goin' to America with me to be with your dad.'

'No!' I screamed. 'She didn't say that. I don't want to live with my dad.'

'Be a good girl now, and do what you're told. What about all them nice things we got you. Aren't you grateful?'

I was very confused. Mum was always saying she would send me to my father if I wasn't good. I searched my mind to see if I had been extra naughty recently. Without Dadda B to help, Mum had to work extra hard to keep us, and she was always tired and grumpy, always yelling that she couldn't afford to keep us and what man wanted a woman with three kids?

I felt terrible and was silent. So my mum didn't want me. It was a lot to accept and I cried myself to sleep in a strange bed.

Early the next morning, I heard banging and shouting at the iron gate in front of the courtyard. I recognised my mum's voice. 'Mum!' I shouted. 'Mum!'

I jumped out of bed, pulled on my clothes, and raced for the front garden. I saw my mum standing at the grille, her face like thunder, arguing with Arlette, who was still in her nightgown. She rattled the bars and yelled that she was going to get the police. 'You think you can come over here, kidnap my daughter? You get hanged in Jamaica for kidnap. You ready to swing for this?'

I can't remember all that was said. Arlette tried to calm Mum down. She let her in, to discuss it, she said. Before she knew what had hit her, Mum punched her in the face and they were brawling in the garden, falling into bushes and flowerbeds. It ended with Arlette staggering back inside, her nose pouring with blood, while

Mum grabbed hold of me and threw me into the waiting taxi. She put an arm around me, and said, 'Nobody steal my daughter – nobody.'

I snuggled into her and thought she was wonderful – the best mum in the world. I was so happy to be going home. I forgot the pain in my life caused by the death of Dadda B and that terrible thing that had happened to me with the gardener.

We had fun that summer. Frankie, our neighbour, kept goats in the back of his pick-up truck. Every Saturday morning he took them swimming in the sea. All of us kids in our yard, me, my brothers, Sierra (before she left) and Ruby's brood, the twins, Cassius and Smokey, and Isaiah – as well as a gang of neighbour kids – would get up at 6 a.m. and hide in the back of the truck with the goats. It was mucky and stinky, but we knew we'd soon be in the waves. When we were on the way, I stood up and chanted, 'Frankie! Frankie!' He stopped the truck, came round the back and told us to hop out and go home.

'We've come too far, Frankie,' I wheedled. 'Oh go on – let us go with you. We love sea!'

'We love sea, we love sea!' the other kids chanted.

It didn't take much to bring him round and we set off again, the goats bleating and frisking their little tails because they could smell the sea and sensed freedom. As soon as we arrived at beach, he let down the tail-gate, unchained the goats and they rushed down, dragging their chains. Then we emerged and ran down while he counted, 'One-two-three-four . . . thirteen.'

'Thirteen of yo brats!' he yelled. 'Where'd yo all come from?'

Laughing, we ran down the beach shouting, 'Frankie – clean up goats – Frankie – go swim –'

While we scrubbed the goats and splashed in the silky, warm waves, Frankie, who couldn't swim, cleaned the bed of the truck and then he went fishing off the rocks. When we tired of swimming, we helped him. The goats wandered off to find shade and some grass by a fresh-water stream that ran across the beach into the sea, and we fished all day. In the evening, as the sun went down, we gathered up driftwood and built a fire in a hole in the sand, to cook lobster and grill fish on sticks. It was a wonderful feast and we were always hungry and then tired.

We came home in the dark, sleepy and happy, carrying fishes and seashells. Mum met us by the yard gate and blocked our paths. 'Where yo comin' from?' she asked, arms on hips.

'We went out with Frankie.'

'Who yo asking?' she demanded. 'When the cock starts crowing, yo up. Paul, yo imagining yo fifteen? And little ones, can't swim, who care 'bout them drownin'? Who you axing? You didn't ax me.'

Paul shuffled in the dirt and hung his head, like he was to blame, but she knew us bigger kids – me, Isaiah, Sierra and the neighbour kids – were the ones who had taken him. We gave her the fishes and beamed, and she said, 'Fish can't buy me.' Then she grabbed hold of us and beat us – and Paul was laughing, watching from a safe distance. 'Yesterday was your day – today it's my day,' he taunted.

Just before I was nine, Uncle Nathan's girlfriend sent down two bikes for Paul and me. Paul's was a shiny blue and mine was red. I adored it. I flew down the Boulevard, pedalling like crazy, shrieking as I hit the potholes. *Wowee!* I was screaming high and excited, like a kettle whistling. *Wowee!*

One day, I was in disgrace. I wasn't allowed out and had to stay in and clean the house, so I let Paul, Isaiah, Cassius and Smokey and some of the neighbouring kids borrow my bike. Enviously, I watched them vanish down the lane, then started to sweep the floor. Mum came home from work and asked, 'Where's Paul?'

Nathan, who was supposed to be watching us, had been idly strumming on his guitar and smoking weed and hadn't noticed that Paul and the others had been gone a long time – six kids riding on two bikes.

'Oh my God, why haven't you been watching them?' Mum shouted at Nathan.

'They'll be OK,' he said.

Just then, here they came, walking home. My red bike was in three pieces.

I started cussing, 'I want my bicycle back like it was!'

The kids walked in through the yard gate into a circle of adults, and got beats from everyone – Mum, Nathan, the aunties, a couple of neighbours who'd heard the row and wanted to join in – they all beat the boys. The boys ran around trying to escape the whacks, then scrambled up into a papaya tree. Thinking they were safe up in the tree, they were all pointing at each other and jabbering like monkeys – he broke Sugar's bike – no he did – the blame passing from one to the other. Mum started stoning them out of the tree and when they fell down, like overripe fruit, they got another beating. I was laughing because they were getting beats – and crying because my bike was wrecked. The boys were muddy from rolling around in the dirt. Mum was fed up with us all. She bathed us in a tin tub of cold water, scrubbing hard until we yelped, and we were sent to bed.

Next morning, Nathan said my bike couldn't be welded, so I got Paul's bike. I rode around grinning smugly – though I really wanted my lovely red bike. Paul was hopping mad and came after me with a knife. He knocked me off the bike and punctured my tyres. I hit him – it was tit for tat. Mum told us to behave and sent us to bed again and went to work. Paul started jumping on the bed, breaking the springs. Auntie was watching us. She said, 'Stop that!' and Paul said, 'Go suck your dad.'

I gasped. I couldn't believe what he'd just said. I said, 'Don't talk to Auntie like that.'

Paul lost his temper and grabbed a cutlass – the same one that Dadda B had used to cut Mum's lip – and came after me. I grabbed a machete and chased him back. The house was getting mashed up, it looked like Hurricane Gilbert had passed by. We lost it completely. It was a real fight, filled with anger and uncontrolled rage. We slashed furniture, hacked at the walls, cut each other. Auntie gave up shrieking at us to stop, and she ran out of the yard to the phone at the bottom of the lane to call Mum.

'You got to get here, get a taxi, come at once!' she screamed so all the neighbours could hear. 'They killing each other!'

When Mum came steaming in like a vampire, suddenly Paul was terrified by what we'd done to each other and the house. He dropped the cutlass on my foot and cut it to the bone. Blood spurted up like a little fountain. I howled with shock and pain, trying to get some licks in with the machete. Mum whacked me with a stick and I dropped the machete. She grabbed me and poured iodine straight onto the cut. My scream split the air like a sharp knife.

'I gonna beat you two till you jelly,' Mum shouted, dragging out the split mattress and the shattered television. I showed her all my cuts, thinking it would stop us being beaten, but the ruined television trumped my wounds and we were beaten so hard we couldn't walk. After a bath, we both got more iodine in all our cuts and lay on the sofa sobbing with rage and pain. Mum was so vexed that she sold Paul's bike.

All this came to an end in the late-summer after I turned nine when Milton sent for Mum and her girlfriend, Yoland, to join him in London. He had got a place for them to stay, and had expanded his business and needed them. Mum came back from the phonecall grinning from ear to ear. For once, she looked happy. 'He's sending us tickets,' she said.

'I don't want to go to England,' I protested. I liked my school now I wasn't bullied, and that summer I'd had so much fun playing in the gully and running wild in the neighbourhood.

'Don't worry, you ain't goin,' Mum said.

I stared at her. 'Who's going to look after us?'

'I got a friend, she said she'd have you and your brothers. It won't be for long,' Mum promised.

'But Mum –'

She glared. 'Don't argue. You want a smack in the mouth? There's plenty of money to be made in England. I can save up. We'll have a better life.'

When it actually came time for Mum to take us to Wilma's – many miles away from our familiar home on Constant Spring – she was sad. At Wilma's shabby little shack, she hugged us and I clung onto her, unable to let go, while my little brothers sobbed. She pushed me away. 'Don't be such a baby. Just do what Wilma tells you. I don't want no bad reports from her. I'll be sending money for your keep.'

With that, she got into the taxi and was gone. We turned around to face our new foster mother. Wilma was a dancer like Mum, and they'd met down the clubs and strip joints. She was getting over the hill and it seemed to have turned her bitter, like Cruella De Vil, the wicked witch from *One Hundred and One Dalmatians* – and what was more, her hair had a wide, snow-white bleached stripe across it, just like Cruella.

'OK, Sugar,' she said, 'let's see how good you are at fixing supper for your brothers.'

That was my initiation into two years of slave labour for Cruella and her kids. Mum had never expected my brothers to do anything – most Jamaican women treated their boys like little princes – but Cruella used me and Paul like servants. My baby brother, Wayan, was little – not even two years old – and couldn't do much. I tried to spare him and was always standing up for him when Cruella bawled him out. Like Cinderella, I had to sweep, and wash dishes, and cook, and scrub our clothes. There was no washing machine – just a cold tap in the cramped yard. Meanwhile, Mum was sending money for our keep as she promised, but Cruella was spending this on paying someone to do her laundry and on clothes for herself and her kids. Her two sons were bigger than my brothers, and bullied them at every turn, so I was always trying to protect them.

I worked the street, begging or stealing money and food. I learned to run like the wind, clutching a bit of salt cod, a yam or some bread I'd grabbed from a stall. I'd seen street kids my age giving blowjobs to pervy tourists, but it wasn't safe. Lots of them were found down wells with their throats slit, or floating in on the morning tide, their toes nibbled by crabs and starfish in their dead eyes. We'd watch the police take them away and I'd be sad that was all the life they'd known.

My brothers missed Mum and cried themselves to sleep at night and, often, one or both of them would soil themselves.

'Goddamn!' Cruella the Terrible shrieked when she came home and smelled the stench. 'Get that boy cleaned up.'

She'd drag me out of bed and shove us outside in the dark. I was always terrified of rats and evil spirits that roamed after midnight, but I'd have to turn on the cold tap, stick Paul or Wayan under the gushing water, and wash them down. Then I'd have to wash their clothes and bedding and put it on the line. In the inky darkness, I'd stumble over stones and thorns in my bare feet. When we got back inside, shivering with night cold and fear, my brothers couldn't get back to sleep. They'd lie there, grizzling and shaking, and Cruella would waken and beat the crap out of us.

In the morning, I had to cook a pot of porridge, wash the dishes and get the kids dressed and to school, while *she* slept. If I let them make too much noise, and she woke, all hell broke loose as, bleary-eyed and hung-over, she charged at me, arms flailing and teeth flashing like an angry crocodile.

I came home from school later than my brothers because they were in a baby class. One day, I found Cruella beating Paul, yelling he was a devil. There was a spoiled black American boy in his class, who was stuffed with sweets by his indulgent parents. We all knew that too much sugar in the blood attracted mosquitoes and this boy was bitten to bits. But Cruella decided my brother was possessed by an evil spirit and had put a curse on the American boy. She was into voodoo and knew a curse when she saw one, she said. First she beat

69

him half to death with a belt to weaken the spirit that possessed him, then she chucked the ashes of burned charms around, things like a cock's comb, lizards and snakes and feathers and herbs mixed with blood. In the middle of her dancing and gourd-rattling, Paul picked up some big stones from the yard, threw them at her and ran off.

I was horrified. He was dead meat, for sure. We didn't know where he'd gone and I didn't know where to look. I was desperate. Mum telephoned to ask how we were and I couldn't tell her because Cruella always guarded the phone. If we let anything slip, we got huge beats with belts and sticks. 'I'm all right, Mum,' I said.

'Let me talk to Paul,' she said.

'He's out playing with his friends,' I lied.

'Did Wilma buy you new clothes with the money I sent?'

'Yes,' I lied again. 'They're lovely, thanks, Mum.'

Mum said, 'Are you sure you're OK? You don' sound right. Let me talk to Wilma.'

'I'm fine. I miss you, Mum,' I said, forcing happiness in my voice.

I handed the phone over to the witch. It was always the same. Cruella talking like syrup was dripping off her tongue and assuring Mum that we were dressed like royalty and eating like we lived in the Ritz. 'Yeah, white shirts an' shorts, and I got her a pretty white frock with a 'broidery frill and pink ribbon jis perfec'. An' after church, I cooked them a big mess of salt cod and ackee with roast yams,' she gushed. 'They ate until they was stuffed. And then we went down road, nice little Sunday perambulation in their new go-church clothes, and I got them ice-creams.' She always ended with simpering demands for more and more cash.

As soon as she hung up, her clunking fist would bash straight in my face and I'd fly backwards across the room.

Paul turned up with our Uncle Nathan after three days. He'd been staying there, but Nathan couldn't look after kids. He talked seriously to Cruella and told her that he didn't care about her voodoo curses, he knew more powerful ones. She'd better treat us good or she'd have a thorn tree growing up her ass and out her eyes.

He must have called Mum about how we were really being treated, because suddenly, a week later, there was Nathan, handing over some cash into my hand. Mum had sent it to buy me a new suitcase. 'I'm getting you a passport, and your mum's sending you a ticket,' he said.

'Brats goin' England?' Cruella said, her mouth dropping open. She could see her meal ticket vanishing.

'Only Sugar's goin' to go,' Nathan said. 'You got to keep the two boys until she sends for them. But you better treat them right. I've got my eye on you.'

'I treat them like they my own kids,' she said. 'Better. Like they was royalty.'

Nathan laughed in her face, but I was walking on air. I'd soon see my mum!

It was a while before my passport and the aeroplane ticket came, but now that Cruella knew I was going, she acted better towards me because she knew I would tell Mum everything, and she was scared of Mum's connections. Time passed so slowly and I was sure something would happen to stop me leaving. I almost couldn't bear it. In August, when it was unbearably hot, Auntie Georgia and Uncle Nathan came for me. I was so happy to see them because it meant I was leaving the hell of living under Cruella's tender care.

But I cried when it came time to say goodbye to my brothers. I grabbed them and sobbed into their hair. 'Take care, babies, Mum will send for you soon and we'll all be together.'

'Come on, Sugar, you'll miss that damn' plane,' Auntie said. 'You said goodbye to Wilma yet?'

'Goodbye, Wilma and thanks for looking after me,' I gabbled insincerely, hate in my heart. I gave my brothers one last hug. 'Wilma will take care of you,' I told them, squeezing hard. They ducked their heads miserably, tears oozing from their eyes. 'Look after my brothers,' I said, looking directly at the witch. I wanted to kick her in the shins. I wanted her to die. But she knew voodoo curses and I was scared she could read my mind and would lay something bad on me or my brothers.

'You take care now, Sugar,' she said. 'Tell you mum how good I was to you three kids. Tell her you bros need some new clothes. They growin' so fast nothing fits no more.'

I dropped my eyes so she wouldn't see the hate. Mum had sent boxes of clothes and she had taken them and put them on her own kids' backs. Some she had sold.

We were still squeezed into the clothes Mum had left us with – and in my brothers' case, they had grown out of them and looked like clowns.

'Well, let's go,' Auntie said.

The sights, pungent smells and lush colours were so familiar to me as we drove away that I didn't pause to wonder if this was the last time I would see my homeland. What about my brothers – would I ever see them again? I stared out of the taxi at the crowded streets, the stalls and the wide boulevards with the big houses of the rich behind security walls. I was filled with excitement because, finally, I was going to see my mum again. The airport seemed huge and noisy and I started to get butterflies. It seemed ages before it was time to board because we'd got there so early. I stood in the glass windows, watching planes take off, wondering how they stayed up – they seemed so big and heavy. I got hungry because I'd had no breakfast, and clutched my stomach. 'You want something to eat?' Auntie said.

I shook my head. 'No, I'm not hungry,' I lied.

'Yes you are,' Auntie decided. 'I can tell you could eat a beef patty.' I licked my lips. I *loved* beef patties!

In the cafeteria, while I ate my beef patty slowly, so it would last, and sipped cola, Auntie fished in her handbag and got out an envelope. 'Yo' mum sent this.' The envelope contained a photograph, which she handed to me. 'That's yo' auntie in England. You goin' to stay with her and she'll meet you off the plane.'

I didn't know I had an auntie in England, and nodded

dumbly, staring at the photo. What about my mum – wasn't I going to be staying with her? I was too scared to ask. 'Her name's Auntie Ellie Jordan,' Auntie Georgia added.

'Like the river?' I said.

'Yes honey, jus' like the river. Now, you got to remember her name and address, 'cause they'll ax you where you goin' be staying, OK?' She read out the address and made me repeat it over and over until she was satisfied I would remember it.

'Why can't I write it down?' I asked. I was in terror that if I forgot the details, I would be lost for ever somewhere in England.

'Cause you can't. Jis remember it. Yo's a clever girl, you won't forget.'

The tannoy announced my plane, and we all got up, then it was rush, rush, rush. Uncle Nathan had bought me a couple of comics and some sweets and he handed them over. 'For a good girl,' he said, and I suddenly clutched him. I was terrified. Travelling so far across the sea was alarming. Why wasn't I going to stay with my mum? I'd heard of aunties in England who bought slaves to work for them. Suppose this Auntie Ellie Jordan turned out worse than Cruella?

'Where my mum?' I whispered and Nathan whispered back, 'She there – just don't mention it to no one, OK?' I nodded, drawing in a great breath in relief. But why this mystery?

'Now, be a good girl on the plane and do what this air steward tells you,' Auntie said, handing me over to a tall man at the gate in a white shirt and a tie patterned with red, white and blue flowers.

He smiled. 'Come along, madam,' he said. I giggled, suddenly feeling excited and gaining confidence. It made me feel very grand. I was going on a plane! I was flying to London! And in my heart, I trusted Uncle Nathan. He had never lied to me in my life – he was my hero.

One of the air stewardesses, in a pretty pink suit, took me to a seat near the window and strapped me in. It was my first time on a plane and I didn't know what to expect. I was scared when we started to take off and closed my eyes tightly. When the sign saying 'airborne' came on, everyone clapped. I looked around. They were all beaming, the women dressed in their best, the men in flash suits. It felt like we was going to Carnival. I joined in the clapping and rich laughter. I was on my way.

Chapter 4

London, 1997

After a long, boring journey, where I've seen nothing out of the window but clouds, the plane banks sideways, into rain. The land looks curved and I feel scared and shocked, sure we're about to crash. I've got no sense of perspective and it looks too small down there to land, let alone live. Then everything gets bigger and bigger and bigger. It's enormous! The nice stewardess tells me to wait on the plane until she can escort me out through customs and immigration to the main hall, where people are milling around to be connected to family and friends. So many white people! I've never seen so many in one place, not even when the cruise ships come in to Kingston. They look pale and cold, like spooks. Then we're walking quickly through the official areas, and nobody asks me nothing. A white man in a dark uniform flicks through my passport and smiles. I fix my gaze on his hair, yellow like a butterfly wing. 'Good morning, Miss Jones. Welcome to England.' Miss Jones – that's me!

I clutch the photo of 'Auntie Ellie Jordan' and my

eyes seem to spin in my head as I look in every direction for her. Is she here? What if she's not? Where will I go? It's all cold glass, reflecting grey skies overhead and shiny grey floors. It's May, springtime in England and freezing. I'm wearing just a thin cotton dress. My bones seem to rattle and snap with cold and my smooth brown skin goes dark and goosebumpy with shock. I'm like a plucked chicken. Then Auntie Ellie's there, loudly saying, 'Well, Sugar, sweetheart, let me look at you! How you grown!'

I've definitely never met her before. Never. I squeak, like a frog's in my throat, 'Where my mum?'

She ignores my question, and repeats, like she's known me for years, 'Yeah, girlie, you sure have grown! Now you all fixed, got you luggage an' stuff?'

The handover is made, and I walk across the concourse with a total stranger, who's dragging my small case on wheels, while I lug a heavy holdall that Auntie Georgia had given me, filled with special Jamaican food for my mum, to remind her of home. We go out into the cold, grey day and for the first time I feel bitter cold wind whip around my bare legs. It's like a black-and-white TV's been switched on. Where's the colour gone? Everything looks flat and dead.

The car park's an echoing dungeon.

Then suddenly, I see my mum, in a spotted fake-fur jacket, climbing out of a big silver car, with shark fins and lots of glittering chrome. She looks very rich – never worn a fur coat before. She's plumper, but lighter-skinned. At the time I didn't know that the sun tans black people and makes them darker. There doesn't seem much sun in England and she's grown pale, like a plant kept out of the light. But she smiles like a sunbeam and holds out her arms to me. I run to her, hobbling sideways like a crab, weighed down on one side by the heavy bag.

'Mum! Mum! You here!'

'Of course I'm here. Hey, Sugar baby, let's have a look at you. You grown, girl.' Why do adults dwell so much on size and height? I drop the bag on the concrete floor and clutch her, breathing in her musky scent, her warmth. I feel I can never let her go. I want to tell her so much, about how Wilma was so cruel, how she beat us and stole our clothes that Mum sent, how we were always hungry, how worried I am about leaving my brothers there – a hundred things.

But she's talking excitedly and Milton gets out of the other side and says, 'The girl bring that stuff OK?' Then he sees my big bag and grabs it quickly, like it's got diamonds and pearls inside, 'stead of jerk beef and chipotle relish. He stows my luggage away, and I get into the back with Mum and Auntie Ellie, and Milton gets in the front, like he's a chauffeur, and we're off. I sit in the back and hug and hug Mum like she might vanish, like I'm dreaming. I love her so much. Nobody ever wears fur coats in Jamaica, but you need one here. I wonder if I dare ask for one for my birthday, coming up June, month away, a nice little fluffy white one.

Milton has the heat on full blast. The motion of the car, tons of traffic, long streets of red-brick houses and blocks of flats on the long drive across London lull me to sleep. Mum shakes me awake when we arrive and for a moment I'm disoriented. Where am I? Then I see Mum and grin, a big happy smile. We're together!

Big eyes wide, I look around as I get out the car. Rain falls and wind still howls, but Mum say it's just a bad day, tomorrow sunshine. She points out the trees up and down each side of the road. 'A few weeks ago, they branches bare and brown, no leaves, no flowers. See how they pretty now?'

'Where they go – did hurricane blow 'em off?' I say.

'Course not,' she laughs. 'Winter comes, too cold, all ice like freezer. Leaves don't like it, they get sick and die. Old ones fall, but new leaves come in spring.'

'Mum, where the birds?' I ask. All the way in the car, through the noise and rush of the traffic, I've watched and listened out for familiar birds, but saw only big wet pigeons, pecking on sidewalks like crouching vultures. No pretty bananaquits drinking nectar from flowers, no hovering doctor bird, long tails streaming behind, no squawk-squawk of parrots. London's mostly concrete and brick, my mum says. No flowers, no sugar cane, no palm trees, no fruit trees – no birds, no butter-flies. 'You'll get used to it,' she says. 'This London. It's a big city.'

I feel I'll never get used to it – it's scary. I want to go home – but where's home? Cruella's not home. I want Dadda B back, I want the fun we used to have in the gully.

Mum says, 'This your new home, where we living now.' She points at a modern block of flats. We're in a leafy street in Streatham, far side of London. The street is opposite a big park Mum calls a 'common', all grass and trees, wet under drenching rain, like a waterfall. Houses made of red bricks and big apartment blocks are crammed side by side. Bricks piled on bricks. There are no tar-paper shacks, no cement boxes, no dirt yards, no mango trees, ripe with yellow fruit. We go into the flats and Milton presses for the lift to come. A steel door slides open on a box with bright lights. I've never been in a lift. I'm scared witless, revert to a baby.

'No, no, no!' I shout. 'Ain't going in there!'

'Don't be silly, girl,' Mum says. 'See, shoot up, shoot down, like magic. I'll hold your hand.'

I grab her hand tight, stand in the metal box. It shoots up and my belly hits the floor. Then it stops. I get out.

'See,' Mum says, 'it safe. You OK, honey.'

Mum and Milton share the flat with Auntie Ellie, who isn't my real auntie at all, and her two sons. It's Ellie's flat, which she rents furnished from the landlord. There's a brown fitted carpet with modern furniture and two red sofabeds Mum says are called put-you-ups. *Put-you-up, put-you-up!* I chant, bouncing on one.

'Where it put you up, Mum?' I ask.

She says, frowning, 'You axing too many questions.'

The room smells of lemons. 'Where the lemons?' I ask.

'It's Johnson Pride furniture polish,' my mum says, showing me the can. Everything's shiny and clean. I love the cream curtains because they have posh gold tiebacks. It's pure luxury. I've never been this high, on the same level as the tops of the wet trees before, like a bird. Milton leaves to take care of business and Mum and I talk for a long time. I tell her all about how wicked Wilma is and how she beat us and made me wash clothes and do all the cooking and washing dishes and sweeping floors.

Mum shakes her head. 'I'm sorry, babe, but I had no choice. I had to come here to make a better life for you. You understand, don' you?'

I nod. 'I s'pose. But, Mum, I didn't like to leave Paul and Wayan with her. They very sad now. They think they been abandoned.'

Mum sighs and says, 'I gotta work hard, raise the money and soon as I do, I'll send for them, jus' like I did you. You here, ain't you, Sugar? I kept my word, yeah?'

'Yeah,' I say, kissing her hands. 'And Mum, don't say nothing to Wilma 'bout what I sayin'. She'll punish my brothers even worse.'

Mum says, 'No, I won't say. Why didn't you say when I telephone what she up to?'

'She there all the time, listening. And she read our letters and tear 'em up if we said anything bad about her – then she give us big beats with a stick. One time, she hit Wayan across the head with a skillet to shut him up, split skin and bone. We call her Cruella. She's a mean bitch. I hate her.'

Mum balls up her fists and says she gonna get back to Jamaica and kill her. But meanwhile, she has to get ready because she and Ellie going West End, earn money.

She says, 'Why don't you have a nap? You must be tired, honey.'

I watch as she puts on a short white skirt and blouse and hangs big chunky gold chains around her throat and big gold hoops through her ears. Red lipstick. She looks really hot and sassy. She picks up her bag and she and Ellie clatter off in white high-heel slingbacks. I undress quickly and get into Mum's bed, pulling the quilt right over my head because I'm so cold.

Sometime in the night, Milton moves me out of the bed so he can sleep. I wake on a put-you-up in the living room when Mum and Ellie return. They're chatting as they make coffee. Milton comes out of the bedroom, scratching and yawning. 'OK, girls?' he says. Through the hatch I hear Mum tell him the cops took their names and they have to stay out of town for a while.

'OK, you can work on Streatham Common,' Milton says. 'Plenty of working girls there. And how about working out of the flat?'

'No way!' Ellie says quickly. 'We can't bring punters back here. I'll get thrown out if neighbours complain. They always looking for a reason to get at me – they all racists.'

Milton laughs because all the neighbours in this block of flats are black. Most are Africans – don't matter where from, Nigeria, Congo, wherever, they're all the same, my mum says. They all no good. Milton says, yeah, he hates them. He tells me not to look at them, keep my eyes down, don' make eye contact. I soon learn that Africans and West Indians don't get on, but nobody tells me why. Then I learn that Milton's a drug dealer and a pimp. Mum calls him 'pimp first class' – and she laughs, mouth open, showing her gold teeth. She think it's funny. Mum and Ellie, they're prostitutes at night; daytime they help Milton sell drugs in Brixton. It's called working 'on street' or 'on road'. At night, Milton stays with us kids while the women go to work.

I hated Milton in Jamaica when he first came to live with us, but then he bought food and gave us toys and clothes and played with us kids, and I thought he was OK. In London I hate him again because I see how he makes my mum's life hell. He makes her and Ellie work hard, but he brings women home and screws them in the big bed when Mum's out all night working her ass off. He don't care if she comes in tired and finds other women snoring on her pillow.

Most of all, I hate his number-one girlfriend. Her name's Vondra. He calls her his sex bitch. He and Mum are always arguing over her and they end up fighting. A man shouldn't be hitting a woman, but he does. He punches her in her head, in her tits, in her belly – it don't matter where. She's always bruised, with a bloody nose or split lip – but she punches him back real hard, so I guess it's equal. She's always shouting at him about neglecting his kids. He's got four sons and Mum makes him spend time with them and give them money. *Yeah yeah yeah*, he says to make her shut up. *Stop nagging me, woman.*

He also likes spending money on me. While Mum

sleeps in after busy Friday nights (men get paid Friday nights, they've got money to burn, she says), Milton takes me shopping Saturday mornings and buys me lunch in McDonald's or Kentucky Fried. The shops are stuffed full of clothes and toys, like it's Christmas every day.

'What you want?' he says. I can choose anything I want. I want Milton and Mum to stop fighting, but I don't say it.

Mum never had much in her life, which is why she fights for everything. It's like her brain's been reprogrammed into one of those fighting dogs who feel no pain and keep going till they die. Fighting's the only way she knows to survive. If she wasn't a scrapper she wouldn't be alive now, but it's not good for a kid to be around someone like her. You just get programmed into being a fighting dog, too.

Most of the summer, I'm bored, just hanging around watching TV. Sometimes I play with Ellie's sons, but they're older than me and go to school. I've got no friends, nothing to do. I don't complain because I know I'll just get beats.

'Don't bother me,' Mum says. 'Can't you see I'm busy?'

I ask, 'Can I go school?'

Mum says it's not worth going for just a few weeks. Summer holidays will soon come and I can go after.

It's my eleventh birthday at the end of June. Mum and Ellie take me to the West End, to the Trocadero in Piccadilly. They let me go on rides in Funland. I tell

Mum my brothers would love Funland – when are they coming?

She says, 'Soon, they come soon.'

'When, when, when?' I ask.

'Stop nagging, you like whining kid, not big girl turned eleven,' she says.

Soon, Milton sees a good way of using me. I'm small for my age and I look younger he says. He says I'm perfect for a street mule and lookout because I can't be arrested. Police will ignore me, no point in picking me up, because they have to let me go. 'Just tell them you're nine years old if you're picked up,' he says, 'and don't give your name and address. If they do pick you up, with no name or address they'll put you in care, but it's easy to walk out and run away, back here.' He laughs loudly, like it's a big joke.

We go down Brixton. I love it there – it's like the bazaar in Jamaica, hot, crowded, dirty, with street stalls filled with West Indian fruit and vegetables, like yams and breadfruit and ripe, golden mangoes. There are piles of salt cod and flying fish, squid and barracuda, pigs' trotters and tails, goats' meat, dried figs, spices and herbs. It smells delicious, but makes me feel homesick.

Milton gives me lots of baggies to hold for him in a shopping bag and shows me where to stand. 'Walk up and down,' he says. 'Look as if you're waiting for your dad or mum. If anyone talks to you, ignore them – or say your dad just coming.' He says when he's sold the small stash he's got on him, he'll come and get more from me. If he has too much and the police arrest him, he can be sent to jail for a long time. He says he'll give me the money to hold. We pile some fruit on the top of the shopping bag, so it looks like regular shopping. 'Hang on to it, don't let anyone rob you. Brixton is full of tiefs,' he notes, wagging his finger in my face. He wears heavy gold rings and a solid gold watch. Diamonds flash around the face and it has an expanding gold strap. I heard Ellie sneer that the rings are fake and the watch a cheap counterfeit, but they look good to me.

Each day we catch the bus down Streatham Hill into Brixton centre, or Milton picks us up in his big silver Pontiac if he spent the night somewhere else. Sometimes the market's so crowded it's hard to find anywhere to park. Milton grumbles and squeezes the Pontiac into a space in a side street some distance away and we walk along the dusty pavements of Electric Avenue to the rambling open market behind the High Street. Electric Avenue itself is a bazaar. Lots of little shops along the way blast rap, hip-hop and ragga, and I skip along to the beat. Sometimes, I hear my Uncle Nathan's voice on dancehall CDs coming out of shop doorways and stop dead. *That my uncle!* I want to shout. *That my boy Nathan! Listen, listen!* Some day he said he'd take me New York. I wish he'd do it soon. I love my Uncle Nathan.

The market people begin to recognise me, the little girl dancing in the sun. 'Hey Sugar – you sure got riddim! Watch that girl go! You wan' iced popsicle, you wan' slice of watermelon, you wan' sarsaparilla drink?'

The shops sell everything from wigs to voodoo, old vinyl and new CDs, sandals and saris, flash suits and cheap furniture. It's a cool place to be. At the end of the day, all my baggies are gone and the shopping bag weighs heavy. We go back to the flat, where it's my job to count the money. Most of it is in coins, fifty-pence pieces or pounds. Milton jokes that it looks like it all come from parking meters or fruit machines. One day, I count out £700 all in pound coins. I have to put it into little bank bags, though they never take any of it to a bank. I make stacks of the paper money, little packets of four twenties, with one folded over to make £100. Then tens and fives. I sit on Mum's bedroom carpet, leaning up against her bed and arrange it all in front of me, like a wall. The bed is covered with a gold sateen counterpane that hangs down with a pleated frill all around and I push money out of sight behind me under the bed, like I'm doing nothing.

Milton never notices. I hate him and nick more and more. One day after I've been his mule for a couple of weeks, I sneak £300. It's more than I know what to do with and I have to spend it fast because I've got nowhere to hide it. Some days I go to the Trocadero in Piccadilly, where I had fun on my birthday. I splurge the money on rides in Funland, gorge my face on fried chicken and burrito wraps, watch a film and then hop on a bus home. Funny thing, my mum is working the streets in the West End, maybe yards away around Piccadilly and Soho, perhaps working all night to earn the same amount that I just threw away. But I can't go to her, give her

£300 and say, 'Here Mum, don't do this – go home with me. I'll give you Milton's drug money instead.' No, I can't do that because she'd kill me – then Milton will kill me and I'm mincemeat.

In July, Mum falls out with Milton and she grabs a ton of money from his stash and we move into a four-bedroom house a couple of miles away. Mum say he'll never find us there. She can't apply for benefits or for council housing because we're illegal immigrants and she's scared of being sent back to Jamaica. She decides to regulate her life. That's how she puts it, 'I gonna regulate my life and get me an education.' She says she's had too many close calls with police and she's damned sure if she's arrested one more time she'll be deported. She uses her friend's birth certificate and goes along to a community college in Lambeth and registers for a course in care work. They help her get a job as a care assistant in an old people's home. It's hard work and she makes very little money, but she thinks it will help her to be legal, go mainstream.

Life's one big struggle. She can't give me spending money and I'm bored, staying indoors, watching TV all day. She falls behind with the rent and she needs another £600 to pay her fees at the college – so she calls Milton on her mobile phone, talking dirty. She tells him where we're living and he comes screaming in his silver Pontiac, chromed grill glittering in the sun like shark's teeth. She's clever – she knows they're like a drug to each other. They get back together and he puts her back working on the street so we can live, buy food, pay rent. He's got another girlfriend, but most nights he sleeps over at our house and leaves his clothes and bags of drugs in Mum's room, his crates of beer in the hall.

I can't wait until I start school in September. Every day I ask, when am I going, when, when? When Mum takes me shopping for my new navy blue uniform, I tell everyone, 'I going to school!' Then I worry. I say, 'Mum you tell me we gotta be careful, we're illegal immigrants. Will they let me go to school?'

She says, 'Yeah, it the law, every kid gotta go school, don' matter where they come from, who they are.'

But just in case there's questions, she gets me into the school system with fake papers. Our culture in south London is very fluid, like clouds changing shape, so it's hard for the authorities to pin things down, especially with kids. But I worry and worry that it might not happen until I'm in my new uniform and on the bus with Mum, going to school at 8.15 a.m., 4 September. She buys me a mobile phone so I can call her when I'm on my way home and she'll meet me off the bus in the evening. Even though I've worked the street as a drug dealer's lookout and I've got loads of common sense, she still worries that something might happen to me. She tells me to be careful 'bout what I say, but I barely listen. When we reach my new school I'm through the gate like a little fish rushing into a big pond.

I'm so happy to be in school – I love it! I love the smell of the freshly varnished floors, and the rooms crammed with desks. It's enormous, so big I get lost inside, but soon I learn all the rooms and names of my teachers. It's the same for the other girls in my class – everything is strange and scary. They have come up from their junior schools with small classes and old friends. Teachers say the first year is always confusing and we're all in the same boat. Most of the girls are black or brown and there are lots of mixed-race girls. The white girls sit at the front, like a barrier. We stick to our own kind and that way avoid fights. Sometimes there's a big fight going on in the playground and the teachers sort it out pretty quick.

Everything's going fine in school and I'm soaking up lessons like blotting paper. I was worried I'd be behind, but so many languages are spoken, so many girls are refugees, some have never been to school, and – teachers say – the standard's so high in Jamaica, I'm ahead, near the top of the class. I bloom and blossom, like a flower in the sun. My school takes girls from a wide area in south-east London, so I don't make friends in my street to hang out with in the evenings or at weekends, but after the first week, I have a couple of good friends in school, Jamaican girls like me. Soon we're thick as thieves, going around the playground, arms twined, telling our secrets, making jokes. They've been here an age, they're proper Brits, so they tell me things I need to know about surviving in a white country. But we've all got family back home in Jamaica and they've been heaps of times, so they know what I'm talking about. My memories are the freshest, so I've got plenty to share.

The following month, October, is an Indian summer,

every day is hot. Skies are bright blue, bright sun, golden leaves. But at night, the city streets are humid and the houses like saunas. Mum falls downstairs and breaks her foot. She goes to hospital and comes home with a cast up to her knee. She's cursing and swearing, hopping around on one foot indoors, hanging onto the walls. She can't go work and is angry all the time because money's in short supply again. After school I help with her bath and clean up after her. I shop and clean and cook before doing my homework, no problem, but she's so irritable I can't stand it – why does she yell at me? I try to help her.

One evening, I've just helped bath her and she's still in the bathroom, getting dressed. Around the house she doesn't bother to wear much, just a loose T-shirt and a G-string. I'm cooking our evening meal when the doorbell buzzes. Mum leans out of the bathroom window and sees her old enemy, Milton's girlfriend Vondra, staring up at her. Mum hates her.

She yells, 'Monkey!'

I'm on my way from the kitchen to see what's going on, when Mum comes hobbling fast down the stairs, an evil grin pinned to her face, like she means business.

'I'll get it,' she says.

Milton keeps his Heineken beer at the foot of the stairs, by the front door. There's full crates, and crates of empties piled up. When Mum reaches the foot of the stairs she grabs an empty bottle and twists the elastic of her G-string around the neck, then another. She does this quickly and expertly, like she's done it many times before. In a few seconds she has six bottles hanging around her hips like grenades. She pulls down her baggy T-shirt so you can't see them, and opens the door.

'Yeah?' she says, arrogantly.

Vondra – who's in her twenties – sticks her big tits into Mum's face like they're the status symbol of her sexiness and fertility and launches straight in. 'Hey, old woman, Milton's my man now, I got his baby in my belly. You too old and shrivelled. He don't wan' you no more.'

I clap my eyes on Vondra's belly. You can see a bulge. She's pregnant all right, maybe five or six months.

'Is that right?' Mum says, and with a smooth movement, she has that long-neck greenie out from under her T-shirt and *whack!* It comes down on the enemy's head. Another bottle, another crack.

Vondra reels, then rallies. She leaps forward, arms outstretched, making like claws. A lethal machine, Mum rains blows down on her – *Crack! Crack! Crack!* Blood flows down Vondra's face, in her eyes, drips onto her low-cut top and those big tits.

By now she's shrieking like a tree full of parrots and Mum's yelling back right in her face. 'Bitch! Whore! Monkey! I hope he give yo clap. I bet yo got syphilis and crabs. Git back in yo cage where yo belong!'

Mrs Ababanjo, the African woman next door, comes running out with her camcorder to film it. 'Ah, my friend,' she says to Mum. 'Are you OK?'

'I'm fine,' Mum says, 'but she ain't. Get off my steps, you bit of trash.'

Mum shoves her hard, right in her fake tits. Vondra falls backwards onto the pavement.

'My baby!' she shrieks. 'You kilt my baby!'

Someone has called Milton, and he comes screaming up in his shark car. He double-parks it with a squeal of brakes, the rear sticking out at an angle into the street. He leaps out and charges along the pavement. Mum punches the air triumphantly. 'Take yo' whore and get going, you shit-faced nigga. We don' wan' trash like you round here.'

'Lulu! What yo done? Yo kilt her,' he yells. He leans over Vondra. 'You OK, honey?'

'She's just fine,' Mum sneers. 'That ho' ain't got any brains – it jis solid bone.'

Milton hauls Vondra to her feet and practically throws her into his car like a sack. He jumps in after her and, as he screeches off, with deadly aim – learned as a child in Jamaica, when she'd pitch sticks at mangoes to get them out of the trees – Mum hurls a brick she keeps on the doorstep for such emergencies. It smashes through his rear window – but Milton keeps going.

Deep inside, Mum is scared of him and knows he might come back and hurt her. She packs up quick and moves us again, this time to a flat closer to my school. It's perfect. I have Mum to myself, I start to make more friends and feel settled at last. The weeks and months seem to pass as if they will last for ever. Sometimes I wake up and think of all I've done since leaving Jamaica and I can't believe it's been six or seven months. Time is elastic. I'm still only eleven. Maybe this is what happens when you're young and have so many new experiences.

Mum works hard and saves money and borrows more so she can keep her promise to my brothers. She sends them their tickets and they come over in December, in time for Christmas. Ellie steps into the breach again as their official sponsor and auntie and, for some reason beyond me, Mum asks Milton to go to the airport with us. I think it's a huge mistake – but she seems to need him. They get back together again.

It's freezing when we go to Heathrow Airport. I remember very clearly how cold I'd been back in May when I flew in, and I know how cold my brothers will be when they step off that plane and walk out the door of the airport. Mum buys two fat Puffa jackets for them and she sits in the car, holding them like they're talismen. We seem to sit for ever in the car park, sick with worry, while Ellie goes inside. I want to go with her, but Mum says we have to keep out of the way in case we're picked up by the police.

'This system works,' she say. 'We gotta just wait.'

Time passes and I want to pee. Mum says I have to hold on in case I get lost. Milton has the radio on and he seems content to do nothing, but Mum is edgy and restless and keeps getting out of the car and walking around. When my brothers come into sight with Ellie, we jump out of the car and Mum runs to them with the Puffas and puts them on. She fusses over them, patting them on their faces, kissing them. My brothers stand still, being zipped up, like they're shell-shocked.

'What's up, devil got yo' tongue?' Mum asks.

I know how they feel. The long flight, the grim skies over London after the bright blue of the skies over Jamaica, the bleak, windswept surroundings had terrified me seven long months ago.

'They're tired,' I say. I give them a big hug. 'You OK?' I ask. They look skinny and exhausted.

They nod silently, then Wayan says, 'You Sugar?'

'Yeah, sure I'm Sugar.'

He's almost four now, a pretty boy with round face and big eyes. Paul is nearly eight. Me, I'll be twelve next birthday. Mum pinches Paul's cheek. 'Yo losing yo' puppy fat, skinny boy.'

I know they're both so thin because Wilma has been starving them, like she starved me, but Mum don't want to hear it – it makes her angry. I'm so excited I can't sit still and finally Mum lets me run off to the toilets at the back of the car park. Then we cram tightly together in the back of the car, me pointing out everything like I'm a tour guide. River Thames, Houses of Parliament, Battersea Bridge. I gabble fast. I say we're planning a great Christmas, with lots to eat and presents. We're going to the Trocadero, do all the rides and see movies and eat Kentucky Fried Chicken and Chinese. We gonna look at the lights in Regent Street and Piccadilly. I'm jumping up and down and telling them this, arms waving like a windmill.

'Sugar, if yo don' sit still I'm goin' throw yo ass out the car,' Mum says. She has her arms around Paul and

Wayan, like she can't let go. 'I said I'd get you and I did,' she says to them, like she's just got gold in the Olympics. But Paul and Wayan are asleep. I keep looking at them, can't believe they're here and we're a family again.

Chapter 5

London, 1998

January. It's the coldest weather in ten years, according to the television news. We think it's colder than the North Pole. When it snows we almost die with shock, it's like nothing we've ever seen or imagined. We know ice, from cold drinks in Jamaica, but not like this. My brothers run around, trying to catch it, saying it's incredible – where's the big freezer in the sky that makes this happen?

Mum registers them at school in Peckham. Paul goes to junior school and Wayan goes to infants. She buys their uniform, says three kids to feed and clothe gonna bankrupt her. She takes them to school on the bus, like she took me when I first started. The boys cry with cold as they wait for the bus. Sometimes, like when it's really cold or raining, or Mum has to go to work early, Milton takes them in his car. I have been to Peckham to shop and know it a bit. It's like Brixton, with lots of different races and there's a huge covered market with things from Africa, the Caribbean, India, China – from all over the world. It's a dangerous place, with gangs from Nigeria clashing with Somalians, Turks and Bosnians, and Mum worries the boys gonna get hurt. Apart from that, as spring gives way to summer, they settle in well and when Milton falls out with Vondra and moves back in with us full time, we're like a regular fighting family.

I turn twelve. I get off the bus one evening after school with my friend Rashona, a tall, thin, mixed-race girl with pale skin, green-speckled eyes and wild, rust-coloured hair. She's coming to my house to do a project with me and we're walking along, talking and laughing, when we see a man and woman slugging it out up ahead. She's got a red wig and those tight pink sateen capri pants like my mum wears. I start to get a sinking feeling. He grabs her wig and throws it into the gutter. She shrieks like a parrot and leaps on his back. Rashona says, 'Is that your mum?'

No, I want to say – and that's not her boyfriend, Milton. I'm embarrassed and ashamed. I want to run away, but we keep walking towards them. They end up rolling around on the pavement, like a pair of dogs fighting. They don't even notice us. Someone had called the police and I hear sirens wailing.

I say to Rashona, 'Maybe you should just go on home. We ain't gonna get no work done.'

'Yeah, OK. Will you be all right?'

'Yeah. They're always fighting.' I act cool, but I'm mortified.

Milton's a big man, bulky with muscles, except for

his belly, which hang over his trousers and spoils the line of his shiny suits. He uses a lot of oil on his hair and has two gold teeth. I'm surprised he doesn't have more gold teeth – he's always brawling, ends up covered in cuts and bruises. He fights so much he's like a piece of beaten steak. My mum's the same, always fighting. She's got curvy big hips and tits and likes to dress real sexy – short, tight skirts, cinched-in belts, low tops, lots of jewellery, wedges or spiky heels.

'Yo' just like yo' dad, that no-good son of a bitch!' she snarls when she's angry, which is a lot of the time. Whatever I do these days, it's wrong. She used to be nicer to me, she used to love me more and protect me more. We were nearly always broke in Jamaica, but she moved heaven and earth and worked long hours to make sure me and my brothers got enough food, and clothes, and I went to school, nicely dressed, with something for lunch. All that changed when we came to England. I don't mean we go hungry. She puts food on the table, and gets us to school and dresses us nice – but it's her *attitude*. That's changed. She's not like my mum no more.

Now I'm watching her rolling around in the gutter with Milton and I want to sink through the pavement. 'Bye,' Rashona says, hovering like she wants to stay and watch the slug-out, like it's a wrestling match.

'Bye, see ya,' I say, wondering how soon this will be around the district. Rashona has a big mouth.

I'm in the kitchen washing dishes when Mum comes in grinning triumphantly. She brushes her hands back and forth like she's wiping off a bug. 'That showed him,' she says. She's still breathless, her hair a mess where it fell down from under the wig and she twists it up into a knot with an elastic band.

I ask, 'Why you and Milton fight all the time, Mum?'

'He axed for it.' That's what she always says, like it's never her fault, she never starts it. Truth is, she loves a good scrap. It fires her up, like a drug. She's angry because she's just learned that Vondra is having another baby. In our culture marriage isn't such a big deal and many men litter up the landscape with babies they have no intention of looking after – but Mum's fuming because he'd said he'd dumped Vondra. Now Mum says she's dumped Milton – she's better off without him. I don't believe her, because she's always dumping Milton and, five minutes later, they're back together again, fighting.

A few days later, Mum and me are walking home, carrying grocery shopping and she's arguing with Milton on her mobile phone. We don't know he's sitting just up ahead with a friend in his flash Pontiac. It's parked behind a lorry and we can't see it. But when we draw level, he jumps out and grabs her around the throat. I scream and drop the shopping and it rolls over the pavement. She falls backwards against the car and her phone lands in the gutter and slides down a drain. She lands a punch full in his face. He goes to smack her in the gob and she opens her mouth wide so one of his fingers goes right inside, and she clamps her teeth shut. She's got gold teeth top and bottom and she chews and gnaws on that finger like it's a bone.

He's like a child on tiptoe with pain, begging, 'Lulu, please let go! Please –'

His friend comes running around the car and begs, 'Lulu – come on – let him go – *please*!'

With that finger still fastened between her teeth she grins, 'Hell no, I'm gonna chew it off. I wish it was your no-good dick.'

Milton's howling and sobbing and my mum keeps on gnawing. Everyone comes out of their houses to watch the fight.

Mum spits out bits of skin and blood, and says, 'You don' taste so good. I'd rather eat a piece of fried chicken.'

His friend drives him to the hospital and Mum says she won't be seeing *him* no more. But Milton's got the guts to come round a few hours later. He walks in on us eating our evening meal in the kitchen, his hand all bandaged up. I sit back, frightened like the devil walked in, and my brothers duck their heads, focused on their food.

'How are you doin', Lulu?' he says, like it's a social visit. He puts a bottle of Lambrusco wine on the table.

'I'm fine, Milton. How are you?'

The big fight fired their passion and, after drinking the wine, they have to go to bed. Sex is always a noisy affair. Me and my brothers, we're used to the banging and crashing, and we take no notice. I clear the table and wash the dishes and the boys watch television, sound turned up loud. I do the ironing, then get out my school-work, and they're still banging away. When they come downstairs, Mum's dressed up in a shimmery dress with a big new blonde wig like Dolly Parton, and giant hoop earrings. She looks very nice. 'We goin' dancing Trocadero,' she says. 'Make sure your brothers get to bed by nine.'

'OK, Mum.'

Mum is happy because Milton pays the rent and some of the bills when he's around.

Six months after that big fight, Milton's son, Delon, by one of his baby-mothers, comes from Jamaica for a long holiday. He's a nice kid, my age. He comes to live with us and Milton pays Mum extra money for taking care of the boy. Everything's very cool, and we're all happy. But again, Mum and Milton fall out big time. They're in her bedroom and he's drinking Guinness from a bottle. She says something to him he don't like and *pow!* – he hits her in the eye with the bottle. She grabs a perfume bottle, breaks the top off and shoves it in his face. Face's a bloody mess, they go to the same hospital to be patched up, sitting side by side.

She comes home in a taxi and says, 'I threw that badass nigga out – and this time, he ain't *never* coming back. No way.'

This time, Milton's too scared of her to come near us for a few weeks, but Mum's taking care of his son, and he has to come by and pay for Delon's keep, give her rent money. They only have to look at each other to get the hots. They make up like they always do, and later go dancing at the Regal in Brixton, where they have a hot hip-hop band. Together, she says, she and Milton got rhythm. Even in their fights they got rhythm.

So Milton's back with us and things are all nice and sweet again. Delon's mum wants him back in Jamaica, and he leaves. I say I'll write to him, but I never do. When I came in from school one afternoon, Milton's in the kitchen in his vest and boxers, getting a beer from the refrigerator. He smirks at me like a cockerel and struts back down the hall. I go up to my room to take off my school uniform. He goes in Mum's room and leaves her door wide open.

'Get off me,' I hear her snap.

'Aw, c'mon, sweetheart,' he cajoles. 'Yo wasn't like this jus' now.'

'Well, I am now. Go on, fuck off.'

He dives on top of her. *Wump!* goes the bed. But she's got her legs coiled up sideways ready, and when he lands on her, she straightens her legs. *Pow!* He flies a couple of yards across the room and crashes on the sofa. She's up off the bed before he can take breath and hurls herself on him, pummelling and clawing.

'When I say no, I mean no. What are you, some kind of goddamn perverted rapist?' she yells.

He's cowering under her, protecting his face. 'Goddamn, yo was all for it just now, what happened?' he yells. 'Yo some crazy motherfuckin' bitch!'

He runs to the kitchen, gets a knife. She chases after him and twists it out of his hand, stabs him in the shoulder with it. Blood oozes on his white vest, like a red rose.

'Goddamn it, yo fuckin' ho'!' he yells.

I go into my room and sit on my bed, hands over my ears. My brothers creep in and sit next to me. We hate their fights because they're so dangerous. I'm always expecting to find they've killed each other, but they always manage to stop before they do any real damage. Their making up is even harder to take. They go at it with no privacy, no sense of decency.

Milton goes to hospital to get stitches put in the wound, then reports our mum to the police. They come and try to arrest her – but we start crying and say it's Milton who started it. He attacked Mum with the knife and got cut. They make notes and look bored but they still take her down the police station and charge her. They let her out on bail, which Milton puts up. It's crazy – even the judge's head must spin. But before it goes to trial, they make it up and Milton drops the charges.

One day, Mum comes home unexpectedly early and finds her bedroom door locked. She can't believe it. She bangs on it, but can't get it open. She gets us kids and says, 'What's goin' on?' We shrug, say we don't know, we've been in school all day.

Mum bangs on the door and Vondra yells back. She says she and Milton have been making it in Mum's bed during the day whenever Mum's at work and Vondra has suddenly made up her mind that this gonna be her house. 'My man pays the rent and I ain't going nowhere,' Vondra shouts. She and Mum scream insults at each other and Mum's half-crazy because she can't get in the door. She runs around, looking in drawers, until she finds a key to fit and boy, she's in.

Vondra's lying in bed talking on the phone, naked, except for her huge gold butterfly earrings. Her things are all around the room, ready to move in. She screams, jumps up and grabs her knife from the side table. Mum smiles and says, nice and polite, 'Don' worry – I ain't staying here with that jackass. Yo' welcome to him and this crap house. I don' want to fight. I'm leaving, but I'd like to take my things.'

Vondra's confused, but Mum keeps talking nice and friendly as she packs up her things. She says she wants to take her bed. 'It's mine, I paid for it,' she says. 'He'll get you a new one, one of them big four-posters with satin sheets like he's always promising me. Here – can you give me a hand?'

She's so matter-of-fact, so casual, that Vondra puts the knife down and helps our mum dismantle the bed. They drag the mattress off, ready to carry it down the stairs. All of a sudden, Mum shoves the mattress against her enemy and comes at her like a devil woman, ready to kill her. Vondra flies down the stairs and into the street stark naked, her big earrings jangling and her tits bouncing. Mum stands at the top of the stairs and yells, 'You're not the first and you won't be the last.'

Vondra screams that she's going to get Milton, tell him to bring a gun, shoot Mum. Mum just laughs – what's Vondra gonna call Milton on, eh? Mum's got her phone. Then Vondra's banging on our neighbour's door to get in, she screams she wants to use the phone, call the cops, have Mum arrested. I hear every word. The door opens and slams and someone's taken Vondra in. I'm shit-scared. Things are escalating in a bad way. I think nothing will stop it until one of them's dead. I sit on the stairs and start to shake.

Mum must feel the same, because she says to me, 'We're moving where that arsehole won't find us.'

That afternoon, she finds us a place near Peckham, rents a van with a driver, and we pack up our stuff in about twenty minutes and we're gone. The new house is horrible, really bad. The man we share with keeps killer dogs in the back garden. They shit all over the place and bark ferociously every time they see us. It's filthy and smelly, the carpets thick with dog hairs. I feel dirty all the time and itch with fleas. It's really bad there and I hate it.

On the grapevine, we hear of gang wars, just like in Jamaica. Police cars go crazy night and day. Sometimes on the TV news we hear there's been a shooting or a stabbing. But most of the time the shootings aren't reported. Mum says she hates Milton, but she's worried, and she's always on the phone checking to hear the latest news in case she hears one day he's been killed. The last thing I expect is to come home from school one evening to find Milton there, helping Mum pack up our things.

'What's happening, Mum?' I ask glumly, though I know. She has that satisfied-cat look about her, like she's just been laid.

'We all moving,' she says. 'To Hackney.'

'Hackney – where's that?' I ask.

'Somewhere, north London.'

I stare. She might as well have said we were moving to Mars. North London is so far off the radar we'll need a compass to get there. I don't know why Milton needs Mum again – but I learn that he's pissed off a lot of people and must lie low for a while, somewhere he can sleep at night without being shot dead in his bed. The house Milton has rented for us is clean, but bleak. It's wintertime and the wind seems to howl down the treeless streets and tower blocks and my legs and hands are always purple with cold. There are only two bedrooms. He and Mum have one room and me and my brothers have to share the other one.

It never occurs to Mum to register us in new schools in Hackney because she thinks we'll be moving back to south of the river again when things have settled down. When you're on the wrong side of the law, you don't rock the boat – besides, I was happy in my school and don't want to go to another one. We're all bored and, with nothing to do, my brothers are always fighting and I get no peace. One day I lure them into the garden and lock them out. It starts to sleet and I ignore their shouts. It's only when they threaten to break the windows that I relent and let them in. They charge in past me, their asses frozen like sides of beef in a freezer, and huddle around the radiator.

'What been goin' on?' Mum asks suspiciously when she comes in.

I grin like the evil bitch I'm learning to be and carry

on watching television. After a couple of weeks, Milton says it's OK for us to go back to school. He drives us south of the river to school each morning and collects us each evening. I don't know where he goes in the hours between, but he probably just cruises around his turf, checking things out.

After some months, when Milton says it's safe, we move back to south London, to a roomy flat at the top of a tower block. It has amazing views, with all London spread out in every direction. Mum says it's too far away from everywhere, and I don't like it much either, because my school is hard to get to and I have to get up early to be there on time. Milton's too busy to take me now, because he's asserting himself on his recovered turf, swaggering with his crew, dealing drugs and working his usual scams.

In the summer, when I'm thirteen, he gets a phone-call from his younger brother, Radd, who still lives in Jamaica. Radd says he's in trouble with a rival gang in Kingston and they're gonna kill him, but Milton says deal with it – it's not his problem. Mum has always said people have to toughen up – fight or die, she says – but for some reason she nags Milton and says it's his duty to take care of his family. He says he tried to bring his brother in once before, but immigration turned him down. Mum won't let it go. She remembers how Dadda B got killed in a gang war. She works hard to find a way to bring Radd over. She manages to get hold of a fake passport and, without telling Milton, she saves up and sends Radd a ticket – to give him an opportunity in life. She says, 'Everyone's got to have opportunity. We owe it to each other.' Her attitude surprises me. It's a side to her character I haven't seen before.

When he comes in late autumn, Radd is quiet and polite. He loves and respects my mum, grateful for the chance she's given him. It's not long before he sees the way that Milton abuses her, and thinks Mum only fights back as a means of self-defence. He doesn't know she just loves to fight.

'She's a good woman,' he tells Milton. 'You should treat her better.'

'Fuck off,' Milton replies. 'It's none of yo' damn bus'ness. She my bitch and she like it rough.'

Radd shakes his head. 'You got it wrong, brother. She want to get on, she want a peaceful life.'

Radd tries to compensate for Milton's brute ways by being extra considerate and respectful to Mum, and I see her sparkle. No man's been that nice to her before. Radd and Mum spend a lot of time together, more than is wise. It's cold for him in England, compared with Jamaica, and he can't stand the wind and the rain, so he stays in the flat day and night, huddling around the electric bars. He and Mum sit and gossip about Jamaica and a whole heap else. They always seem to have some topic on the go. Whenever Milton walks in, Mum and Radd are chatting and laughing. They play music and drink beer and it's all very cosy. Milton's paying most of the bills and he finally sees red. He yells that Mum's treating him like a fool.

It escalates until Milton hits Radd and Mum joins in.

It's a three-ring fight club. The flat's wrecked. Me and my brothers are screaming and the neighbours bang on doors. Someone calls the police. Mum grabs us kids and her bag and we rush out the door with nothing but what we're wearing and go to stay with one of Mum's friends. Next day, Mum goes back to get our clothes. While she's there, her mobile rings and someone tells her she better get going – Milton's hired a contractor to kill her and he's on his way round. She can't believe it.

'That bastard, I gonna have him killed!' she rants when she gets back to her friend's flat. She's on the phone, trying to get her own contractor to kill Milton. She tells him it's got to be done cheap because she's got no money. When she hangs up, she's laughing, her eyes glittering like she's crazy. 'Yeah, I sorted it out, innit. I'm gonna get that bastard, fix him permanent.'

It's a nightmare. We left Jamaica to get a better life – and all this violence is happening over here. I beg Mum to cancel her contract killer, say she can't do this. I tell her she'll get arrested and locked up for years, but she's determined. Nobody gets the better of her, she says. 'No guts, no glory' – that's my mum through and through.

Someone tells Milton that Lulu has a contract out on him and he goes bananas. He decides to kidnap me as a hostage. He comes to my school to get me, but he don't know it's a parent-teacher meeting and the hall is packed when he shows up outside. He hides around a corner in ambush and when the meeting wraps up,

Mum and me leave early to get ahead of the crush. We're heading for the school gates when Milton jumps out and grabs hold of me. I'm wriggling and screaming and Mum's hitting him and yelling when a load of parents and teachers come streaming out of the school and surround us. They watch amazed as Milton tries to drag me along the pavement towards his car.

'Police are coming!' someone shouts. Milton drops me, jumps in his big shark car and shoots off.

Mum's friend is worried. She doesn't want a shoot-out at her place. She locks the doors and windows like it's Fort Knox and we have to stay shut inside, nothing to do all day. Soon, Milton comes banging at the door, yelling that he's gonna set fire to the flat, burn us out. He making such a noise that he doesn't hear the police turn up. It's the armed squad. He tries to throw away his gun, but they grab him. He's charged and banged up in jail. He gets a sharp lawyer, who quotes his human rights, and he's freed on bail. Soon as he's out, he gets hold of a fake passport and flees to America.

All Mum thinks of is how we are going to live. 'Who's gonna protect us, who's gonna pay the rent?' she raves. She finds a low-rent house in Camberwell and we move in. Our new house is in a street just behind the main road leading down to Camberwell Green, not far from the big hospital where Mum and Milton have been so many times to be patched up after their fights. The houses in our street are all the same, with three storeys and three steps up to the front door. There's a sub-basement that the landlord lets cheaply to one of his relatives and we have the two upstairs floors. Most of them are council houses, but ours is privately let. We have to pay through the nose for everything and life is a constant struggle.

We're used to hopping about all over the place like refugees. My brothers and me can still get to our schools and we just carry on like normal. Each day I fix breakfast, pack lunches, do all the chores in the evening, and Mum gets more bad-tempered and stressed out. I dread going home. I dream of going to a boarding school, where the girls come from nice homes and everything runs as smooth as clockwork.

Mum has decided that she's going to try to get a regular job again, and applies to many companies, but she doesn't have the right status, and isn't hired. Finally, she finds work as a care assistant for an agency, looking after old people, cleaning up their mess, giving them their meals. The pay is poor, but the agency is a bit flighty and they don't ask for any documentation. She doesn't earn enough to pay the bills, nowhere near, and all she does is moan that if she was legal she could get benefits. Christmas is coming round again and she's got nothing put away to make it nice for us. The landlord comes for his rent every week, but she's been avoiding him and we're two months behind.

When I get in from school one day she's standing at the bathroom mirror, fixing her hair. She says over her shoulder, 'There's food in the refrigerator. Fix your supper. And I don't want yo' brothers going out, playing in the street tonight. After they eat I want them bathed and glued to that sofa watching TV. Then bed at nine.'

I saw the pile of little plastic baggies on the kitchen table when I walked in and I know she's going out to sell crack. Suddenly I get a bad feeling in my gut, and say, 'Mum – don't go out.'

She stops fixing her hair and stares at me in the mirror. 'What?'

'Don't go,' I beg. 'Can't you stay in? I'll make a real nice supper.'

'Who's going to pay the rent? Not that bastard, Milton.' She finishes fixing herself real foxy, and leaves. I sigh and get on with my evening chores. She's not there in the morning, or the next evening. A week passes and I'm sick with worry. I call everyone I can think of – 'Have you seen my mum? – but nobody has. By the end of the week we're hungry, there's nothing for breakfast and nothing to make packed lunches with. The electricity and gas have run out and the house shuts down, all cold and dark like it's the North Pole. We wear our coats indoors and wrap ourselves in our duvets.

Paul says, 'Let's chop up the furniture, light a fire.'

'Yeah, very funny, wiseguy,' I say. 'We don't have a fireplace. What you gonna do – light a fire in the middle of the carpet, burn down the house?'

Paul whines, 'Is Mum dead?'

I walk up to the hospital to see if she's there, but the woman at the desk says no, she's not listed, she's not been admitted. Then she asks if I want her to call the police or Social Services, and in a panic I say no, and leave. I walk back down through Camberwell and the smell of food drifting out of McDonald's by Coldharbour Lane makes my mouth water. I can't stand my pangs of hunger and clutch my stomach. I want to run in, grab a big bag of burgers and fries – and some chocolate shakes! When I reach home, the landlord is banging on the door. The curtains are closed and I imagine my brothers shivering with dread inside. The house looks very bleak and shabby on the outside, like all the other houses in the street.

'Hi,' I say, coming up to him.

'You live here?'

'Yeah.'

'Well, tell your mum the rent's overdue. Is she in?'

I shake my head. 'No, she's out.' I stand there, staring at him, wanting him to go. If I open the door, he'll be in through it and take possession – that's a term I've learned from Mum when she talks about bailiffs – only she calls them 'the fuckingbailiffs' like it's one word. Eventually, the cold gets the better of him, and he leaves and quickly I let myself in. Now I'm shaking from fright, as well as cold. He's a slum landlord, with strong-arm boys. Soon, he'll just evict us and throw us on the street. I tell my brothers to go round to one of their friend's houses, where it's warm. Maybe their mum will give them some food.

I shut the door behind me and walk to the end of the road, debating where to go. Maybe I can steal some food. They have dumpsters behind the supermarket – I could find something there, maybe. If it's still wrapped, it will be past its sell-by date, but fit to eat. When you're hungry, you don't much care about sell-by dates.

I walk along the road and bump into Tawni heading for the bus stop by the green. She's a little older than me, but goes to my school and we're friends.

'Hi, Tawni, how you doin?'

'OK, I guess. Yo girl, you look in the dumps, innit? What's up?'

'Nothin'. You going West End?'

She grins cheekily. 'Nah, just going to river, to hang out. Your mum back yet?'

I shake my head. 'Not yet.' To my horror, I start to cry. 'Landlord want his rent and we got no gas, electric. No food neither.'

She grabs my arm. 'Come on, let's have a coffee. You wanna make money?'

We go to the coffee bar a few yards away and she orders two coffees and a kebab for me. We sit down, and then she tells me about her 'job' as a hooker. I'm shocked and sit up straight. My voice rises to a squeak. 'You gotta be kidding. Yo' only fourteen.'

'So what?' She laughs. 'They like 'em young. I got a good gig going.'

She says she gets out there and only acts like a prostitute. 'I just lures men, but I rob 'em before I gotta do anything, like sex or blowjob.' I look around to see if anyone's listening. She seems high, laughing and waving her arms around like she's on speed as she describes how she grabs their wallets and then runs. She makes it sound so easy. She points to her leather jacket. 'How you think I got this? Come on, Sugar, it ain't hard – you just got to be quick, keep your wits about you.'

We talk some more, and I take a deep breath. I must do something – my brothers and me, we can't go to bed hungry another night. We just can't survive without money. In Jamaica, we can pick fruit, run through the ghetto being fed by everyone – in England in the winter, there's nothing.

'OK,' I say, 'show me the ropes, baby.'

We burst into laughter. We go back to my freezing house. Tawni lends me some money to feed the meter and the lights snap on. I've been unable to wash up for days and the kitchen is piled high with dirty dishes. The place is a tip, and I'm ashamed. Tawni looks about. 'Hey girl, you should have come to me sooner. You can't live like this.'

We root through my mum's things to find something sexy that will fit me. I choose a pair of her high heels and get dressed as quickly as I can. We hop on the bus to London Bridge and, within half an hour, we've walked the route, worked out what to do – and I'm ready for my first sucker.

In a night, I can often make two or three hundred pounds – sometimes more if a wallet is stuffed full of cash. Even if I don't get their wallets, I always get the cash they get out in their hands to pay me. Days pass, and the money begins to pile up. I love it when my brothers and me can go shopping down Rye Lane and come back laden with good things to eat. I load up the meters so they won't run out, and we make the place warm and cosy. I pay a week's rent and tell the land-lord we'll catch up soon as I can. I know he'll accept – he can't throw us out when we're paying the arrears. He still doesn't know – or care – that my mum's not around.

Tawni and me, we vary our venues so there's no pattern, no return visits by enraged punters, no police stake-out. Sometimes we do it along the river, or in church graveyards. After a week, by London Bridge, we're chased off by pro hookers and their pimps and move to ordinary pedestrian streets, taking men back to dank city gardens, hidden behind hedges. On winter nights nobody ever looks to see what's happening behind dense bushes just a few feet beyond brightly lit pave-ments. Each time, we've planted a weapon of sorts – usually a brick. So far, I've only had to use it that first time because, after that horror story, I became like greased lightning. I have the money off them and I'm gone before they realise. I've even learned that I can ask some of them for money for a cheap hotel room, one of those shabby places by the Elephant or Waterloo station. I tell them to wait on the pavement and I go in and 'fix it up' with the desk. Instead I stroll out through the back door, or down a fire escape, and I'm gone. I'll even walk out of a side alley and see the poor saps, standing yards away, patiently waiting for me to beckon them in. I think it's hysterical.

Chapter 6

London, 1999

Thump, thump thump. Ghostface Killah raps Assassination Day. 'Mothafucka, motha-*fucka!*' shriek my brothers, Paul and Wayan, leaping from the sofa to the chairs.

They're mad with excitement and speed. I don't know when the back broke on the sofa, when the cushions split on the chairs, who pulled the wallpaper off the walls so it hangs down in long strips. Food and pillow-stuffing flying. Across the room, my best friend, Rashona, is shrieking down the phone, all the way to Jamaica. I hear my name. 'Have yo seen Sugar's mum? Yeah, her, Lulu, she's gone.' How would anyone in Jamaica know where she is? But they always seem to know everything – they always do. The jungle drums beat back and forth across the wide gulf of the Atlantic with gossip like we're neighbours just across the street.

It's fun! Free-*dom*! No adults, no rules, money starting to flow in every day from scamming those men. Serve them right! I shriek with laughter, remembering some of the near escapes. Gaining a sense of release from the awful risks I take almost every night, I leap after my brothers, bouncing from chair to sofa like a gazelle. I can do anything.

Our living room's a mass of heaving kids, dancing, fooling around, smoking pot, drinking Milton's beer and Southern Comfort we've shoplifted. He's gone, Mum's gone, Dadda B's dead. I can't even remember my real dad. Fuelled by a mix of unfamiliar drink and drugs, suddenly waves of pain and sadness wash over me and I start to cry so hard it hurts.

I can't live like this. Mum will kill me when she shows up. I never drank, have never used drugs before. And the mess. Our house is wrecked. How could I let it happen? I moan and start to shake and my stomach cramps in tight waves of pain. I just make it to the bathroom and throw up. When I've got nothing left inside to throw up, I wash my face and rinse my mouth, then I lean my head against the mirror and snivel miserably. I just want it to end, to get back to my crazy mum running the house, telling me what to do – and me going to school and doing my homework. I love my school, I love my lessons. I love my teachers. I want a regular life like any other girl.

Where has she gone – where has she *gone*? I almost fall down the stairs back into the living room where it's still a crazy zoo where the animals have all gone mad, screaming and gibbering. My brothers are still jumping and screaming, 'Mothafucka, motha-*fucka!*' The loud beat vibrates through my skin and bones. I've got to get out. Gotta to get out. Sobbing, so I can't see, I stumble to the door, tripping over sprawling legs, slipping on bits of pizza and chicken bones.

'Get yo' ass over here, Sugar!' Rashona yells over the din. 'Yo' Auntie Georgia says she want talk you.'

In the hall, I push back the bolts of the front door, shut against the world. I have to escape, I don't know where, but I can't stay.

A long arm reaches out to grab me. 'Where yo think yo going?'

I shriek, then stare. 'Mum? Where you been? You went off without a word. You been gone for ever.'

'Well, I'm back now.' She holds my arm in an iron grip and pushes me inside. The hall is a mess, dirty garbage bags spewing rubbish, the stairs full of junk like a junkyard you have to clamber over. The music is so loud, nobody notices our arrival in the living room.

Mum stops and stares. 'Holy shit. What the hell been going on?' She raises her voice into an angry bellow. 'Get the hell outta here. Get out.' By now, she's kicking and hitting, pulling and dragging at bodies. 'Get outta my house before I kill yo.'

She unplugs the CD player and hurls it. Bottles fly. Broken windows or broken heads, it's all the same to her in her fury and frenzy as she clears the room.

'Mum! Mum!' I protest, as she picks up a chair to use as a weapon. She's red hot, like a volcano that's blown, her rage so incandescent you can almost see smoke and flames flashing from her eyes and mouth. 'Yo little whore, I'll deal with yo in a minute.'

One moment there were fifteen kids in there, the next, they're flying out the door, and me with them.

'Sugar! Git back here, yo black bitch whore nigga!' my mum screams. 'Git back here now, or yo dead.' She comes after me like an express train. When she's in that mood, she's dangerous. I keep going.

It's November, raining and cold. I hunch my head into my coat and pull the hood forward, over my eyes. I'm glad I won't have to do the thing tonight. Every time, there's the same level of fear, the same risk. Sooner or later I know I'll come up against someone faster than me. I close my eyes. I don't want to think about it. Where shall I go? Tawni is probably out there, working on her own. Later, she'll go to a crack house, burn up some of the money she's stolen. Rashona's probably home now, and her mum always has some food cooking. I lick my lips over the idea of something good. Man, I threw up everything and I'm *hungry*.

Mum is always dangerous, like a tiger, always into scams, trying to survive, but when she's without a man – like now – she's really, really bad, one mean, badass woman. She scares me half to death. To start with, she's obsessed with money. Not just enough to get by, but more, much more. It's all money money money, making money, having it, planning on getting more. And it's about being illegal. 'We can't do this, or that, better watch out or we'll be arrested and sent back to Jamaica,' she nags us all day, like it was some big black cloud permanently hanging over our heads.

Yes, that's what bugs me. It's the change in her. We go from being happy, always having fun in Jamaica – except when those gangsters came looking for us after they kilt Dadda B – to being scared all the time in London. Moodily, I trudge along, shoulders hunched. My only security is school. School is my anchor. My brothers don't care if they go or not, but me, I make sure I get there, no matter where we live. I'd dodge paying my fare, or walk if I had to.

Where's Mum been? She just walked back in, yelling like a banshee, but she didn't say where she's been for six weeks. Man, is she *angry*. Then my mood darkens. Where *has* she been? She couldn't disappear just like that and not phone, not get us a message, not say a word. We're her kids, she should have let us know. It wasn't like she'd been hit by a bus, was it, and lost her memory? I didn't want her to go, I begged and pleaded with her, convinced something awful was going to happen. 'Don't go, Mum – please don't go.' But she'd ignored me, and left.

She looks the same, but thinner, more tired and a bit battered. She's wearing the same clothes she left in, too. It's not like my mum to look so gaunt and scruffy.

Walking in the rain through the drab back streets of Camberwell, I shrug inside my fleece. I wish I could feel more, respond more to pain and joy. My mum's hardened me. She's a tough woman – nothing and nobody scares her. She likes to fight, and I don't mean argue. She likes hard, physical scraps, just like a female wrestler. She either gets in somebody's face and snarls, 'Yo wanna fight?' and then she backs off an inch, sort of crouches, her hands open like claws, talons out, and her eyes narrow. There's that teeth-baring smile, like a tiger, and if you're staring right back at her your blood freezes cold. Or she just launches herself straight at her enemy, using knees, teeth, nails, and they're at it like a couple of spitting cats or bitch dogs. I hate to fight, but she's taught me that you have to be tough to survive.

Having been brought up by her, I'm not scared of violence or the sight of blood, because I've always known it. I've seen people die and been left cold. It just meant that person wasn't coming back. Nothing touches me – except my mum. She has power over me because I want her to love me, and I am beginning to realise that she can't. Tears mix with the rain, and I wipe them away with the back of my hand.

Who was I fooling? I knew I wouldn't make it to Rashona's house. My mum is waiting for me like a boil about to burst and if I don't get back, it will be worse. I know she'll beat me – but it's better to get it over with than to put it off. I turn and trudge back. When I creep in through the back door – suspiciously left unlocked – hoping to sneak upstairs to bed, she's sitting at the table, drinking beer, that crazed look on her face. She has the phone bill open in front of her. The belt she keeps for beats is lying on the table, coiled like a black snake. She's been waiting – and the longer she's waited, the more riled she's got.

'Where the hell yo been?'

It was the question I've wanted to ask her these past weeks. Instead I say mildly, 'I just been walkin'.'

'I'll give yo walkin' – you won't be doin no walkin', you ho', when I've finished with you. How you expect me to pay this bill?'

I hadn't opened the envelope when it came, stuffing it out of sight and mind – but I know it would be stratospheric. In my mum's absence, every kid we knew had called friends and family in Jamaica or the US, often chatting for hours. Our house had become a free call-box and hangout.

'A thousand pounds,' Mum says. 'What kind of phone bill is a thousand pounds? You been phoning Jupiter and Mars?'

She stands up and drags my fleece off. She's strong. Soon, I'm down to vest and knickers. I close my eyes. Here it comes. I hear the whistle of the leather. Thwack! Thwack! *Thwack!*

I cower under the blows, try to cover up my head as the belt and heavy buckle descend. I make myself a small ball on the floor. She wants me to fight back, to get into a wrestling match with her, but I know I could never win. It's better to take the whipping and get it over with. The pain numbs me, and I drift off.

After a while, she stops. 'Get to bed,' she says, disgust and tiredness in her voice. 'Go, get out of my sight.'

I uncoil myself and run for the stairs before she changes her mind. Upstairs, my brothers are wide awake. In Jamaica, beats could be fun as we danced out of the way of Mum's blows, often screaming with laughter. She'd been more fun, too, even when enraged. But now, a good beating means heavy business, real pain and humiliation.

'You OK?' Paul asks. He's a short, skinny boy. Wayan is younger, but bigger and fatter.

'Yeah, sure. I didn't feel a thing.' Pain courses fiercely though me and my vest sticks to my back where the skin has broken.

In the bathroom, I soak a cloth in cold water and hold it to the weals on my face where the edge of the belt flicked around and bit into my cheek. One eyebrow is split and seeps blood. The heavy buckle has torn me, my skin is streaked with bright blood. I dab some cream on the wounds I can reach and crawl into bed, worn out and hurting. I think of Tawni, out and about somewhere in the dark night, scamming men into promises of sex and running before she has to deliver. She says if she can't get away in time, she gives the men what they want. I worry about her because she's so young and thinks she knows it all. Man, some of those men are brutes, and if they think you're trying to scam them, they can turn on you.

I'd be out there too if Mum hadn't come home, and I shiver. At the time it seemed a crazy, brave, delirious thing to do. I was psyched up on adrenaline, hungry to get in the money. But now that Mum's back, I feel flat and depressed. I can't believe the risks we took – the risks Tawni is still taking. 'Man, she crazy,' I say aloud, staring at the ceiling.

I have to get up early the next morning to clear up the mess in the house, while my brothers loll around in bed upstairs, but I can't move. In the night, my skin has stuck to my sheets, and the wounds have puffed up. One eye is closed, my lips are split.

Mum tells me that as the girl I'm responsible for it all. 'They made the mess too,' I try to say through my swollen lips. I resent it that my brothers never helped. I'd cooked and cleaned ever since I was just six or seven years old, but my mum pampers them like they're little princes. She seems to hate me and love them, yet I try so hard to please her.

She hates it when I answer back. Not once has she said where she's been, or asked how we managed. There's food in the refrigerator and the electricity meter has a few pounds in it. I paid last month's rent, but this month is overdue by a few days. The landlord is still being a pest, coming around and banging at the door. I hope he comes while I'm at school, so she has to talk to him. He'll show her the book and she'll see how much I paid.

When she sees the state I'm in, Mum says, 'Yo axed for it.' Then she considers, and more gently says, 'I'll rub some medicine in. Get back into bed.'

I lie there and listen to her resentfully bang and clatter downstairs as she cleans up. Some things she won't be able to fix, like the torn wallpaper or the wrecked furniture. I hear the vacuum cleaner. My mum likes a clean house. No wonder she's so angry.

I'm too bruised to go to school for three weeks. My

friends come round when Mum's at work to see what's up. I show them my bruises and cuts. 'Mum beat me over the phone bill,' I explain.

Tawni's eyes widen. 'She done this to you over a fuckin' phone bill?'

I defend my mum. 'Yeah. It was my fault. How she goin' pay it?'

'How much is it?' Rashona asks.

I shrug. 'Almost a thousand quid.' I've been pulling in that much working with Tawni – yet all that seems a long time ago, now that Mum's back, and I haven't a clue where all the money went. I got in a lot more than I actually needed to survive. I should have saved some, but didn't bother. My brothers and friends were just helping themselves. Easy come, easy go.

The school principal writes to ask Mum why I'm not at school, and when she tears up the letter, he asks my friends where I am. Rashona tells him about my mum beating me because she thinks my mum will just get a lecture. She doesn't expect the police to come around. Mum pushes me under the bed and tells them I'm not there. She says I'm always running off. They don't let it go at that, and I'm put on the 'At Risk' register. Mum is livid and blames me, as she drags me out from under the bed.

'You nothin' but trouble!' she rages. She rants that she wants to be invisible, under the radar, and instead she's getting known by the authorities. 'We'll be deported an' then you'll be sorry,' she raves.

I don't point out that she's brought most of this on

herself. It's her fault I can't go to school because she beat me.

Things settle down again, as much as they can. Mum won't tell me where she vanished to, but she always seems to be living on a knife edge and I know she's worried sick. I return to school and everything seems to go smoothly for almost a year. Mum manages to make a living at doing care work and night work on the street. She runs a risk, but is careful. Then she's arrested in a crack house at Tower Bridge during a police raid. She's charged with dealing Class A drugs – an offence punishable with at least two or three years in jail and deportation at the end of it. Once again, she disappears, but this time, it's just overnight, before she gets word to Nero, a drug dealer she knows, to go to court to see if he can bail her out.

Nero comes to get us first thing in the morning before we go to school. We're alarmed, but he explains where Mum is. He says, 'Come on, get in my car. Your mum thinks the judge won't bang her up if he sees you lot in court.'

'What will happen to us if the judge sends her down?' I ask him, feeling sick. The three of us are alone and vulnerable. She's all we have.

Nero shrugs. 'Depends on the judge,' he says. 'Some are easy, some hard – and your mum's already wanted by police.' He tells us what happened when Mum disappeared before and left us on our own for all those weeks. She was arrested for soliciting and possession of drugs. She was held on remand for so long because she refused to give her name or address, or call anyone. Eventually she gave a false name and she was charged and bailed to appear in court.

'But she didn't go to court, did she?' I say, nervously.

'I guess she didn't,' Nero says. 'I guess that's a big strike against her.'

His words make me feel very insecure. I'm shocked when I see Mum come into court with a policewoman, and I look to see if she's in handcuffs. She doesn't look like my mum. She's stressed, there's pain in her face and dark circles under her eyes. My brothers and me run forward and hug her and we cry and she asks if we can stand in the dock with her, but the judge say we're too young and he orders us out. We have to wait outside in the marble hall. My brothers get bored and start to fool around, and I have to grab hold of them, make them sit still in case we all get into trouble.

Maybe we impress the judge after all, because he releases Mum on bail of £1000, and Nero drives us all home. Mum has to sign on each day at the police station. She rants about it being a waste of time – but the one thing she's scared of is being chucked out of England and sent back to Jamaica. It eats away at her, day and night. She hates going to the police station because each time she walks in through the door, her bones are rattling with panic. She's sure she'll be grabbed and locked up when they've done some checking into her background. For her walking into that station day after day is like walking into the mouth of hell.

Then everything goes wrong big time when a Nigerian

boy at my brothers' school in Peckham is murdered. It's in the news every day and everywhere is crawling with the press. The police interview all the kids in this dead boy's class. Paul is questioned, like he knows something he don't, like he's gonna spill the beans on boy crews. The police say Mum's got to be there when Paul is questioned because he's so young. Sitting there with two policemen taking notes, she gets the heebie-jeebies. She's out on bail, still signing on each day – are they gonna say she's a no-good woman and send us back to Jamaica?

She's convinced that someone has put a curse on her and she blames Milton, then she blames Vondra. She writes out a list of her enemies and takes it to the Obeah-man, a secret witchdoctor in Brixton. 'Who's my enemy, who's put a curse on me?' she asks him. He tells her, listing a handful of people. 'Yeah, that my enemy, and that one,' she says.

She goes to a voodoo shop in Brixton Market, where she buys amulets and charms and a big bottle of Katanga limewater. Back home, she uses all kinds of cleansing rituals she gets from the Book of Psalms. It all costs tons of money that she borrows and gets into more debt over, and she's vexed that she's been inflicted like this. 'Why me?' she moans. 'All I want is a quiet life, innit?'

Next day, I come home from school and she's packing. 'We're moving,' she says. 'Get your things.'

'Where we goin', Mum?' Paul asks. He looks fed up. We're always doing moonlight flits.

She won't say, just keeps on cramming things into suitcases. There's too much for us to carry and we leave a lot behind. I know I'll never see half my things again. In her heart Mum knows you can never flee from a curse, it follows you wherever you go, but she's determined to run and hide. We go to Victoria Coach Station and catch a coach to Bristol. I've never heard of Bristol. I'm apprehensive.

Chapter 7

Bristol, 2000

'Look, Mum, a castle!' I exclaim.

We all look out of the window. It's huge, with a round tower and high, grey walls. None of us knows its name, and the lady in the next seat says, 'That's Windsor Castle. The Queen lives there.'

'She lives in Buckingham Palace,' Wayan pipes up.

'Yes dear, but she has many homes.' The lady is elderly, with permed white hair and a soft blue jumper that reflects the colour of her eyes.

'She must be rich!' Wayan says.

The lady laughs. 'Well, she's the Queen!' During the two-and-a-half-hour journey she chats to Mum and tells her she's going to Bristol to help care for her new grand-daughter. Her daughter's a teacher. She had her family late in life and finds it hard to cope with three children.

'Yeah, I got three kids,' Mum says. 'They a handful all right.'

The lady smiles at us. 'They look a lovely family, so nicely dressed and well behaved. Do you have family in Bristol?'

'A cousin,' Mum says. 'We're going to visit her for a while.'

A cousin. This is news to me. She's probably as much Mum's cousin as Ellie is my auntie. Mum always thinks claiming some kind of family relationship makes a dodgy situation more respectable.

'That's nice,' the lady says. 'Will you be visiting for long?'

'Maybe a few weeks.'

'And will the children be going to school in Bristol?' She probably means well and is just taking a friendly interest in us, but I can feel Mum growing tense. *Oh no!* I groan inwardly. Mum is just as likely to take a swing at a total stranger as at someone she knows. She's embarrassing. But she controls herself.

'Yeah, I guess they will be, if we stay long enough. I ain't seen my cousin for a while, and we might not get on no more.'

I don't take anything Mum says seriously, because, as far as she's concerned, we're on the run and lies have to be told to aid the subterfuge. But I can't help wondering. Have we left London for ever – *will* we be going to school?

The woman nods. 'Very wise. It's best to be flexible.'

They continue to chat about other things, like the scenery we're passing through. The lady tells us about Stonehenge that's out there somewhere on Salisbury Plain, and some of the little old villages scattered across the landscape, and places in Bristol we should get to see if there's time. She's a retired teacher herself and

133

knows a lot about history. There are historic docks in Bristol, where old sailing ships used to moor.

'They brought slaves,' she says.

'I know about slaves,' Mum nods. 'My great-granddad was a slave. He married a white woman and that's how come I'm light-skinned.'

Mum is proud of this fact. I wish I was as light-skinned as she is. Perhaps she'd like me more. Already, having been out of the hot Caribbean sun for a while, I can see that I'm growing paler. When I'm older I'll buy a wig and hair extensions – then I'll look *real* good and get myself a rich boyfriend who'll stick with me and buy me nice clothes and my own house. My man won't have no other baby-mothers, hell no. At the back of my mind though, a little voice is starting to tell me that I can change things if I want. I can make my own destiny – I don't have to do what everyone else does. With a good education, anything is possible.

We catch a taxi from the coach station in Bristol to the house where Mum's friend Bertrise lives. She shares with three other families, so it's already crowded. The four of us cram into one room. Bertrise has dragged in two mattresses, which are leaning up against a wall, and there's an old brown plastic sofa, a table and some chairs. It's not grand, but Mum says it'll do until she gets some money together. It turns out that she knows Bertrise from London when they both worked the West End.

'How's bus'ness down here?' Mum asks.

'Busy,' Bertrise says. 'Yo'll make money.' She laughs

– but Mum frowns. She's stressed out and has too much on her mind to see any humour in anything.

Mum works hard, she's out day and night. Soon she gets an entire three-bedroom house and finds some basic furniture from somewhere and makes it look nice. It looks as if we're staying and my heart sinks. Christmas soon comes. Mum makes a big coconut cake and we soak fruit in rum and she cooks a ham and goat stew – but we don't have many friends down here and it's very cold and boring. Christmas was hot and exciting at home in Jamaica – not freezing cold and miserable like here. I miss the parades, going shopping at Halfway Tree in the bazaar, where pedlars sold bright trinkets and knick-knacks. I miss the rich cooking smells wafting over Constant Spring, sharing food with friends and neighbours. Everyone went from yard to yard, eating and singing carols about baby Jesus and shepherds in the snow. I loved to sing those carols, even though I'd never seen snow.

In Bristol I'm so bored I could scream. My legs and arms keep moving to do stuff, to have a direction, go down Brixton Market, or up Trocadero – but there's nothing for me here. Mum refuses to let us go to school in case the police find her that way. If we register, we'll go on a list, she says, like Interpol. She's constantly paranoid. The police want her and she's heard that Nero is out to get her because he's lost that thousand quid bail money he put up for her. 'Fuck him,' Mum says. 'He fucked with me, so screw him.' But she's worried because Nero's a big man with powerful friends. I know she's just talking big and will have to find the money to pay him back eventually. It's all a big mess.

For weeks, my brothers and me roam about, feeling fed up. Most days I like to jump on a bus going down to the harbour and when I get out, I walk over the cobbles to the marina. There's tons going on. There's cranes and boats and a museum in a great big old sailing ship that's painted black, like it's covered with tar, and lots of fat gold carvings. Across the water a hill rises up to a tower on top. At the bottom of the hill, like it's growing out of the river, is a tall red-brick chimney and a ruined church. I stop to watch a man painting at an easel on the docks. He's wrapped up in a thick coat and hat and he's wearing gloves without any fingers. There's crowds of sailing ships in his painting, with all those spars and high masts and sails jostling for space, but I tell him I only see one in the docks. He laughs, and says, 'I'm using my imagination.' He points downstream and says, 'In the summer, you can see old sailing ships, coming into Bristol for the tall ships festival. You can stand here and see them. It's like an armada.'

I want to see this, but I don't know where we'll be in a few months' time. My brothers want to go to arcades and stuff like that, but it bores me now. They learn to steal, so they can play on the games. They're happy not having to go to school, but I'm frustrated. I loved my lessons and learning new things. I want a good education – I want to better myself. I nag Mum half to death. 'I want to go back to school.'

'If you want something to do get your ass out on street and earn yo' keep like I got to do.'

I clamp my mouth shut and go to my room to write in my journal. I started keeping it when we moved to Bristol. It passes the time and gives me something to focus on. I write down my memories of my childhood – just fragments – because I read in a magazine that if you write down bad memories, they go. I have so many flashbacks that at times I can't write them down fast enough. Sometimes I lie on my bed, my pillow drenched with tears. It's a good thing Mum's out so much, because she would hear me crying. The neighbours think we've got a cat. I tell them it's seagulls.

But soon, I'm back on the same topic. I keep on at Mum until finally she snaps, 'How the fuck yo' goin' school? It's in London, hundred miles away. Don't be such a dumbass nigga all yo' life.'

'I can take the coach,' I say stubbornly. Mum doesn't know I've been to the bus station and looked at the timetable and the fares and worked out how I could do it. It's a tight squeeze, but not impossible.

She laughs derisively. 'The coach, eh? All the way to London and back every day, five days a week? You dreamin', girl.'

'There's a coach at six o'clock in the morning that gets into London at eight-thirty. I can get to school by nine-seventeen.'

She stops laughing and looks at me thoughtfully. 'Oh yeah? And what about evening? I want yo here evenings, look after yo' two no-good brothers, so I can work. Yo' think I can lounge around doin' nothin' like yo' majesty?'

I have the answer ready. 'There's a coach at four-fifteen, I'll be home by seven.'

'And what about the fares? Money don' grow on trees – or haven't yo noticed?'

I persist. 'I can work weekends, in a shop or something. But you'll have to give me my fares until I find a job. A child's fare is cheap, day return.'

She caves in. 'It's on your dumbass ugly head. Only don' tell anyone where we's at, OK? I don' wan no police down here hauling my ass to jail.'

So each morning, I get up at four-thirty, wash and dress in my uniform, pack a small lunch, and run all the way to the coach station in the city centre.

Chapter 8

London, Early 2001

Now here I am on the early morning coach, heading back to London. Somewhere past Swindon, I nod off and revisit the past, like watching a film about someone else's life. None of it seems real. I open my eyes and watch the landscape pass by. The rolling downs of Wiltshire billow like the smooth waves of the sea.

The coach pulls into Victoria at 8.30 a.m. and I'm out of it, down the steps like a rabbit, running for the tube. Out the tube at the Oval, onto a bus and hoping it won't get stuck in a traffic jam. I rush into school at 9.17. I'm late, but I try to act casual, like I'm not late, like I've not been away for over four months. But my ass is hauled up before the principal.

'So where you been, Sugar?' he asks.

I hang my head and mumble Mum took me back to Jamaica for holiday, but he's not impressed. He looks at me severely. 'She should have written a note,' he snaps.

I keep my mouth shut, and he scribbles something in

a ledger. 'Very well. Next time, tell her to write a note. We could have given you some lessons to do, but as it is, you're behind in everything.'

'I'll catch up,' I say.

'Yes, I believe you will, Sugar. You're one of our most promising students.'

I'm overjoyed by his praise and walk on air for the rest of the day, but I know I've got to run out at 3.15 to catch the evening coach. The last lesson is maths – my favourite. I used to be top of the top set in maths, but now I'm too far behind to catch up. The bell rings to change classes and while the rest of the girls in my class go to maths I'm running out the school gates. I hop on a bus. Back to the Oval, dive down the underground, arrive at Victoria at four o'clock for my coach. There's a later one – but I promised Mum I'd be home by 7 p.m. I do my homework on the coach, so when I get in I can do my chores, clean the house, fix supper, wash, iron clothes.

I'm late for school each morning and leave early. I'm tired all day but stick it out because I want to learn. It's important. In some crazy way, it's my sanity, my way of leading a normal life. My friends in class welcome me back. They ask where I've been and I just say we moved house. They think we're back in the district – I don't tell any of them that I'm living over a hundred miles away in Bristol because some of them are big fat gossips. I dodge Mr Jenkins, my maths teacher and think he don't notice. Immigrants are always shifting around, coming and going. Some of the kids – especially from Pakistan or India – are taken home for extended holidays to learn their culture. Some girls as young as thirteen or fourteen disappear for arranged marriages.

But one afternoon I'm flying by on the stairs on my way out of school when I bump into Mr Jenkins heading for my maths class.

'Sugar?' he says, surprised. But I take to my heels and run. Next day, he comes looking for me in the lunch break. 'Ah, there you are, Sugar. It is Sugar, isn't it?'

I nod. 'Yes, sir.'

'It's been such a long time, I've almost forgotten what you look like.' He sits down next to me. 'So – what's the problem? Don't you enjoy maths any more?'

'Yeah, I like it,' I say in small voice.

'I'm pleased to hear that, because you're my best student – or you were, because you're hardly a student of something when you're not there to study it, are you?'

I don't answer.

'Look, Sugar,' he says kindly, 'I know your life might be very tough at times – but there has to be a reason you're bunking off my class. Try me – I'll understand. Let's see if we can fix it.'

I want to tell him, I want to pour it all out, how we had to leave London, how I've been commuting from Bristol for months – but I can't do it because I'd get Mum into a load of trouble. They'd say I couldn't go to that school any more because I didn't live in the school district. I'd probably end up in care. We've got girls in my class in care and they're always fighting, always angry.

In the end, when I don't say anything, he sighs and stands up. 'Very well, Sugar. I'm going to have to report you to the principal and he'll ask your mum to come in to see what's to be done. When you're at school, you have to obey the rules and that includes attending all your classes – not just the ones you fancy. I'm disappointed. I really thought you had a chance with maths. You're very bright – but it's GCSEs soon and you won't pass unless you've done the work.'

I want to cry but hold back my tears. I'm stressed all afternoon and instead of doing my homework on the coach home as usual, I try to work out how I can sort it all out. My head spins and I feel motion sickness, but I know I can't fix this problem and I close my eyes and, eventually, nod off. My life is a yo-yo, up and down, backwards and forwards. My childhood in Jamaica rings in memory as sweet as a mission bell. It was bad a lot of the time, but we also had a lot of fun – and I knew for sure back then that deep down Mum loved me as much as she loved my brothers.

With so many students who speak so many different languages and a constantly shifting population, the wheels move slowly at my school, but finally, I get hauled up before the principal again and he tells me I'll be suspended if I skip maths any more. I gotta confront Mum at the weekend and I'm dreading it.

Nothing tried – nothing gained. I pitch in first thing on Saturday morning, when Mum's sitting at the kitchen table looking a wreck after the night before. 'Mum, I've got to live in London,' I say.

'Yo don' gotta do no goddamned thing, except what I tell you,' she snaps. For some reason she's got a real mean look about her. I wonder why – and I soon find out. She smiles that crocodile smile of hers, when she seems all sharp teeth and glittering eyes, and moves aside the magazine lying on the table she's been pretending to read. Underneath is my journal. I almost die. I stare at it, mesmerised, as she picks it up and fans through the pages.

'What you doin' writin' all this crap?'

'It's nothing,' I say quickly. 'It's a project for English class.'

I know it's the wrong thing as soon as the words leave my mouth. 'Yo a fuckin' lying bitch. Yo writin' 'bout private things for yo' class to read and giggle over – like that time yo let that no-good nigga rape yo – and yo sayin how I beat yo senseless, 'stead of listening. Yo' a lying cunt.'

I don't see the blow coming as she almost knocks off my head and sends me crashing against the wall. 'Yo taking a conflagatory document like this to school and lettin' the goddamn teachers read them lies? Are you out of your mind, yo little ho'?'

She drags me up and punches me full on again. I try to twist and cower away. 'Ho'! Nigga! Fuck you bitch!' she screams like she's gone demented, hitting me with a chair. When she's done I can hardly move. I drag myself to my room. I lie there moaning for most of the weekend as the pain comes in relentless waves. I have to take two days off school at the start of the week, but eventually I get up and dress and tell her I want to move back to London.

'Mum, I got to,' I say desperately. 'I can't bunk off the last class any more.'

I think she regrets hitting me so hard. Her expression softens and she focuses on me, like she's seeing me for the first time. My jaw is still swollen and she reaches to touch it with an open hand, as if stroking a cat. 'Yo' jaw ain't broken, is it? Put some cream on it,' she says.

'Mum, you got to listen. They want you to go in for a parent-teacher conference. I told them you was away working and couldn't go, but they say they'll send a truant officer around –'

'Goddamn it!' she yells, 'Yo ain't nothin' but trouble. Fuckin' trouble from the day yo was born. I shoulda jis let his whoring bitch take yo. Yo' no-good dad wanted you, more fool him. You'd've been brought up in America, outta my hair.'

I'd never forgotten the time my real dad's girlfriend had tried to kidnap me – but Mum had saved me.

She yells at me and picks fault for most of the day, until she runs out of steam. I don't argue back – that will get me into worse trouble. Eventually, she simmers down and gets on the phone to Olivia, Rashona's mum, and arranges for me to stay with them during the school term. She says she'll pay for my keep. Summer holidays are coming, but I can stay in London from September. I'm ecstatic, and try to give her a hug, but she brushes me aside. 'I still paying back that useless nigga Nero one thousand pound for my bail money – and now I got to pay Olivia for yo' keep.'

'Mum –' I say, feeling guilty.

'Yo ain't nothin' but trouble,' she mutters.

'No, you're the one who's going to get into bad trouble,' I think – but don't say it. Her new boyfriend Leo has got friends in the housing department at the council. Now she's got a big brand-new four-bedroom house and she's got a weed factory going upstairs. There's rows of seedlings and plants in big pots, and she's installed some big halogen lights that burn up tons of electricity. Leo, a badass drug dealer, has jumped the meter so she don't have to pay no big bills. My brothers are out in the street, selling baggies to the students at the university. They're both still kids, Paul not yet ten and Wayan's a little boy, only six years old. She knows if they get caught they'll just get a lecture from the cops.

Rashona doesn't know I've been hiding out with Mum in Bristol – she just thinks we moved to another part of London. People like us are moving around all the time, either on the run from the police, or because we're behind with the rent. But one night when we're chatting and I feel she's my true friend, a girl I can trust, I tell her how I've been commuting all this time. She's astonished. 'Why didn't you change schools, go to one down Bristol?' she asks.

'Mum say I can't, ' I say. I don't tell her my mum's on the run. It's not her business, even though we're good friends. I tell her a lot, but not everything. I share her bedroom with her and her little sisters and we spend the night talking girly talk and giggling, until her mum, Olivia, blows a gasket and comes and switches off the light and says she'll send me home unless I'm quiet. After that, I try to fall asleep quickly and just whisper under the covers when Rashona and me are in bed.

But gradually, I notice a cooling in the atmosphere and a lot of hostility, and I think it's because I've outstayed my welcome. But I've only been there for three months and often kids like me stay with other families for years on end – like we stayed with Cruella when Mum went to England. Sometimes, Olivia forgets to put my dinner money out, or she passes me over when we're sitting at the table eating a meal. I have to pick up my plate and hold it up to her like I'm begging, and she slaps food on it with a sneery look. It's not always bad like that. She's a kind woman, but has a lot of mouths to feed and I feel like a burden.

One day I hear her on the phone and I know she's talking to my mum. 'So when are you gonna pay for her keep, like you promised?' she asks. Then she says, 'You been promising for three months. I ain't seen a penny yet.'

Now I understand that Olivia's grown cold because my mum's not sent any money for my keep. I've been living here all this time, rent-free. They talk some more, but I'm humiliated and put down the slice of bread and peanut butter I'm about to eat. I look at Rashona, who I know has also heard and say, 'I'm goin' walk.'

'Here.' Rashona picks up the piece of bread and gives it to me. 'Eat it.'

But I put it down and walk out the door, hot tears of shame burning my eyes. All Mum has to do is stick some money in an envelope and post it to Olivia. But Mum is always bitching about how she can't apply for no family allowances and benefits like other women do, how she's got to pay for everything, it ain't no free ride for her. Then she goes on about paying Nero back for her bail money – but it's been months. How long can paying back a thousand quid go on for? She says people don't understand what it's like to be illegal. But I understand too well because it rules our lives every single day and makes us do things decent people don't have to do. I guess the difference between me and my mum is I have a great big conscience and she doesn't.

I haven't got anywhere to go and it's cold. I turn back and slowly climb the stairs to Rashona's flat, wishing I didn't have to go back there. Her first excited words to me when I walk through the door are, 'Your mum's coming up London to pay your rent!'

I'm amazed. 'Mum's coming here? When?'

'Sunday. She's coming Sunday. Mum's gone market to get a big chicken and some goat meat. She's goin' cook a big dinner.'

My mum doesn't come on Sunday and, although we have a feast, I feel like a criminal eating it when Mum still hasn't paid my keep, and I try to make myself small. Everyone talks and laughs, and the adults drink lots of wine or beer, but every now and then, Olivia sucks in air through her teeth in a little hissing sound and says, 'So, Lulu didn't bother come. Look what she missin'!'

They all laugh and drink some more, and then someone else says, 'Goat stew damn good. Bet Lulu would've enjoyed it –' and they laugh again.

That's bad enough, but at school, Rashona moans about me living free off them with her friends and they start to say spiteful things and call me names. I can't call Mum because I've got no credit on my phone and don't even bother to carry it around with me. I feel alone and abandoned, a parasite in a family who don't want me. I drag my feet going home in the evenings and try to creep in and be so quiet and small nobody notices me. Sometimes the smell of food from the kitchen gets my juices going and I clutch my stomach and drink some water from the bathroom tap to fill me up. Instead, just to eat, I start to shoplift and pickpocket. Sometimes, when I've stolen enough money, I sit in McDonald's or Kentucky Fried, and fill my face, cramming as much in as I can until I'm bloated. Then I chuck up in the gutter outside.

I put credit on my phone and call Mum. 'You said you was coming,' I accuse her.

'Yeah, well, something came up,' she says. 'How yo doin'?'

'You know I ain't doin' well. You owe Olivia three months for my keep.'

'Yo think I'm doing' well? Yo think I'm OK?' her voice rises. 'Yo said you'd come at weekends, but I ain't seen yo neither. I need you here to help with your brothers. They running wild, out of hand. How the hell yo expect me work, send yo money?'

'I haven't had the money for my fares. How could I come?'

Our conversations never get anywhere and always leave me feeling miserable. I snap my phone shut and walk quickly down the street, as if walking away from her. Now that I know Mum's not coming, I can't stay with Rashona any more. Quietly, I cram my school uniform and several changes of shirts and knickers into my pink backpack and sneak out. I don't bother with a note – I feel they won't care if they never see me again.

In my head as I walk, I plan how to survive on my own and be able to wear clean clothes to school each day. Romantically, trying to make a bad situation better, I decide that I'll be like a butterfly, alighting on different flowers to sip a little nectar before flying on. I drop casually in on two or three friends and ask if I can leave a change of clothes here, a change there. Then I get on a bus at Clapham and take it to the end of the line, north of the river, having no idea where I'm going – it could be to the moon. I want to get far away where nobody knows me. I guess I'm acting like a martyr, feeling sick and sorry for myself. I get off the bus at Finsbury Park bus station, where it terminates, and cross the road to the park, wondering what the hell I'm doing.

I've never even heard of Finsbury Park, and I've not been this far north for a long time, not since we moved to Hackney with Milton – and I hated it. Like Hackney, Finsbury Park feels cold and hostile after my familiar territory in south London. I roam around the park. It's a dank November afternoon, and almost empty. I look at ducks on the lake, and big brown geese eating grass on the empty bowling green. Some people walk dogs, there's a couple of kids in buggies, but it's a big park and the wind blows cold. I sit on a bench and wonder how long it will take for me to freeze or starve to death. Some winos shuffle by and sit down next to me. I shift along to the end, but can't be bothered to wander off.

'Hey girl, you wan' a drink?' one of them asks. He's got long grey hair and a blue beanie hat. He offers me his bottle of hooch in a brown paper bag. I shake my head. I'm frightened of catching disease. The winos seem happy. They laugh and talk about what's wrong with the world and I start to listen. They're not as daft as they look. Sometimes they get up and stagger about, waving their arms. They seem harmless and don't bother me. I wonder how they have ended up here, and then I wonder if I'll end up like them, another homeless person. By the time night falls, I'm hungry and colder than I can ever remember being before. A parkie bicycles past, ringing his bell. He shouts out, 'Closing time in ten minutes.' A distant bell rings and I stand up. One of my new wino friends, Blue Beanie, says, 'Where you going, girl?'

I shrug. 'I don't know.'

'You run away?'

'Yeah.'

'Well stick with us and you'll be safe,' he says.

They get up and beckon. I follow them slowly, then stop when they dive into a shrubbery. Blue Beanie pops his head out of a bush. 'Come on, girl, you gotta hide in here until the park is closed or they'll make you leave. Cops check out at closing time.'

I step through a gap and crouch down inside a dark cave under a rhododendron bush. The leaves are still dry and smell comforting, of earth and mould. I could sleep here, like *Babes in the Wood*. Sounds are distant – another bell, then silence. The winos shuffle out to light a small fire of twigs they collected, but I stay in my cave. I bank up some leaves to make a nest, using my backpack like a pillow. After a while, despite the cold, I drift off and wake freezing some hours later. To get warm, I pile my school blazer and skirt over me, and pad out my jeans and sweater with spare clothes. I'm awake early in the morning, as the thin wintry sun rises mistily over the East End. The wet grass sparkles with heavy dew and the winos sleep obliviously on their benches, like logs wrapped in newspapers.

I swear I won't do it any more – that one night was enough – but I've got nowhere else to go. I wash in the public toilets at the bus garage, trying to make myself look tidy, and make my way to school. I'm starving, but at lunchtime, I shoplift a packet of chocolate biscuits from Mr Patel's Sunshine Grocery. To wash the biscuits down, I help myself to a can of Coke and an apple from Eli's Soulfood Store.

I sleep rough for a couple of weeks, jumping on the

bus or the tube without a ticket, washing and dressing with the girlfriends I left some of my clothes with. They share their breakfast with me and don't seem to care where I've been. Lots of them stay out all night with their boyfriends anyway, and their mums don't seem to know or care. Sometimes, I stay with strangers, people I just bump into that I drift home with. There's one group I fall in with – don't even know their names – and I end up back at their squat for a couple of weeks. It almost feels like home, like I belong there. They do so many drugs they never seem to notice I'm there. I'm always one of the first at school and hunger makes me lean and focused. Some kids have vouchers for free lunches, and I wonder if I dare ask. I decide it will be too much of a problem, and instead, I carry on shoplifting. I always go in with a fat black lady if I can, so it looks like she's my mum. As she pays and chats to the shopkeeper, I'm shoving stuff up my sweater. I walk out with her and it works just fine.

But after a while I look like one of the tramps in Finsbury Park, with that same grey look of sifted ashes. My head itches, my hair sticks up like a dusty mop, my socks smell and I wonder if I stink. I wash carefully every day, always making sure I wash my armpits, fanny and face, like Mum taught me, and I've stolen some toothpaste, but people shift away from me when I sit next to them. Some of the girls in class turn up their noses, but my school's in a poor district and there's lots of other kids at school who come looking like they've not been washed, or got clean clothes, so the teachers don't say anything.

I long for a hot bath and a deep soak, with loads of bubbles. I want to wash my hair and rub in coconut-oil conditioner. I want clean, ironed clothes. I want a bed with clean sheets and a soft down pillow.

I grow bitter towards my mum, blaming her. She doesn't seem to care about me. I wonder if she's tried to get in touch. Rashona and me, we're not talking, so I don't know if my mum has tried to send them any money. Lots of girls in my class don't talk to me any more, but I don't care. I wrap myself in a shroud of misery and just keep focused on my lessons. I learn that I can do my homework in the public library and it's a good place to stay until closing time at nine in the evening – there's even tramps in there, reading the news-papers and keeping warm, just like me.

But eventually, it all gets to me and I know I have to sort things out, or I'll end up demented. One morning, instead of going to school, I get off the tube at the Elephant and walk down the Walworth Road to the Social offices. I'm the first one waiting outside the door when they unbolt it. But even though there's no one else in off the street that early, they won't deal with me. They say I need an appointment, they say I'm too young to be there on my own and to come back with my 'parent'.

'Do you have a mum or a carer?' asks a skinny Indian woman in a blue sari.

'I got a mum, but she won't come. She ain't no carer because she don't care shit about me.'

A tall man with a goatee points at my school blazer with its badge and says, 'I suggest you go to school.'

'I want to talk to someone. I need help,' I say.

'*Do* you go to school? How old are you?'

I'm fifteen, but I'm small and look about twelve. 'I need help, I got nowhere to live,' I repeat stubbornly.

'I'm sorry, this office can't deal with children off the street.'

'It's Social Services ain't it?' I say, jumping up. 'It says "Social Services" on the door outside. I need Social *Services*, not a kick up the ass.'

'We won't accept abusive language. Do you want us to call the police?'

'Yeah – if it gives me a place to stay and some money to buy food.'

That was a mistake. I'm a beggar now. Their faces close ranks and they go about their important work of helping deprived and hurting people who have appointments. The place fills up with a lot of riff-raff. No wonder they're tired of helping people. One by one, they disappear into offices and cubicles to be dealt with. Everyone's being dealt with, except me. I ask politely to use the bathroom and say if they don't give me the key, I'll pee in their plant pot. So they let me go into their area. I drink from a cold tap but I've had nothing to eat. I watch Goatee dunk his biscuits in his tea. He watches me watching him, then silently beckons me over and hands me a single digestive biscuit.

'Thank you,' I say, and nibble it slowly so he can see I'm no animal, though I'm dying to stuff it all in and swallow it whole. In the afternoon, he disappears. Maybe he didn't like me staring at him. A breezy young blonde Irish woman with a ponytail comes from the back and asks if I want to telephone my mum.

'She ain't goin' help.'

She sighs. 'What is it you want us to do for you?'

'I told that man –' I point at Goatee's desk. Oh, he's gone. 'Well, I told him I wanted a *home*. That's all, a home.'

'We don't provide homes. Your mum has to go to the council and get herself on the list for a council house, or emergency housing. It's up to her – not up to you.'

I sit there all day. By late afternoon, there's nobody left in the waiting room – just me. In the evening, the staff get ready to go home. Goatee is back and jangles the keys at me. 'You have to leave now, miss.'

'I'm not going. I'll sleep there.' I point at the carpet, under the potted rubber plant. He sighs and indicates that I am to follow him to the back. I sit at a desk and Irish Girl, who has her coat on, picks up her pen to write. 'Give me your mum's phone number,' she says.

I laugh inwardly. I can hear Mum's reaction now. Irish Girl punches in the numbers and Mum's mobile rings. When Irish Girl tells Mum that she must come and get me immediately, we all hear the explosion echo out of the phone. 'That little bitch! What she done now? I'm goin' beat her so hard you'll need a shovel to scrape her up.'

When Irish Girl puts the phone down, she stares at

Goatee and Sari. 'Mother of God, did you hear that? She'll be here in four hours.'

I jump up. 'No, no! My mum's coming here?'

'Yes, that's what she said.' She says to Goatee, 'I can't stay here until ten o'clock tonight.'

'I can't either. I have to get back to my family,' Sari says.

I start to scream. 'Don't make me go, don't make me go!' I'm running out of the room and down a long echoing corridor with rooms off, banging at the doors to find a place to hide, and I'm screaming, 'Don't make me go – don't make me go!' and they're running after me, trying to catch me and calm me down.

Goatee shouts, 'Stop that!'

Sari says, 'Are you frightened of your mum?'

I gabble, 'She scares the shit out of me. She almost kilt me one time and I was put on the At Risk Register.' My voice rises like a boiling kettle. 'She's psycho! Don't make me go with her.'

At Risk Register. I should have used that magic pass-word earlier in the day. They check the records on the computer, call my mum to tell her not to come, listen to more of her abuse, and call around their emergency numbers. Within an hour I've got my own social worker and I'm in foster care. I've finally got a room of my own and a mum who won't beat me and tell me to get on the street and earn my keep. It feels incredible.

Chapter 9

London, Late 2001

My foster mother, Jessica, is Jamaican. She has a tall, skinny house near Peckham Rye, close to the smelly doggy place where we'd lived once. Like her house, she's tall and skinny. She's very houseproud and her home is immaculately clean – but it's soulless and bleak and filled with polished brown furniture, brown carpets and brown curtains. She reminds me of the Wicked Witch of the North in *The Wizard of Oz* – the one who has warts on her long, skinny nose and chin. Jessica would be upset if she knew how I see her because she's a good woman, a strong Roman Catholic. She goes to early morning mass every single day and wants me to go too.

'It will do you good,' she says, all prim and proper in her grey pleated skirt and twinset. She fiddles with a little gold brooch with seed pearls on her collar.

I want to say a bit of affection will do me good, but I don't. I've chosen this and I can hear my mum saying, 'It's your bed, lie in it.'

'Where are your things?' she asks when I arrive. My

stuff was in a black bin bag, all rags and dirty because I hadn't had a chance to wash any of it. I dumped it in the bin outside the Social offices. 'I don't got nothin',' I say.

'I haven't got anything,' she corrects.

'Yeah, that's what I said, Miss.'

'Call me Jessica. Nothing at all? Dear me, I'll have to get some money from your keyworker and we'll go shopping. That will be fun, won't it?'

So we go shopping and she gets me a new school uniform, shoes, changes of underwear, a pair of jeans and some tops. She tries to stop me buying the jeans, but I don't want the frock she chooses.

She's always trying to guide me and direct me along what she calls 'the right path' in life. 'Now, Sugar, what is your ambition in life?' she asks me, in one of her heart-to-hearts. I hate people asking me that. I am struggling to get through school – that's enough for me for the moment. 'Do you have any ambition?'

'Dunno,' I mumble.

'I don't know,' she corrects.

'What?' I stare at her.

'I don't know,' she repeats. She's always correcting me and the way I speak. 'It's no good speaking Jamaican patois,' she says. 'One is in England now. No one will employ you unless one speaks good, clear English.'

I'm shocked to hear a Jamaican woman talk like that. One – who the fuck is one? 'Yeah, well I know how to talk,' I say sulkily.

'How to speak. I know how to speak.'

'Yeah – proper,' I say, jumping up and flouncing out of the room.

'Come back, Sugar, where are you going?' she calls, raising her voice, but I pretend I haven't heard.

There's a park opposite. Instead of sitting in her living room under her disapproving gaze, watching the educational TV programmes she selects, I run across the road, dodging the buses. I see some boys I recognise from the school my brothers used to go to, and I wave to them. They come over and join me and we hang out on the swings. They're smoking puff and brag how they buy it in the playground. They pass the spliff to me. I pretend to inhale and choke and they laugh. They ask me about my brothers and I say they're with my mum in Jamaica at the moment. We discuss the little Nigerian boy who was murdered, and even though it's been a year since he died – a whole year since we fled to Bristol – they say the fuzz are still buzzing around like flies on shit. Nobody will talk to the police. We laugh, although it's a shame a nice little kid was stabbed to death. They say there's always stabbings and shootings and only some get into the news. They brag about their weapons.

'You got guns on you now?' I mock.

Instead, they show me their knives. One boy can't bend his leg because he's got a sword down his jeans. He pretends to walk with a wooden leg. We all laugh again as he circles the tarmac under the swings. 'Pegleg!' we shout. We discuss the boy gang in Camberwell, which rules the roost in that postcode and won't let other boys go into McDonald's unless they're in their gang.

'That's silly,' I brag. 'If I want a Big Mac, I'll have one. Won't be nobody will stop me.'

'Yeah – you a girl,' they say. The gang patrols the pavements in Camberwell, checking to see who's wearing their colours. If you're a boy and you're not one of them, you're chased and beaten up. It's hard sometimes just getting to school.

'Sugar!' I turn in mid-swing and see Jessica standing there. She has approached silently across the grass in the darkness. *Oh shit.* I wonder how much she's heard. But we were talking in patois, so maybe this prim woman don't get it. She nods to the boys. 'Sugar, it's getting late. Your supper is ready.' She speaks pleasantly, so I don't think I'm in trouble.

I jump off the swing and I say, 'See ya,' to the boys. Casually, I slouch over to Jessica, like she hasn't just embarrassed me. Doesn't she know you just don't *do* that?

She takes my arm. As we walk back across the grass, she says, 'I don't think it's a good idea for one to play in this park. It's dangerous. A pretty girl like you could attract all the wrong kind of attention.'

I'm stunned. She called *me* pretty? My own mum says I'm so ugly she don't know where I got my looks from. I sure didn't get the ugly gene from her, she says.

Jessica continues, 'And, Sugar, please don't speak to strange boys again. Not while you're under my roof and in my care.'

'They ain't strange boys. I know them.'

'They're not strange boys,' she corrects me. '*Not.* We don't use ain't.'

She is a good woman, but very controlling. She thinks she knows what's best. I want to tell her that I'm not a delinquent. I'm in care because I've been abused and I'm homeless. I bite my tongue and don't tell her what I think, because it's disrespectful for a girl my age to argue with an adult.

My social worker comes around only once to see how I'm doing. I'm doing just fine, I say. She makes her notes and leaves. Jessica nods. 'I'm glad you said you're happy here, Sugar. I think we'll manage well together and you will grow up into a fine young woman.'

Gradually, the rules are laid down. The state gives me some pocket money, but Jessica wants me to save most of it. She lets me have some to spend on myself. I can go to the cinema down Rye Lane, but only to the afternoon 3.30 viewing at the weekend or on holidays. I must come home straight from school, do my homework, and be in bed by 10.30. The social worker doesn't make me go to church, but Jessica says I must go two days a week. I don't mind church – I loved it in Jamaica – but she goes to the Catholic church and I find it very dead. Even at Christmas, apart from a dull little crèche with a white Jesus and Mary, nothing happens in their church.

I remember the exuberant carols we used to sing, and the fantastic masses, with clapping hands, dancing and praising. I can almost taste Mum's coconut cake and our traditional Christmas dinner of rice, gungo peas and curried goat. I yearn to be back with Mum and my brothers and wonder if they miss me. I want to go home for Christmas, but in my heart I know Mum will find a good reason to beat me to a pulp, like she said she would next time she sees me. Jessica won't even hang a few paper streamers in case the house sets on fire. I walk down Rye Lane and see the tinsel and the coloured lights and get excited, then I go back to Jessica's house and feel deflated.

When I tell her I'm not Catholic, she insists I must go to church with her. 'It will do you good,' she says.

Do me good? I'm not a bad girl, so why does she treat me like one? Rebelling against her rules, I start staying out late with friends. It gets so I won't speak to her. I grow depressed and unhappy and think about running away – but what would be the point? I've slept rough and hated it. Instead, proud of myself for doing the sensible thing, I return to Social Services and tell them I don't get on with Jessica. I want another family.

They shake their heads and tell me I can't hop around on a whim like that. We discuss it, until finally they sigh and ask me, as if it's a fate worse than death, 'Would you like to go to a children's home?'

'Yeah,' I say quickly. I'm not even sure what I'm letting myself in for, but there's girls at my school in children's homes and even though they seem angry most of the time, they have plenty of pocket money and a real cool, screw-you attitude. I want to have some of what they've got.

The home I'm sent to is small, with only six or seven girls and the same number of staff, working in shifts. It's in a once-handsome Georgian terrace house near

Elephant and Castle, in a row of other terraced houses, many divided up into flats and bedsits for immigrants. Some are offices. When I walk in through the door, noise ricochets off the painted walls – but it's not shouts of pain, it's the girls yelling and screaming and shrieking with laughter. They all seem to be running up and down the stairs, hysterical, slamming doors. The staff are oblivious. I stare around with big eyes. How can they stand this noise?

I'm shown to my room. It's nice and pleasantly furnished. There's a bed, a desk, a dresser and a cupboard. I even have my own TV. I have to clean my room and make my own bed, but apart from that, it's like being in a hotel.

'Come down to the office when you've unpacked,' I'm told, 'and we'll sort out your allowance and pocket money.'

I'm astonished when I'm told I am to get all my own spending money – as well as everything else, like clothes, fares, books. They offer me a laptop and a loan to get a CD player. I have never been so rich. I should be delirious – but the girls are so boisterous it makes my head hurt. There's no peace, no respite. Why do they all shriek and clatter every waking hour? They're as hyperactive as monkeys. They are so disrespectful to the staff I find it hard to understand why they're allowed to get away with it. I soon learn that however badly the girls behave, there are no parameters, no rules, no punishments. The staff are scared of being accused of abuse. They let the girls run riot, they do their jobs and escape gratefully at the end of their shift. I can see it in their faces. 'Oh Lord, let me get through the day in one piece,' is what their eyes say.

As the weeks pass, I can't stand the noise and confusion, and I complain. The girls turn on me and call me Goody Two Shoes. They say I'm geeky. They trash my room and rip up my homework. My clothes are chucked out of the windows and hang on railings and off ledges. I feel I'm in a nightmare and my work suffers. I'm tired all the time, I get purple rings under my eyes and I start to throw up each time I walk in through the front door.

Stress, says the nurse. I ask if I can be sent to another home and wonder if I am always going to be shifted around like this. At night I cry myself to sleep and dream of the old days in Jamaica, when we lived on Gully Bank and Mum was with Dadda B. He was a bad man, a gangster – but he loved us. Here in England, no one loves me.

I drift into patois and dream of lazy Sundays, when after church, during the mango season, we went hunting for mangoes. Until you've tasted a ripe mango, freshly picked in the sun, you've tasted nothing. *Mmm-mm!* Pure honey and nectar, juice oozes down your chin, it tastes like paradise.

The posh people who live on the Boulevard have big mango trees, heavy with ripe fruit. The air is rich and cloying with sweet scent – so sweet you can taste it. We walk along knocking on doors – 'Can we pick mangoes, sir, madam?'

No, no no, they say. Go away, slum kids, you don' belong here, get lost. We're tired of asking, sit on a low stone wall. One big house has a mango tree right in the front garden near the gate. There's no car in the drive, the place looks deserted. A huge white stone statue of a dog, alert, pointy ears, sits by the front steps. Is it real? Nah – it don' move. Chuck rock at it – no, you chuck rock at it. Go on, Louis, get up that tree, fill bag, we keep lookout.

Up the tree goes Louis, picks mango, turns and grins at us, peels mango with his teeth, fills his gut. Ho, Louis, we here, we *hongry* man! Throw dem mangoes down! He grins, and slowly, deliciously, sucks the mango. *Louis!* Pick us dem mangoes! He picks a few, drops them to the grass, stuffs some in the bag, and skins down the tree. He trots for the gate – and that's when the statue moves. Like an Exocet missile, with deadly aim, straight for Louis.

'Watch out! Run!' we shriek. Louis don' hear, brags, 'This my bag, no one goin' get my mangoes –'

Big dog flattens him. 'Oh-oh-oh! Help! Help!' This is Louis shrieking.

'Dawg eatin' Louis, dawg eatin' Louis!' This is us jumping up and down and yelling.

Fat maid comes running out of the house with a broom. Dawg lying down, massive paws on Louis's back. '*Tief! Tief! Tief!*' Maid beats him like she's beating a carpet.

Everyone running to see.

Louis's mum, Ruby, running from her stall right there

on the Boulevard, 'My boy, my boy, bein' eaten by dawg. Save my boy! Call off dawg.'

Louis scrambles out from under dawg, runs for tree, skins up it, mango bag dangling, mangoes falling. Dawg leaps up, great jaws at Louis's feet. Maid drags Louis down, grabs hold of his clothes. *'Tief! Tief!'* she's yelling. Louis wriggles out of clothes and runs. Dawg rolls on grass and grin, bushy tail waves like banner. Louis walks home naked. We all laughing, Ruby laughing. Street laughing.

Wednesday nights were bingo nights. The lane was blocked off with a big tarpaulin, there were speakers and a stage. All the mums and aunties were there and us kids could do whatever we wanted on bingo nights! A water tank up on the roof of the stage drew us with its forbidden delights. We climbed the spiral stairs, kicked off the lock from the gate and jumped in. We could swim and splash and the sound of the loudspeaker drowned out the noise we made. As each kid leaped into the tank we yelled out our names.

'Power Ranger!' – that was Dwayne.

'Pink Ranger!' – that was me.

'White Ranger!' – that was Paul.

'Penguin!' Louis shrieks, opening his mum's big umbrella, jumping off the top of the tank towards the stage. Airborne! We stare in awe. Umbrella turns inside out. Rocket man! Louis falls splat on the tarmac.

'Me hand! Me foot!' he moans.

Shriek from Ruby, ' Louis! Gawd, he kilt hisself.'

They pick him up off the tarmac and we run, go hide.

They put him in a taxi and rush him to hospital. Next day, home from school, we slapdash chores. Race about, sweep yard, put chickens in, feed chickens, fetch water.

Mum looks, frowns. 'Do it again, you slapdash. You kids too turbo.'

'Mum, can we go hospital, see Louis?'

'He soon be home, go see.'

Turbo-fired, we rush down the lane. Ruby's paying off a taxi, Louis comes waddling on two crutches, a big grin on his face. '*Yo Penguin!*' we shout.

In my bed at the children's home in south London, I wake up, giggling, remembering. The fun we had. I miss it. I miss the gully and Constant Spring. I miss my brothers and my mum. I miss Dadda B. I fall asleep, my pillows wet with tears.

Chapter 10

London, 2002

Just before Easter, I ask to be moved again, and end up at another home a couple of miles away. This one is a mixed one, with about twenty teenage boys and girls aged thirteen to seventeen. It's a big converted house like a B & B hostel and we all have our own rooms over four floors. Downstairs, there's a big kitchen, common rooms where we can sit and watch TV or play games like snooker, and there's a dining room, where meals are served at set times. It's quite well organised. They even take us to our various schools and for outings in brand new cars known as people carriers, that seat seven.

I'm happy that I can carry on going to my old school. Ever since Jessica's, when I started to be clean and tidy again, and didn't act so spacey, my old friends came back – I even talk to Rashona, though none of them know I was first in foster care, then at children's homes. I'm too ashamed to tell any of them that I'm being looked after by the state. It has a stigma that says you're undesirable, no one wants you. But my schoolwork is going well – Mr Jenkins says I'm doing brilliantly at maths and have caught up – and I'm told I can sit for all my GCSEs in the summer. The only sadness in my life is that I miss my brothers. I often think of them and wonder how my mum is doing. I'm too nervous to call her and she never tries to get in touch with me. She didn't send me anything for Christmas or my birthday. It's like I don't exist.

The kids in this second home are very off-key. They fight, yell, steal from each other and do drugs. They're abusive to the staff, whom they treat like crap. I wasn't brought up to be disrespectful to staff. I never argued or was confrontational, was always patient and polite. But here, I feel pushed to one side. I'm like a little deer in the forest, charged by a herd of trumpeting elephants. I feel there's no point in asking to be moved again, because I've worked out that all these places are the same. The staff are too scared to discipline the kids in case they lose their jobs, the children are in control, and act like spoiled little monsters.

I must be like them if I'm to fit in. After six months, I've changed. I start smoking and being loud and argumentative. Instead of asking for my pocket money politely, I slouch into the office with an attitude, demanding things with an aggression that often scares me. Who is this rude, angry girl? I don't recognise her. It's just as well that I haven't lived at home for over a year, since the previous summer, because my mum would kill this uncouth girl I've become. I don't cry myself to sleep very much any more. I'm as hard as nails, a tough cookie, determined to do my time and get out. It's not jail – but I feel I'm a criminal because I've learned to behave like one. The more criminal I feel, the more criminal I become. I'm trapped in a rat wheel, spinning out of control.

Many of the kids are crazy and shouldn't be here. They're dangerous. There's Tilda, a suicidal, mixed-race girl. She attaches herself to me, like I'm her best friend, or her auntie. She comes into my room all the time and won't take a hint. I'm revising for my GCSEs and need time to concentrate. I ask her to go, say I'm tired and need to get some sleep for the exam next day.

'If you make me leave, I'll kill myself,' she threatens, and giggles. She has long ginger pigtails that curl out at the ends and widely spaced, sharp teeth.

'Yeah, well kill yourself,' I say, offhand. I push her out and close the door. I get up in the morning to dress and get ready for school and when I open my door, I almost trip over her. She's lying across my door like a guard dog. There's a clear plastic bag over her head. Her face is purple and her eyes are wide open, staring up at me. I stand there like a moron, screaming, until the staff come running. They bend down over her, snatch off the plastic bag, pump her lungs, breathe into her mouth. I slide down against the wall and I'm sitting on the floor, sobbing and hiccuping. Everyone ignores me. I return to my room and crawl back into bed, pulling the duvet over my head. Two weeks pass in a daze and I have abandoned my exams. Does it matter if I pass or fail? I'm not going to university or nothing, so what's the point in anything?

When she returns from the psychiatric hospital, I try to be nice to Tilda. She tells me that she's going to kill herself. I ignore her, but she tells me every day, until I want to hit her. 'Do what you want,' I snap, each time she says it, and she looks at me with those crazy eyes the colour of pebbles under water. 'Yeah, well I will.'

'Yeah, OK,' I say.

One evening after school I come in up the front stairs, past her and Joelyn, a new girl who's recently arrived at the home. They're sitting on the steps, drinking something from a bottle.

'What that?' I ask.

'Vodka. You wan' some?' Tilda offers it to me.

I'm about to take a big slug, when the smell hits me at the back of my nose and I choke. It's bleach. Thank God I didn't swallow any. I'm so angry I snap. I start hitting them and screaming. The staff come running from the front office and sort us out. They empty the bottle and call for medical help for Joelyn and Tilda. I don't care if they both die, but I wonder if they really drank any of the bleach – or did they just pretend to? Their throats don't seem to be burned. They were playing games and I can't stand that kind of fooling around. After that, whenever Tilda tells me she's going kill herself, I'm angry and hit her. She seems to enjoy being hit by me, which makes me even angrier. I am so frustrated I want to hit her when I see her and knock that mad look off her face.

One time, she has a long shoelace around her neck and she's pulling tight, twisting, twisting. There's that purple face again and popping eyes. I don't care no more about rules. I bash in the glass on the fire alarm and staff come running. They always come in a mob because they're always hiding, drinking coffee in the front office, never seeing what's going on all around them. Roof fall in, they'd never know.

I say, 'You want for to kill yourself, let me help you.' I bang her head against the wall. The staff separate us and have a meeting. Big deal. They decide to make us swap rooms. My old room is closer to the office and I had to share a bathroom down the hall. Tilda's is a nice room, with ensuite. I'm happy, until I move in. I'm putting my stuff away when the room falls to bits around me. The bed collapses, then the chairs, the desk, the cupboards – even the skirting board and the picture rail. It's like matchsticks, like I'm in one of those crazy, rocking houses in a fairground. I go mad, run screaming down the stairs. I feel like I'm on angel dust.

Tilda laughs like a maniac, rolling around, choking with laughter. 'Ooh!' she screams. 'Oooh-oh!' She clutches her stomach. 'This girl screwy.' She laughs so hard she shrieks like a monkey. I want to hit her again, but they call an ambulance and she's gone in a jangle of bells and sirens.

They X-ray her. Doctors faint. She's eaten every single screw and nail in her room, every druggy, junkie needle she can find, every pin, every needle in sewing class. The girl's a mess, stomach torn up. Needles migrating, in her kidneys, in her lungs. She's gonna die for sure. They cut her up, root around. She lives.

She loves to hang out around Trafalgar Square and along the river, and when she asks me to go with up town with her and Joelyn, I agree, although I'm dreading what she might do. A little voice tells me that she's planning something, because she has a wild and manic look. So we walk along the Embankment. Casually, she says, 'You wanna jump off Westminster Bridge with us?'

I laugh. 'Yeah, sure. Can you swim?'

She hands me a joint. Skunk. I know it does me head in, but I puff. Joelyn takes it. Deep puff. We walk along past Ancient Brit queen Bodicea in chariot, towards Big Ben and Houses of goddamn Parliament. Tony Blair – what's he done for me? He lets terrorists in, gives them tons of money, but won't even let my mum in legal, so she can claim benefits, be happy. Be a together family. I'm laughing, raving, walk on benches, jump on parapet, wobble along. River deep and dark. Run down to sea, sea run to Caribbean. Run to Jamaica. I float on fast current, carry me home. Wash in on mornin' tide like them little dead kids, starfish in eyes.

Big Ben strikes ten. I stomp along parapet, shout out bongs. *One-two-three-four-five-six-seven-eight-nine-TEN! Attention! Curfew!* Should be home, should be in bed.

Me good-girl conscience on automatic pilot, I hop on a bus, can't pay fare, driver shrugs. 'Black kids,' he mutters, 'think they fireproof.' I get home at 11.30, door locked, I ring bell. Sign register, sent to room.

Next morning, wake with headache. Place in uproar. Look at alarm clock, 5.30 a.m. What in hell's going on? Kids and staff downstairs, talking. The police there. Hall full of people. Big news. Joelyn arrested. Tilda jumped off Westminster Bridge last night.

'She dead?' I ask. Memory floods back – we were there together. I'm about to blurt it out, but I keep my mouth shut. Who wants trouble?

No, she's not dead. She land on concrete, break arm. It's a miracle.

'She got nine lives like a fuckin' cat,' I say. Police stare at me. 'Me, I'm going to bed,' I say.

Saturday, no school. The police are thick. They should try smelling the air. It stinks of crack. Place reeks.

Lazing in bed, listening to radio, stench of crack strong under my door, like smoke seeping. Is place burnin' down? I take off earphones and hear boys on landing, fighting over a deal. Who cares? It's like, all the time – bad deals, bad fights, disputes. There's no peace. The staff come and break it up.

'Sugar – you know what it's all about?' they ask. I yawn, shake my head. I don't want to be a grass. Last time, a grass had shit and diarrhoea spread on all her clothes, all over her room. There's too many changes of staff. No one cares – they just do the job, go home, switch off. I overhear the manageress say it's like taking care of animals in London Zoo. Yeah, well, she's right – only animals in zoo better behaved.

One day, at school, year teacher says to me, 'You OK, Sugar?'

'Why you ask?'

He hesitates. 'You've changed. You used to speak good

English in class at least – now, you've reverted to patois all the time. What's happened?'

I want to say, 'Don't you read my record? Me, I'm fitting in with my peers, with kids in home, so I don' get hit, don' get picked on. In pack, animals gotta conform. You wan' I be murdered?'

Then he takes the wind out of my sails. 'We're putting your name forward to represent the school in a gifted student competition.'

I'm shocked and stare at him. For once, I'm speechless.

'It's a national competition. We think you have a good chance.'

Wild with excitement, I walk on air, and decide that I am different. *I don't have to fit in. I can be myself, I can shine.* My name has been put forward with another girl, Sally. Seems we're very bright. We enter the heats, win, enter the next round, win. I want to tell my mum, but dare not. After her threats, Social Services won't tell her where I am. They tell me I mustn't contact her, for my own safety. I know if she learns about how well I'm doing, she will try to fuck it up – it's like she's jealous of me. Once, until I was about nine or ten years old, she was proud of me. She worked hard to make enough money to send me to school – then she stopped caring. I've had to fight, I've had to do it on my own. I tell myself I don't need her. But I miss her all the time.

The final is held in Oxford. As the coach drives through the streets and I look in awe at all these ancient colleges, the huge gatehouses and the spires, I'm in love. I vow that some day I'll come here, I'll be one of them students walking through the gates with books. One of *those* students. Lord, Sugar, you can do it – you can! I vow.

I don't win, but I'm second. A boy wins. He goes to a big public school, speaks posh – but I talk to him and he's a real nice, polite boy. He wishes me luck, shakes my hand. Everyone cheers and I'm happy. I'm the second smartest schoolkid in England! Wow.

If you work hard you can achieve anything, my teachers say. I nod. Yessir! I can. I will.

When the kids in the home learn about the competition some of them want to bring me down. Tilda makes a bong with a Ribena bottle and some crack on foil. She offers me some. 'Oh, Sugar, it makes all your problems go away.'

I don't have no problems. Me, I'm a smart kid. I'm smarter than you, Tilda. I'm going places – you just going into a hole six feet deep in ground.

I don't know what demon gets into me, but I take the bong, suck in deep. All my pain seems to come together to try to destroy me. It's like the competition and the praise has acted like a catalyst to show me that I'm fooling myself. I'm just a girl who's been rejected by her mother. What's the point of trying hard, doing well at school – what future is there for me? I'm an illegal black kid. When I'm eighteen, if I don't hide under the radar like my mum and brothers, they'll just toss me back to Jamaica. I'll be like my mum, working the street, having to find a man to protect me.

I want to shout, OK – you don't care about me, Mum – you don't even know I won a competition in Oxford! You never ask me how I'm doing, you don't give a shit. Well, I'll show you that I can hate myself too. I feel rebellious and a bit crazy and suck in more smoke.

Soon, I'm smoking tons of crack and weed every day, spending all my pocket money. At the children's home they give us tons of cash, like they're the Bank of England. Older boys make more, dealing. I'm no longer floating on air – now I'm floating in a cloud, a haze of smoke. My clothes stink of weed and crack. School-work's gone to the dogs – who cares? The teachers aren't in a children's home – I am. Not one person in the whole wide world loves me. Not one. Who do I belong to? Nobody. Who cares about me? Nobody. I'm like the fuckin' Lone Ranger without Tonto.

I find myself a little boyfriend. He hangs out in the park where me and my friends go sometimes to have some blow. He's very cute, with dark almond eyes and long braids. His name is Angel. I love him too much for my own good. I sneak out at night by climbing down a tree outside my window and running like hell for the all-night bus. When the staff check my room they find my bed empty, and I'm in trouble, but he's worth it.

He's scared of his strict Jamaican mum and dare not let me in through the front door. Instead, I creep into his room through his window. We lie in bed and smoke a spliff, then have sweet sex. He's a good kid and doesn't want any babies. He buys a box of condoms and hides them under his mattress. One Saturday when we think his mum's out shopping, she walks in and catches us. She hits the roof and says she found the condoms when she made his bed. She knows he's up to something. She calls me a little whore.

'Go home, you leading my boy astray,' she says. 'He's a good boy and he don't need a no-good, worth-nothing girl like you.'

My confidence takes a bitter blow and I go home, crying. I stay away for two months and lie in bed at the home, dreaming about him. 'I'll wait for you,' he tells me when we meet in the park. 'You're my girl, Sugar.'

'I love you, Angel,' I tell him. And I do – I'm dewy-eyed like a silly sheep over him – until I find out he's cheating on me. My heart's broken, but there's nothing I can do – we're just two fourteen-year-olds. OK, mistah wise guy, screw you, I say. I get this bitch attitude and cheat on him. I'm searching for guys to give me comfort, but they're bad men, gangsters and pimps and dealers. I'm in a lot of fucked-up situations. I get a terrible reputation and know I could be hurt or killed if I don't stop.

One day, there's a fight on the lawn outside the home between a shy boy, Danny, who lives in the home and Kane, a kid I've seen hanging around the street in Peckham. Kane's an older boy, a casual friend of Angel. Everyone says he's no good, though he's as good-looking as a movie star, with black curly hair and long, girly eyelashes. I like the way he looks, but hate his bad attitude. The fight's over drugs. I break it up, and Danny thanks me. 'That's OK, Danny,' I say. 'Kane's just a bully.'

I see Kane more and more, hanging out, and without realising it, I start to talk to him. Late one night, I see him hanging out outside, just sitting on a wall, looking miserable, and on a whim, I go out to talk to him. 'What's up?' I ask.

'I've run away from home,' he says, 'I've been sleeping on street. Is there a spare bed in the home?'

I shake my head. 'Place is full,' I tell him, 'it's so crowded they've turned the upstairs gym into a bedroom.' He nods and starts to mooch off – but he looks so pinched and cold I feel sorry for him, even though I don't like him. 'You can sleep in my room, on the floor,' I tell him. I sneak him in, and find some food from the kitchen. In my room, we sit smoking weed, listening to music and talking a bit. He doesn't say much. My door opens and Tilda slips in. Oh shit, I think, she'll report me. I glare at her, but she sits on the floor and rocks back and forwards, her head in her arms. Time passes, and we're in our own little world, smoking and listening to music.

I wash and get ready for bed, but when I pull up the covers I think, they can't stay there all night, and I let them climb in with me. I'm in the middle. It's crowded, but OK if we stay still – and I'm used to sharing beds. Kane's on the outside, and he turns off the light. There must be something about the dark, because we start talking. Kane starts to tell us about his life. He starts slow, talking in small bits, but after a while, it all comes tumbling out, how his mum got together with another man, his step-dad, who's been raping Kane for years. 'It started when I was six,' he says. 'It's never stopped.'

'What, he's still doing it?'

'Yeah.'

'What about your mum – didn't you tell her?' I say.

'Yeah, I did. She don't give a fuck. She lets him do it.'

Soon, Kane is crying, and I put an arm around him, and tell him about how I was raped, and how my mum beats me, and how I can't figure her out – and I'm crying too. Then hesitantly, in the dark, Tilda says, 'I was born in prison.'

She has never told anyone her story, and I almost hold my breath to hear what she will say. There's a long silence, and then she tells us how her mother has been in and out of prison all her life. She is so dangerous and violent, her sentences are very long. Tilda was taken away from her at once, and put into foster homes. Her final home was a place where the 'parents' already had daughters of their own. 'I don't know why they wanted me,' she whispers. 'They never stopped reminding me that I was born in jail, that my mum is a sinner, and that I didn't really belong anywhere. As they grew older, the girls used to torment me and call me names – said I was devil spawn. In the end, I ran away.'

She hung out in the street with junkies and street kids, doing whatever it took to be accepted in the gang. 'I was always looking for love and attention. They treated me like shit – and I let them. Some attention was better than none. Being the outcast of even the outcasts was so horrible, I started to self-harm.' One day, she stood outside a children's home until someone noticed her, and she was taken in.

'Like me,' Kane says.

'Yeah – like you,' she agrees.

'Do you think they'll let me stay here?' Kane asks.

'You don't want to come here, it's horrible,' Tilda says.

'There's nowhere else wants us,' I say. That realisation is almost more than we can bear.

We're lying in bed, our arms around each other crying, until we fall asleep with exhaustion. In the morning, we're crying again with the memories. One of the staff knocks and comes in to see why I'm not up for school, and finds us there. He stares, and says, 'Who's this? What's going on?'

There's something about the pain and pleading in my face, I guess, that stops him in his tracks. I see him nod, then he says, 'OK, the boy can stay for breakfast, but he's got to go afterwards.' He closes the door and leaves us. I get out of bed and tell Kane that he should go to Social Services and get some help, like I did. No one has to put up with what he's putting up with. Now that I know her story, I'm OK with Tilda, too – but she still drives me crazy. We've all had some pretty crappy things done to us in our lives and that's why we've ended up where we are.

I don't talk to the staff at the home – none of us kids

do – because at the end of the day, they just don't care. I can't talk to Mum. She'd laugh and say, 'I told you so. Now get your ass down here to Bristol and get paid for laying on your back, 'stead of doing it for free.'

One day, there's a room search. The manageress calls me to her office. 'Are you soliciting, Sugar?'

I'm angry. 'You mean like on street? A tart?'

'Yes, that's what I mean. You have too much money.'

Silly cow. You give me too much pocket money. I buy weed, sell it. I have weed and cash hidden all over my room. I didn't realise they do room searches.

'No, ma'am. I don't solicit.'

I return to my room. Dammit, they've taken everything. Place reamed out. I don't want to say they've taken it because I'd have to admit having it – but I want it back.

John, a member of staff, is on duty that day. I know he took my weed and used it. His eyes are buzzing. I know it's him. I'm angry. I want to do a spliff in the park after school. It makes me feel good.

I stand in front of him on the stairs. 'You a tief. You stole my shit. Give it back.'

He grins. 'Fuck off.'

I run into my room, turn on the tap, fill a glass, throw it over him. He reports me. I'm told I'll get no pocket money that week. Big deal.

Jasmine, the girl from the room next to mine, sees I'm angry. She says, 'Lets go clubbing Peckham, yeah?'

'We can't go clubs. We'll get into trouble.'

'They can't do nothing, innit. What they goin' do –
lock us in our rooms?'

I'm angry and don't care no more. Jasmine is gorgeous
– big eyes, long legs like Naomi Campbell. She dreams
of being a model and being rich. We fix our hair nice,
I pull on a black bra, a satin halter-top and some skimpy
little shorts that show off my bum, and we run for the
bus. Dancing, dancing, having fun, wild in the club
Chicago. We meet these American Yardies, Sammy, John
and this older guy, says his name's Delta. They buy us
champagne. So cool. The bottle comes in a bucket,
clinking ice. First time I've drunk champagne. I'm giggly,
feel soft like melting butter.

Come to my senses. This path leads to having babies.
No sir! I say, 'I gotta go home.'

Delta says, 'I'll drive you.'

'Yeah, thanks. I'll get my friend.'

Jasmine's gone. I look in the ladies' room, she's fixing
her hair again. She's always fixing her hair. 'You comin'
home?'

'Yeah, OK.'

I return to Delta. 'OK, you can drive us. You know
the way?'

'Sure thing, babe.' We all pile into his big Ford car
glide through south London. I lay back, gaze at the sky
through sunroof, lights flashing and shimmering. We
drive and drive. It's a long way. 'You sure you know
where you going?'

'Sure. We going home.'

I wake up on motorway. 'Let me out! Let me out!'

'You'll be OK, babe. Don' you want some fun?' The boys laugh. They pass a joint. The car stinks of skunk and I drift off.

'Where are we?'

'Oxford.'

I think he means Oxford Circus. Where shops? Where lights? They laugh. Oxford, they say, Oxford in Oxfordshire. I say, Oxford where I won second best in the competition? They don't know what I mean.

Delta says, 'Yeah, you won the competition, babe. The horny girl competition.' They all laugh. He say, 'And I goin' win the horny man competition, whoohoo. You want big jig-a-jig?'

They're drug dealers. They have a rented house in a place called Jericho. It's a name from the Bible. They say it's by the river. John sings, 'Joshua fought the battle of Jericho and the walls came tumbling down.' We all join in, clap hands. '. . . And the walls came tumbling down.'

We share one bedroom. Jasmine pairs up with John. She strips off in front of me. I'm embarrassed. Where's her modesty? As soon as they get into bed, he starts to fuck her, hard. She's wooing and squealing and he's panting, like they're a pair of hogs in season. I get into bed fully dressed, and Delta gets in with me. He's naked. He pulls me to him. Man! He big, got big muscles.

'You know what they doing?'

'I guess.'

'We should do it.'

'I'm tired.' But I take off my shorts, kiss him back. Seems I lost my will.

He forces himself deep into me. 'You my girl now.'

Next morning, I have a bath, put my dirty clothes back on. He doesn't use protection – no self-respecting Jamaican man does. They believe it's an insult to their virility. But me, I'm too young, I need to leave. Instead, Delta pulls me back into bed, and without thought, I let him do it. I don't know him, but look like I got myself a man. Will he be my first baby-father? I'm stupid to let this happen so easily, to just go with the flow, no condoms. Am I worth so little? I'm weak and stupid.

He bangs me hard all day and night for a week like I'm a real woman. I'm sore. He's got a dong like a donkey – hell, his mum must've thrown him at a whole forest of little-boy pee-pee papaya trees. The curtains are drawn all the time so nobody can look in, it's like a nightclub. We feed on takeaways and listen to music and smoke dope. People come to the house to buy drugs. Sometimes they go down to colleges in town, sell shit. Money flows in from all them rich students. Delta's got so much cash, his wad fills his pants pocket like he's got a giant banana stuffed down there. They all got guns, they got machetes and swords in the boot of the car, there's an axe by the front door and a sub-machine gun in the wardrobe.

I rinse my undies in the bath and wear his shirts, but I want a change of my own clothes. I tell him to take me home. He says, 'You got me babe, I'll look after you. I'll take you shopping, buy you what you want.'

'No,' I say. 'You want me to be your woman, you got to give me my own money.'

He laughs. 'You learning fast, honey,' he says admiringly, slapping me on my ass. He gets out his fat wad and peels off £300. 'Get some sexy things.' He winks.

He drops me off in the centre of town, right near the train and bus station where the big shops are. 'I'll pick you up here at two o'clock,' he says. 'Don't get lost.'

I give him a big smile and watch him pull away. As soon as he's gone, I go straight to the bus station and buy a ticket for Victoria. I'm back in London in just over an hour. When I walk through the door of the home, the manageress grabs me.

'Where you been, Sugar? We've reported you absconded. The police are looking for you and Jasmine. Do you know where she is?'

'No, I ain't seen her,' I lie. Let Jasmine work it out for herself. It's her life.

The manageress says, 'I have to report this. You do know you might get into serious trouble – perhaps be sent to a secure unit, where you can't run off for a week when you feel like it.'

We've heard all about secure units. It's a fate worse than death, nothing but cold showers, restraints and abuse. For two weeks I am good and go to school every day. I do all my homework and give up smoking weed. But the £300 is burning a hole in my pocket and I can't resist going out one Saturday with Joelyn to East Street Market. I'm happy. I'm not pregnant. It's like I've been given a second chance to get my life back on track. I've seen the good and bad faces of Oxford. Some day, I might go back and be a real scholar and get a real degree. I smile. Mum and my brothers would die. I'd go back to Constant Spring, waving my degree. 'Look what this girl done! Look what little Sugar achieved! The first one in the ghetto ever get a degree – and from Oxford University!'

There's a great big silly smile pinned to my face when I move the clothes on a rack and there's my mum. Our eyes meet. My blood runs cold. My smile freezes. Then I whirl around and run.

She chases me, yelling, 'Stop that girl! She my daughter, she a runaway. She a tief!'

Nobody helps me. Joelyn runs off and tells no one. People stop me. 'No!' I shout. 'She ain't my mum. She kidnapping me.'

She's grabbed me and they stand back. 'Let go! Let go! Call the police!' I yell.

Mum drags me off to Bristol. Somehow she's got another big three-bedroom council house. She's got a friend in the housing department. 'There's lot of Jamaicans on the council, we help each other,' she says. My brothers have started school down in Bristol, using fake names and she says, 'You can go school Bristol if you want, but you old enough now to help me. I was working streets at your age. You can earn good money. I want to build house in Jamaica.'

'I'm not your sex slave,' I say angrily. 'I'm your daughter.'

Without warning, she punches me in the face. 'Hey, listen, girl, I did things you don't even know about to support you and your brothers. Don't you dare talk to me like that. I'm your mother. You better not disrespect me again.'

I resign myself to a way of life I had thought I'd left. But someone must have called Social Services – perhaps it was Joelyn after all. The police come looking for me, down in Bristol, banging on the door, and Mum freaks. Upstairs it's so full of pot plants, it's like a plant nursery. Mum could be sent to jail for ten years – and she's still on the run from that previous arrest. Social Services get hold of her phone number and call her and she freaks again. I have to return to London, she shouts. 'Get on the bus, you going today.'

I smirk, then laugh. 'Good!' I say.

'You'd rather be in a children's home than living with your own family?' she sneers.

I think, 'Yeah, Mum, I don't want to go hooking or sell drugs for you and your boyfriend. I'd rather go to school and not be beaten so bad I can't walk for three weeks.' Instead, I say, 'It's better for me, Mum, you know that. I'm smart. The school says I can do well if I apply myself.'

She and my brothers take me to the bus. I kiss my brothers. They're growing so fast, they'll soon be taller than me. Paul is like a sapling, Wayan is like a young ox. I turn to Mum, then suddenly we're hugging and kissing goodbye. I'm crying.

Mum says, 'Look honey, tings ain't good between us, but I'm your mother and you my daughter. I'll come up London, come see you, yeah? I'll call you.'

I nod and sniff and get on the bus, wave to her and my brothers. It shouldn't be like this.

Back in London at the home, social workers come

and finally try to sort out my legal situation. It's like they've suddenly woken up to the fact that I'm an illegal alien, with no right to be in England. They say it will all take time. I'm shit-scared and cry a lot. What would I do if they sent me to Jamaica soon as I hit eighteen? Was I a fool to desert Mum? She manages to stay below the radar and is thriving, using her wits. Someone tells me she's done a moonlight flit and moved house again. I don't know her new address, but she might keep her promise to get in touch.

A few weeks later, she does call and we arrange to meet down Brixton Market, at her friend Millie's hair-dresser's shop. Millie's in her forties or fifties, fat and cheerful, except when her feet hurt at the end of the day. Her bouffant hits the sky like a chocolate soufflé. Everything's fine between us. We have our hair fixed – Mum pays – and we sit side by side, chatting, laughing like we've never been apart. Whenever she comes up to London on the bus, we secretly meet by a prearranged appointment. She sells drugs and stays with friends, so I don't kid myself she's coming just to see me. She never wants to hear about my problems. If I say anything, she gets impatient. 'We all got problems,' she says.

Eventually, Immigration decides that, as an underage child, I'm entitled to stay and be taken care of by the state until I'm eighteen. I'm safe for now.

Chapter 11

London, 2003

I'm down Chicago when I meet Dillon. He's a street man, quite old – maybe forty or fifty – not even good-looking, got a barrel chest and short legs. I don't fancy him, not even a little bit. But he fancies me like crazy and this new hard me soon sees how I can take him for a ride. Testing him, I ask for £500 and he gives it to me – doesn't even ask what I want it for. I stare at the wad of cash, then flash him a big smile and put it away in my bag. I think, he's gonna ask for sex, how will I get out of it? But he doesn't. Just as well 'cause I've got a jealous toyboy on the side I'm having sex with. I don't know how I don't get diseased or pregnant, 'cos I should, banging away like rabbits. I wouldn't even care. Nothing seems to matter. Nothing but school. I'm still studying hard.

When I phone Dillon, he comes every time, like a puppy, tail wagging. He gives me lifts and so much money, I'm careless with it. I buy clothes that I give away or throw out when I've worn them once, and I get drugs to share with everyone, throw it around like confetti. I'm a popular girl, me. One night he's driving me around, and he says he wants to be my permanent driver.

'Sure,' I say carelessly. I mean, he's got a brand new blue BMW – a girl can look good, win respect, being driven around in a car like that.

He drops me off in Peckham and says he'll call me on the new mobile he got me, he'll come, take me home, or anywhere. Thanks, I say, and like the Queen of Sheba, I flick him under the chin, strut off, shaking my tight little ass. The sauce of that girl, I laugh to myself. He's an idiot, more fool him.

One night, he sees me raving, out of my head on crack, flirting and French kissing all these boys. Oops, I think. Then I think, 'So what – what's he gonna do to me? I don't want no old man anyway. Screw him.'

In the club, flirting hard, sitting on strangers' laps, kissing in corners, buying all these pretty toyboys drinks, I look up and see Dillon's watching me. I shiver. His face is nasty, like an attack dog. He calls me outside and, like a lamb to the slaughter, I go. I'm nervous. I've seen how the other men look at him, like, with respect, and suddenly I see he's not some dickhead old geezer I can wind around my finger, no, he's Mr Big and I'm a silly little girl in big trouble.

Outside in his car he's angry. 'You're coming home with me tonight,' he says, grabbing my arm. 'You take me for fool, spending all my money on you, nothing in return. Tonight I'm going to screw you, like you been screwing me.'

I say, cute and sulky, 'You no fool, but I ain't going home with you. You too old. Old enough to be my dad.'

'I been treating you nice, like you was a virgin, I been saving you for myself – but tonight's the night, bitch. Your number's up.'

'You can't make me. I'm going home –' I yelp, going to open the car door.

Click. Oh shit. Gun to my head.

I'm drunk, head spinning. Giggle. I still don't take him seriously. He's good old Dillon, just fooling around. I'm argumentative, tell him I don't love him. Then my phone rings. It's my mum.

'Hi Mum,' I say, gun to my head, like it's all normal. 'How you doin'?'

He grabs my phone. 'You this bitch mother? What kind of daughter you raise? She take me for a fool. I spend thousands on her – she give it all away to no-good losers. Gigolos with bum fluff on their chin.'

He nods and says, 'Yeah, I'm telling you – that what she done. Yeah, I agree, she damned fool whore.'

I grab the phone back. 'Mum? What you saying? He got a gun to my head.'

My mum says, 'Well, he sounds a nice man. You lucky to have him.'

'Mum!'

He grabs the phone, chuckles, 'Yeah – you told her.' Then his voice changes. 'Lulu, that you? Yeah, this is Dillon. Hey doll, how you doing?'

I sit there, my mouth open, while my mum and a

gangster who has a gun to my head chat away like they're old friends. He clicks the safety back on and puts the gun away. Then he hands the phone back to me. 'Here, she wants talk wit you.'

My mum snaps, 'What you doin' wit a murderer?'

I mumble, 'You jokin', yeah?'

'Girl, he from Jamaica. Get with it, girl. You fool wit him, you put yourself in danger. Now I talkin' nice and easy to him, we old friends, but you better watch out. He kill you, dump yo' body, sure as eggs is eggs. He a mean motherfucker badass man. You gottit?' By the end, she's yelling.

I sober up quickly. Suddenly very scared, I tell him I'm just a prick-tease, I ain't never done it – I'm just fourteen. I sweet-talk him into taking me home. He tries to deep-throat me when we reach the children's home, but I give him one quick thrust, pink tongue in his mouth and I'm gone out the car, like a slippy little fish. *Night,* I wave, running up the front steps. *See ya!*

I start avoiding him, but he comes, sits outside in the BMW all the time, uses the street like his office, runs his business right where he can keep an eye on me coming or going. Shit, he's stalking me. I can't leave by the front door and walk to the bus stop as usual every day. I have to go to school in the home's people carrier. I hide in the bottom of the car in the well between the seats. Sometimes, he telephones and says, 'I'm outside. Come out, bitch, and talk to me face to face or I'll kill everyone in there.'

No signal, I gabble, no signal. I'm terrified and hang

up. I telephone Angel and beg him to run away with me. I've got money saved, I tell him. 'I love you, you gotta help me, baby – he gonna kill me.'

Angel knows Dillon's reputation. 'You crazy? I can't go with you, he'll kill my mum and my sisters.'

I decide to run away on my own. *Where to?* Don't know nowhere. Then the TV news says there been a shoot-out in a pub in Brixton. Dillon's photograph is onscreen. His mugshot stares out at me. I sit bolt upright. Holy crap! He shot a couple of men from a rival gang – and they pumped him full of bullets. He's hurt bad, in hospital.

Shit. I stare at the screen. He's in the big hospital just up the road from here, guarded round the clock by armed officers. They say they're taking no chances, he's a dangerous criminal.

My phone rings. It's my mum. 'Did you see the news?' she asks. Her voice is excited, yet nervous. 'I told you, you tangling with dynamite.'

'I hope he dies,' I say.

Then I hear he's getting better, they're moving him to prison. Before he can go to court, he escapes, and runs off to America, still swathed in bandages. I breathe a sigh of relief and feel I've won a reprieve. I have to straighten up. I start to behave, do the right thing, get serious. I'm top of the class. My teachers are pleased – they tell me the sky's the limit. I wish I believed them.

Chapter 12

Croydon, 2003

I turn seventeen at the end of June. I'm a moon baby. Cancer, a crab. Soon, I'll be thrown out into the world on my own. It's drummed into me that I have to be ready, have to be prepared for the future. My social worker says they're putting me in my own flat, all paid for by the state. She says nothing about me being illegal, throwing me out of England. I don't ask her any questions in case it wakes up the sleeping dog. Fingers crossed they've forgotten.

'We'll be supporting you to make the adjustment, there's no need to be nervous, Sugar,' my social worker says, kindly. Poor woman looks tired, too big a caseload.

I'm beyond nervous, flying on automatic pilot. I take life as it comes, one day at a time.

'We will supervise you twenty-four-seven, someone will always be there for you. We'll pay your rent, give you an allowance, give you a loan for a new bed, sheets and so on,' she nods, checking off the list. I can't believe all the things this country is doing for an illegal girl.

What for? She continues with her checklist, 'Help you get a job –'

What kind of job? My dream fades. I knew deep down I would never go to Oxford University like them rich white girls with stable homes, never get that degree, never go back home to Constant Spring and wave it at them. No big party for me.

'We're allocating you a three-bedroom house in Croydon –'

Croydon? Where the fuck is that? Maybe Outer Mongolia? And why do I need three bedrooms? I've got no plans to be a baby-mother or run a B & B.

'Yeah, OK,' I say. As an afterthought, I add, 'Thank you.' I've been taught to be polite, and I'm grateful, they don't have to do this. I expect nothing from anyone.

But she's still talking. 'When would you like to see the house?'

I look puzzled, and quickly she explains that I must inspect it and agree to take it. I'm still puzzled, and she says, 'The choice is yours, Sugar. You don't have to live there. But I'd advise you to do so. It's in a very nice area. Some of the other accommodation available is not as nice. I think you'll like it.'

I'm amazed. Not only am I offered a free place to live, but I have a choice. I think back to Jamaica – tar-paper shacks and cement blocks. Nothing's free there. Britain is the land of milk and honey, if you know how to play your cards right. But for a girl like me with no family and a mum who can't cope, like the Bible says, it's a bitter harvest.

I move in a month later. Another girl will be joining me, but for now, I'm the first one in the house. I get a job at a big store in Oxford Street. It's nice to be independent, but if I earn too much they'll reduce my allowance from the state, charge me rent. It makes no sense – why penalise people for working hard?

But none of that seems important. I love my own place! I walk from room to room, stretching out my arms to feel the space, to get a sense of ownership. It's mine! My name's on the lease and I have the keys. The walls are painted magnolia, a pretty creamy colour, like milk. There are gauzy curtains at the windows, and blinds in the kitchen and bathroom. The floors are polished woodblock, easy to keep clean. I visualise rugs, pictures on the wall. I can do anything I want! But I won't have wild parties. I'll enjoy the space. I'll be happy here, no noise, no crazy suicide girls, no eyes watching, no ram-raids on my room. I decorate in my free time, get a twenty-inch TV and stereo, a radio. I go to Argos, buy a nice duvet and matching curtains out of the catalogue. I make it homely and comfortable. Everything's new and clean. I love it – it's my very own place. Every weekend, I wash and scrub and polish – it's the cleanest house in the street.

But as the weeks pass, I feel lonely. I have a friend in care, like me, though at a different home from the one I've just left. Marina's a mixed-race girl, just turned seventeen, who I met through Milton. She's got a big bottom, pale skin, wild, bushy hair, bleached blonde like a mop. Very pretty face, but dumb. She has to get out of her children's home soon. I bump into her in Brixton and tell her about my place, how happy I am. She looks envious. 'Can I see it?' she asks.

'Yeah, OK – come on over tomorrow, hang out.'

She comes over next day, Sunday. 'You so lucky,' she says, looking around. 'All these big rooms, paid for by government. What you done to deserve it?'

I giggle. 'Nothin'. Man, they crazy.' We laugh like hyenas. She begs me to let her share. I say I'll think about it. I like my space, but it's lonesome in the evenings. I ask my social worker if Marina can share. Fine, no problem, she says – it's too big for you and you knew we were going to give you a housemate. I hadn't remembered that, so I'm glad I found Marina before I ended up with a total stranger. I give my social worker Marina's details and leave it to her.

One day, I come home tired from work. I've done a little shopping on the way, got vegetables and fish for my supper, there's rice and beans, hot sauce in the cupboard. I lick my lips. *Mmm-mm.* I can taste it already. I'm happy, and sing as I put the key in my door. The chain is across it, I can't get in. I ring the bell. What the fuck's going on? Marina opens the door, smiling. She's piled her hair on top of her head, like a cockatoo. She's happy to be there she says. Come on in.

Come on in? Into my own house? Who does she think she is?

'Why the fuck you put the chain on?' I say. Not a good start.

She glares and shifts her shoulders aggressively. 'You want to fight about it?' Definitely not a good start.

'Look, I'm tired, goin' cook something to eat. You want some?'

'Sure.'

We start again, have a laugh, share a bottle, have some puff. Say we'll get on. 'We'll be sisters,' she says, 'look out for each other.' For a while we're good friends, have a load of laughs, go clubbing. I know she could be a bad enemy. Her dad, Cardinal, is a member of the Brixton 28s, the heaviest black gang in London. These are serious guys, very dangerous. Nobody tangles with the 28s. She's from one of Cardinal's baby-mothers, but mostly he ignores her, leaves her alone to fend for herself. But I know if anyone insults her, he'll have to sort it out.

One Sunday, lying in bed, yawning, deciding what to do, it dawns on me that I'm grown up. My mum's not there to order me around, there's no teachers, no one. I can do anything and no one can stop me, say lights out, clean this, do what I tell you. It's scary and exhilarating. I'm a strange mixture of confidence and panic.

That night, I go to a party and the first person I see when I walk in is Kane. He's grown taller and broader and looks so cool. I go up to him, smiling.

'Hi Kane, how you doing?'

His gaze is admiring, friendly. 'Hi Sugar. How you been?'

We stand grinning at each other, and he asks me to

dance. He's a great dancer, really moves and he holds me close. I love the feel of my body next to his, love his smell. When I look up into his face, I want to kiss him all the time. That night we spent sobbing in my bed seems a long time ago, as if it happened to other people. I'm getting my life together and it looks like he's been doing well. He tells me that he's got a job in building, earning good money and he's going to college as well.

I say, 'Yo man, you're a JET!'

He laughs and denies it. A JET is in a Job, in Education, or in Training. At school it was banged into our heads that a boy should be a JET and girls should go out with JETS until it was a dirty word. Boys wanted to rebel, girls wanted bad boys. Neither side wanted to have anything to do with a JET. But Kane's a cool JET and when he asks me to go on a date, I agree. We have fun and soon are sleeping together. But I hear on the grapevine that he's two-timing me and I'm really upset. He's no different from anyone else. I'm pissed off, but keep going out with him. When I'm out clubbing with Kane one night, we bump into my sweet Angel. I haven't seen him for a long time.

'Yo, Angel – how you been?'

'I'm fine – you? How you been?'

We grin goofily at each other. My, he's such a pretty boy! He says to Kane, 'I didn't know you know Sugar.'

'Yeah,' says Kane, 'we friends.'

I look from one to the other. 'Do you know each other?'

'Sure,' says Kane, 'we work for the same company. Small world.'

With Kane playing around on me, I decide to pay him back, and I start two-timing him with Angel. It gets so intense that I can't make up my mind which one I really want. I love them both. I'm on the point of dumping Kane when I hear on the grapevine that Angel is two-timing me. He's playing the field, he's sleeping with half the girls in south London, flying from one to the other, like a butterfly sipping nectar. Furious, I rush round to Angel's place and bang on his door. When he opens it, I'm in his face.

'We're through!' I yell. 'You a two-timing rat.'

'Hey, baby, calm down,' he says. 'You going with Kane – what's the big deal?'

He takes the wind out of my sails. I didn't know he knows – but it makes sense. Just like girls compare notes, boys do, too. 'Yeah, well, guess we better split up,' I say. 'Our relationship is toxic.'

'C'mon, baby, no need to be like that,' he wheedles.

'Yeah, there is,' I say. 'You boys all run around, your dick in your hand, like you God's gift to women. I don't need it no more. '

I split up with Kane and Angel, go through a succession of short, quick relationships that get me out of my house and stop me dwelling on how bad things are there. Marina has become a thorn in my side. I come home, find my bedroom a mess, my clothes used, bath dirty, kitchen squalid. Her friends come around, stay up until 6 a.m. *Boom-boom-boom*. All night, loud music, TV on full volume, I don't get no sleep. Tired at work all day. Place stinks of weed. Neighbours complaining. I'm worried I'll be arrested or evicted. I get up in the morning, go downstairs, and find mixed-race twins eating my food from the refrigerator. Marina's invited them to stay without discussing it with me first. They cook, don't wash dishes, use my coffee, leave puddles of milk and sugar all over the counter. No milk left for me to have some breakfast before I go to work.

'Fuck off!' I shout. 'Get out my house.'

'It's not your house, you can't tell us to go.'

'OK, but you eating my food, watching my TV, listening to my radio.'

'So what?'

My bedroom is above the living room. They're keeping me awake with my own things. I unplug my TV and radio and take them upstairs, panting with the weight. I might be selfish, but they're mine, I paid for them. When I come down, the twins call me a bitch. I don't look at them and run to catch the train for work.

Soon as I've gone, Marina steals my stuff from my bedroom. She brings down my TV, plugs it in and turns it on loud, so the neighbours complain when they see me. I have a nice pair of white satin trousers, they really make my bum look nice and tight. She steals them. I rant and yell when I see her wearing them. She offers them back, dirty. I shout she's a slut.

She says, 'Keep your cool, they only cheap. Plenty more down market.'

I say, 'Screw you! They from Topshop.'

She washes them and I grab them wet and lash them in her face. 'If I want second-hand clothes, I'd go to a second-hand shop.'

I demand money to replace them. She refuses. There's no manageress living in to sort out our disputes like at the children's home. We're on our own, we've got to sort it out ourselves.

I come home one evening, find a man in boxers snoring on the sofa. 'Who the fuck you?'

'Chester.'

'Yeah, well, Chester, you can fuck off home.'

'Hey girl, no need to have dat attitude. Dis mah home. I live here.'

Marina found him on the street, nowhere to live, so she's rented the spare room to him and pockets the money. But she also makes him her lover, more fool her. She sleeps with him in her bed. He gets arrogant, stops paying rent after a week, pushes her around, swears at her, thinks he's boss. Then he comes on heavy to me, like we're his harem, like we're his baby-mothers. I tell him if I want a boyfriend, I'll go find one of my own. I don't want no second-hand goods, no scum like him.

I don't tell him that my next boyfriend is going to be nice-looking and with money to spend on me, not the other way around. I'm waiting until the right boy comes along and, meanwhile, I'm quite content to spend my spare time with my girlfriends.

I pack a bag and leave my own house, to stay with my friend, Tawni. I'm complaining to her, asking 'what can I do', when the doorbell goes. Marina's standing there crying, black eyes, split lip. Sure enough, it's all ended up bad. She and Chester have had a big fight. She soaked all his clothes in the bath, he punched out her lights – she slammed the door on him and ran, no money, nothing. She walked all the way to Tawni's house. 'What am I goin' to do?' she sobs, pulling combs and pins out of her bushy hair, making it stand up like a halo around her pointy face.

She's got a nerve, asking me. I tell her it all rebounded on her, more fool her.

'Yeah, I know,' she says, hanging her head. 'He like cock of the roost, taken control of chicken house. He say he going to let out our rooms, make money.'

I feel sorry for her. She wasn't brought up properly and has no common sense. Maybe we should ask Cardinal, Marina's dad, to sort it? But he'll kill Chester and it could rebound on us. We need a softer approach. Tawni's boyfriend is boss of a south London crew, he's the man in his district, everyone's scared of him. Tawni calls him. He goes around and evicts Chester with just a bit of gentle persuasion, not too violent. We know we will never see him again. I pay to change the locks and then I sit and talk long and hard with Marina. 'You can't just live off me. You need a job. We got to share costs, I ain't no benefactor to the world.'

She agrees. I say we can make our little house really nice, turn it into a palace, a comfort zone. So Marina gets a job and starts paying her way. I save for a microwave for the kitchen and tell her she has to pay half.

'I want to get some clothes,' she says, sulky again. 'I got none.'

'That's because you spend all your money on no-good bums and drugs,' I lecture, like I'm her mum. Big mistake. She starts to treat me like I'm her mum and she's a badass delinquent teenager rebelling against me. I become the enemy. In the end, every bad thing she does to spite me is a victory for her.

I buy a microwave from Argos and put it in the kitchen. 'It's mine, don't use it,' I tell her. After work I find it splattered. I say, 'You used it.'

She says, 'No, I didn't. You left it like that.'

'Well, you gotta clean it.'

'Why should I?'

We argue over everything. It's getting out of control, soon there'll be blood on the carpet. Tawni calms the situation down and gets us talking. 'You're both being silly. You have to be more mature. Split the cost of food down the middle and keep your personal things separate. Respect each other's property.'

'What about if I buy a toaster?' I ask.

'If you buy it and you don't want Marina to use it, keep it in your bedroom.'

I say it's crazy, but Tawni says, 'If it keep the peace, it the only way, innit?'

Marina and I shake hands and agree to a truce. She says she will try harder, try to budget better. We start again. I get a kettle and a toaster and put them in my bedroom, like Tawni says. I'm angry that I have to bring them down to the kitchen when I want to use them.

It's crazy. I go grocery shopping Saturday down Croydon market and ask Marina for her share of the money. She says no, she don't eat nothin'.

I call her a fucking liar. She eats like a horse. I grab all the food, all the pots and pans and put them on my side of the cupboard. Her side's bone-dry, empty. I glare at her. 'Use any of my stuff and you're dead,' I say.

She says, 'You want to fight?' She rolls up her sleeves. She's in the kitchen, knife drawer open behind her, mad look in her eyes. Holy shit. I run out the house.

I go to stay with Tawni for the weekend to keep out of the way and give Marina some space she doesn't deserve. When I come back early on Monday morning before work, there's no food in the house. She has cooked it all, had a party and left the kitchen a horrible mess, pots, pans, dishes everywhere, sink overflowing, food all over the floor. We have a huge fight and batter each other black and blue. I'm late for work and crying. I telephone the social worker from work and say Marina and me, we're getting at each other all the time. She has to come and help us sort it out. She gives us the usual social worker spiel, very ambivalent, and says we have to try to do better, we're old enough to respect each other, we're both entitled to live there and it's not her job to sort out minor domestic disputes.

'If she stabs me, then I guess you'll help,' I say.

'Is that likely to happen?' she asks, sighing. 'If it is, call the police. It's their job.'

To my astonishment, Marina suddenly gets a regular, boring boyfriend. He's a good boy, a JET – yet here's this useless bitch, Marina, with him. I'm laughing. But Tawni says, 'Good thing. Maybe she ready to straighten up and settle down.'

Just as suddenly, Marina ditches her JET for Shed, who's only fifteen, a little man in big man's shoes. I hate going home in case he's there, he's such a dick-head. He sits sprawled in an armchair, legs apart, eating with his mouth wide open, scratching his crotch. Scritch-scratch, scritch-scratch, like he's masturbating.

'For fuck sake, Shed, stop that,' I say.

'What you say?'

'You got the itches or sump'n?'

'Yeah, bitch. You wan' 'em?' he leers.

We never stop bickering. He knows I despise him and tries to act big and fails. A little while later, Marina comes crying to me. She went to the STD clinic Saturday morning, walked in and Shed was sitting there. He's seen her so she can't leave. She sits next to him. They don't say nothing, she says. Next thing, the JET walks in, sits on the other side of her. Boy gave her the infection on the left, boy she give infection to on the right. She's in the middle.

'What am I supposed to say?' she moans. 'I look complete fool.'

'You don't need me – you've got enough support,' I snigger, walking out of the room in stitches.

She dumps Shed and the JET, or they dump her. Next thing, she drags home this guy called Jelly. What kind of a guy is called Jelly? I say she changes men like her underwear. She says he's a good man, very sexy, ooh-ooh!

She rolls her eyes, rubs her big bottom. Ten days later, she's moaning because she has pimples, like she's shaved. I'm laughing.

'Get back down the clinic,' I say.

'Yeah? Why?' she says.

'Trust me, girl, you got problems.'

So she goes and finds out she's got the clap and herpes. That bastard, she complains, I'll never trust a man with a name like Jelly again. I'm rolling around the floor laughing. What a dumbass is that girl. But she doesn't learn. There's another little boy, nice kid, I've known him since I first came to England. He's distantly related to me and we all meet up every Christmas, Carnival or christenings, when a new baby's born. His family is legal and been in England a long time, right back to the Windrush ship that came long ago. I've always called him Cuz. He's only fifteen. It's Carnival and there's lots of house parties around Brixton and Peckham. Everywhere there's West Indians, there's a party going on.

Marina and me, we bump into Cuz at a party. 'Hi Cuz – this is Marina.'

'Hi Marina.'

They chat. She tells him she's seventeen – so I tell her he's seventeen too, to keep his face – I don't know she's gonna fall for him.

'Oooh, he so cute, such a pretty boy, think I'll go out with him,' she says.

'No, Marina. You don't need to give my relatives your infections,' I say it straight out. We argue and she flounces off. Later, I warn him not to have sex with her. I don't tell him what she's got, it's not fair. I just say she's a bad girl, she's real trouble.

Three hours later, my phone's ringing. It's him. I say, 'You still at the party with Marina?'

No, he says, 'I'm at home –'

I'm thinking, Good –

'Back at the party, we go into bedroom, I put on a condom, just about to fuck her, but she stop me and say, "You're Sugar's cuz, I mean, like her real cousin, innit?" Yeah, I tell her, that's right, and she say, "OK, I gotta own up. I got the clap and herpes."'

Now I'm laughing, hand over the phone.

'Holy fuckin' shit. I went soft and ran home.'

Thank God, I think.

But he tells everyone that she's diseased. She was robbing the cradle, so she got what she deserved. Marina's so ashamed, she finds a new place to live. I'm relieved she's gone. A few weeks later, out of the blue, I get a phonecall from her.

'Hi Sugar, can you come round?' she asks, nice and sweet like honey. 'I'm having a party, just girls. I've given up boys.'

'Yeah, OK.'

I go round, find six girls there – Marina and five others. All five are good friends of mine. They're grinning like cats. She's called them round to duff me, but they don't tell her they my friends. When she tries to get them to rush me, they won't. Instead, they rush her. She runs from the house, realising she's made a big mistake and we all run after her whooping like crazy. Before we catch her, there's an African man walking by. We hate Africans. They hate us. Our energy changes, we forget our fight with Marina, she's now in our girl gang. We sidle up. 'Hey man, you got any cigarettes?'

'No, girls, go away.'

'Go on – give us your cigarettes.'

'Fuck off,' he says.

Six girls rush him, frenzied, beating him, kicking his head, his belly, all the soft places. He lies on the ground moaning, clutching privates. But his friend is in the phonebox at the end of the street and runs to help him. Big burly Africans, heads hard like coconuts, we can't knock them unconscious. Tables turn. They start bricking us.

'You fucking bitches, we going to kill you.'

My friends and me run, leaving Marina on the street, being bricked by two mad gorillas. Her face all bloody, she's yelling, 'Help! Murder! They killing me!'

Twelve Jamaican boys hanging around on the street corner watch. They don't move.

I scream, 'They gonna kill her! Go help her! Help!'

Four of the boys slouch towards the Africans, they're in no hurry. Get knives out, real slow and casual. One of the Africans runs off. I run back, pick up a brick and hit the other on the head. He's a hard nut to crack. I bang down hard. He jumps up, charges after me, I run into an estate and hide in a bin.

Later, I see Marina. Her face is out there, battered

black and blue. Swollen mouth, big cut in forehead. My back is bruised, I walk like a duck.

'You were going to jump me,' I say. 'What you playing at?'

'Your cuz been bad-mouthing me.'

'So? That my fault?'

I don't talk to her for a month. Next time I see her, she and another mixed-race girl are standing at a bus stop. I join them. 'Hey, going Brixton?'

'Yeah, you?'

'Yeah. Going shopping.'

Big white guy walks by. Marina throws her drink over him as he passes, no reason. She's laughing.

He stops, comes back, looks her up and down. 'You bitches think you're so tough because you're a bit black.'

'Yo can't talk to me like that,' Marina shrieks. Before he can answer, she hurls herself at him. *Bang!* He's not even winded. She's a crazy dumbass whore, he's big like a rugby player, built like a rhinoceros. 'Come on!' she yells. 'Kill him!'

We leap on him, so I guess that makes us all crazy dumbass whores. Clawing and scratching, pulling hair, biting, punching mouth. He kicks me hard in the knee with a steel toecap.

I scream, fall over, think knee is broken. He runs off. Marina runs after him shrieking abuse – man, is she crazy?

I shout, 'Come back, you can't manage him on your own.' I grab a stick, run after them around a corner. He's against a wall. Pulls out a knife. *Shit.*

Marina backs off slowly. White man runs into flats. Someone calls the police. They come, car sirens screaming. I throw stick behind bin and stand quietly, shy girl doing nothin'. They question us, but we ain't armed, got no weapons. They give us lecture, let us go.

I go home and sit on my own, staring into space. I see it's no way to live. Marina, that whore, she's nothing but trouble. I have to change, I just have to. One day I'm gonna be killed. I'm worth more than being another statistic, another worthless black girl who come over here, causing trouble.

Chapter 13

Brixton, 2004

I work hard, go straight, stay away from badass gang girls, stay out of trouble. Six months later, my social worker tells me I've been supported long enough and I must start to adjust to standing on my own feet. I lose my nice three-bedroom house. The rent is £800 a month and Social Services won't help me to pay it. *You're on your own, baby.* I ask my social worker if there's anything she can do to help, and she offers me a hostel in Brixton, a halfway house. It's free if I go into further education. I discover that I can take a skills course at a community college. Great! Sign me up.

When I move into the hostel, which is close to my old stamping ground, Brixton Market, I find Marina is already living there. Warily, we stare at each other in the hall. I'm happy she's there because it's good to know someone – but I know she's real bad news. I smile, say, 'Hi, how you doing?'

She smiles back. There we are grinning at each other, still not sure if it's gonna be war or peace. 'I'm good,' she says.

'OK, see ya around.'

My next shock is when I'm coming home from college one evening, and a car toots me. I ignore it – men are always tooting me because I've got a cute ass and tits.

'Ho, Sugar!'

Shit. I recognise that voice. I turn and look. Goddamn, it's Dillon, sitting in a brand new silver Lexus. He winds down the window and beckons. I walk across to the kerb and lean in the window.

'What you doin' here?'

'Hey, darlin', I been looking for you. Your mum gave me your address. Get in.' He reaches across to grab me.

Furious with my mum, I run, shoot around the corner to the hostel, punch out the entry code on the door, race inside. My heart is beating frantically. I run down the hall, banging on doors. 'Don't let him in, don't let him in.'

In my small room, I fall onto my bed and close my eyes, my head full of angry questions. Why can't I trust my mum – why is she playing games with me? I told her I was avoiding Dillon. Why did he have to come back? Why haven't the police locked him up for ten years? I'm entirely on my own, no family, no nothing, and I'm scared.

There's a knock at my door. I open it. He pushes his way in. Oh God. My worst nightmare.

'How'd you get in?' I say.

'I buzzed, said I was your uncle, and your good friend, Marina, let me in.'

Yeah, she would. 'What you doing back here? Police

station is just down the road – if they catch you you'll go to jail.'

'Nah, I got a good lawyer. He got me off. I got probation.'

Probation for a shoot-out at the OK Corral? It's crazy. 'Yeah,' he brags, 'I'm banned from Brixton, have to live in Croydon.'

Shit. Good thing I moved from there. 'So what are you doing here?'

He smirks. His old car, the one he's not allowed to drive in Brixton, is registered with the police. But this is a new car, registered in another name, CCTV cameras won't catch it. 'Hey baby, you don't look pleased to see me.'

'I'm not. You're a gangster.'

'I've gone straight.'

'Yeah? You got a job?'

'Nah, I'm living on my savings.'

I laugh.

'Aw, come on, baby, all I want is you. You're my girl.'

We sit and talk and he asks me out, but I say I've got an essay to write and I'm tired. 'I'll see you tomorrow,' he says, as he leaves. He kisses me. 'You can't keep fighting it – we're meant to be.'

I try to ignore him, but he learns my timetable and he's coming to my room every day. Within a week, I'm in bed with him. I don't even enjoy it. He's too old, there's no buzz. His pee-pee is three inches long, he's never been near any old papaya tree. As I lie under him, I close my eyes and wonder what I'm doing. A voice in my head says, 'Sugar, you like your mum. You're nothing better than a gangster's moll. Next thing, you'll be his baby-mother. Is this what you want?'

I find out he's married and has children, but it don't bother me none – you can't change history, so it's best to accept it. I'm just drifting along. I give up college, don't work. He buys me clothes, gives me money, wants me hang out with him at clubs and places, looking good. Night and day merge. He promises he'll set me up in a house of my own.

'Mm-mm. That nice. A rented place or one you gonna buy for me?'

'I'll buy one just for you, babe, wherever you want, sign over the deeds to you. It'll be our love nest. I'm in property, I have houses,' he brags, full of hot air.

He's got no property portfolio. All I see are his drug deals, his prostitution and extortion. I hadn't wanted a protector – I was fine before – but now that I have one, I'm actually in danger. If I stop being his woman, like my mum all those years ago in Jamaica, I'll be a target for his enemies.

He gets me in deeper, into all kinds of scams. There's the credit-cards scam, like an industry, run out of flats down the river. Piles of stolen credit cards, buy goods mail order. The goods pile up and we sell 'em quick. Moonlight flit before the cops catch up. It's happening all so fast, there aren't enough cops to check it out – and we're closed down and long gone. We work shops, buying high-end expensive goods, sell 'em cheap. Stolen cards are nothing on fake cards, piles of blanks, numbers copied from cash machines, garages and restaurants. All these deals going down, money flowing in like confetti – but girls like me, we don't get to see it. Mr Big just gets bigger and fatter, bloated on cash.

I hate myself, and feel depressed. I'm a zombie, a dead soul. I'm nearly eighteen and my life has come to an end.

I keep saying I will do better, that I'll snap out of it, but I'm too depressed. Then I find Dillon has a baby-mother and he lives with her. I use that to end our relationship. When he picks me up in his silver Lexus, I shout at him, 'Screw you. You jump from her bed to mine like a louse in pubic hair. Where's my house, my deeds? You're a fucking liar.'

'Oh, baby, don't be like this,' he wheedles.

I'm a crazy woman, throwing things, waving a knife. 'Screw you. We're through.'

I yell I'm not going to depend on anyone – definitely not a criminal like him.

I turn eighteen in June and decide it's a good key day to change my life. Mum telephones me.

'Happy birthday, Sugar.'

'Thanks, Mum.'

She sighs. 'Has it really been eighteen years? I'm forgetting how you look – send me a photograph.'

'Yeah, OK.'

I don't bother to remind her that I visited about six months ago – she's always trying to make me feel guilty. I'm surprised she has remembered the day – but she hasn't sent a card or present. Although I didn't expect anything, it still hurts, and I am casual with her. But I have a wonderful birthday present – my own council flat in a leafy district near Crystal Palace. It's in a small block on the end of a cul-de-sac. I've got one big bedroom with a kind of storeroom off and a nice bathroom, a living room and a kitchen – and best of all, there's a small fenced-in garden with a patio.

'Uh-huh,' I say to the council officer who shows me around. 'I like this garden. I can have barbecues, lie on my sun lounger, shades on, listening to radio, like it's Venice Beach.'

She laughs and hands me the keys. 'Good luck, Sugar.'

My social worker helps me with new furniture, but I have to pay my own rent, so I get a job in a call centre in the country north of London, out near Elstree Film Studios. It's a long way to travel each day, and I'm too worn out to do much. I want a quiet life with a nice boy. I hook up again with my sweet Angel, only he's still sweet on every girl in south London, still plays me for an idiot. Even when we're together and having sex, he's jammy with girls, just come from another bed. But he's my playboy, one I can't do without, and I forgive him almost everything.

One weekend I go away and I leave him with my keys so he can hang out in my flat. More fool me. When I get home, there's no DVD. He tells me he's lying on my nice black leather sofa, listening to music, when he hears the buzzer. It's Marina and some girls. 'Hiya, Angel,' she says, batting her lashes. 'Sugar said I could borrow her DVD, innit?'

I rant, 'So you gave it to her, just like that? How the fuck could you let them in and let them take my stuff?'

Angel looks embarrassed. 'She said it was OK.'

'Yeah? She's a fucking liar.'

I go to Marina's house. 'Where's that DVD you stole? I want it back and I want it now,' I say. 'That DVD ain't even mine.'

Sulky, she says, 'Well you ain't never going to get it back, 'cos I lent it to a boy and he's dead.'

'You're a lying bitch.'

'No, it's true. He got murdered at Balham Race Track.'

I look at her and don't know whether to believe her or not. Tons of black boys are being murdered, one gang against another. It doesn't even hit the news. In the end, I say, 'Well, that DVD's not the only one in the entire world. Go get me another one from a shop.'

She says, nose in air, 'You fucking bitch. Go suck yo' mum.'

'Yeah, go suck yours,' I shout and she slams the door in my face. I kick it a few times, but there's not a lot I can do. The argument festers for a month. One evening, I have two girls round my place and I'm bitching about that slut Marina when the front door buzzes. It's Marina and her foster sister, Yolanda.

'Hi Sugar, can we come in? We got some weed.'

I say, 'Yeah, OK,' even though I don't trust them. I know they're up to something. I go in the kitchen and quickly fill a pan with oil and set it on the stove to heat up, ready to throw over them if there's a problem. They follow me into the kitchen and Marina starts to insult me. Suddenly, they punch me, and run, tearing out of the front door. I open the door wide – and there's seven more girls hiding around the corner.

I say to Yolanda, 'You're a dickhead. You have three children – why are you fighting her fights?'

Marina's standing right there, making faces at me. Before she realises what I'm doing, I dart in and grab her long hair and wrap it around my hand. I pull her face down and knee her in her big mouth. She screeches like a cat set on fire. My friends come running and hurl themselves at the other girls. A big man comes from next door and tells them all to back off, he's called the police, we'd better be gone before they get here. We glare at each other and they run off. We're all bloody, battered and bruised. I know it won't end there – it's building up into a girl-gang vendetta.

A week later, I'm on the bus when I see Marina walking along. I jump off the bus and grab her, *whack!* – she starts running. I scream after her, 'You're dead meat!'

When I get home, there's a letter from the council under my door. They say Marina has complained I'm intimidating and bullying her. If it doesn't stop, I could be evicted for antisocial behaviour. I get on the phone at once and tell them I'm not the troublemaker here. 'Look at the CCTV. You'll see she came to my front door with nine people ready to start a riot.'

I'm still talking on the phone, when out of the corner of my eye I spot Marina coming round the back. She's climbing over my fence. She jumps down and crosses my patio towards the French windows. I slam down the phone and jump on her and start fighting. She's a bloody mess, with handfuls of hair ripped out, a cut eye, a split lip. She runs away and I'm shrieking after her. The neighbours hang out of windows shouting. I remember my mum fighting Milton's baby-mother in the street and I think, 'What am I doing? This is crazy. Do I want to turn into my mum, a street fighter?'

I'm cleaning up when the door buzzes. Uh-oh – is she back, maybe with reinforcements, weapons? But I see it's just four girls on their own. I keep the chain on and talk to them through the gap.

They say, 'Marina don't want to fight with you. She want go truce.'

I say, 'Why does it take four of you to bring a message from her? Where were you when she came with nine to attack me? Why can't she tell me this herself?'

'Yeah, well, she just want to be your friend.'

'She ain't my friend. She a lying whore bitch.'

That's the end of our friendship. We keep out of each other's way. I'm sorry it has turned out like this, but I should have known better. I decide that I can't hang out with losers and troublemakers, but it's difficult to break free, because it's where I live. We're part of the same wide community. Jamaicans hang out with each other, West Indians fight with other West Indians. African tribes hate other Africans. We all have our groups and gangs and it's hard to keep aloof.

The final straw is when I'm visiting a friend in a big block of flats. We hear this yelling and screaming coming from the hall and open the door, peer out. Everyone knows Marina's been having an affair with a married man, my friend's neighbour. Now Marina's banging on his front door, telling him she's pregnant in front of his wife. He loses it and beats her up real bad. She tries to run off, but he chases her down the hall and jumps on her belly. She screams and crawls away and he grabs her and hangs her over the stairwell, six floors up.

I get on my mobile phone to her dad. 'Hey Cardinal, you need to get round here quick. That your daughter you can hear screaming –' I hold the phone out so he can pick up the fight. I yell into the hall, 'Pull her up. Her dad's coming.'

Cardinal lives around the corner and he's there in a few minutes. When the man sees him, he's gone green and jumps out of the window, down the balconies and over the fences. Marina, she's gone to the hospital in an ambulance. Her baby's dead. She just shrugs and says, 'I didn't want his baby anyway.'

Chapter 14

Kids Company, 2004

David and Annie are two friends of mine. David's got a junkie mum, Annie's an orphan. I've known Annie since the children's home and David grew up in another one. After they were told they were on their own when they reached eighteen and cast adrift, like all kids in homes are, they led really screwed-up lives, living on the street, into drugs, stealing, totally without direction until they got together and tried to make a family life for themselves. I haven't seen them for a while, then I bump into them out shopping down Brixton Market.

'Yo, what's up?' I ask.

'Hey Sugar, where you livin' now?'

'Still living Crystal Palace, I got that little flat.'

'Oh, yeah, nice place. You workin'?'

'No, I go college, innit. You going college?'

'No, man, we go the Urban Academy.'

'Where's that?'

Annie says, 'London Bridge. It's a kinda club run by Kids Company, where kids like us can talk, hang out, do stuff, whatever they want. You should come, you'd like it.'

'Maybe I will some time.'

So time passes, and each time I see them, they tell me more about how this Urban Academy place helps them get better organised, but I say I'm doing just fine. In fact, I'm getting more fucked up. Nothing matters, I drift from one disaster to another, one boy to another and I'm always doing drugs – mostly weed, but sometimes crack or a line of coke, or uppers and downers – and fighting with gangs of girls for no good reason other than that fighting's what we all do. It's like I want to live on a constant destructive adrenaline high. I feel completely rootless.

I never imagined that a T-shirt would change my perspective. It happens when I'm walking past Brixton Tube station, and David and Annie come out, wearing really cool T-shirts. They tell me they made and designed them themselves at this place they go to near London Bridge.

'I want to do that,' I say. 'I'd love to make a T-shirt.'

They invite me along with them next time they go. 'You'll have a good time,' Annie says. The following week, I meet them at Brixton tube station and on the train they tell me about the woman who set up Kids and Urban Academy. She's Camila, they say, and they tell me a little bit about her. The way they talk about her is awesome, like she's some mysterious, legendary figure, and I'm curious.

We go to London Bridge, then walk through an old

district. This is the same area where all those years ago me and Tawni conned punters and stole their money. They are not happy memories. I can't believe that I did so many dangerous and foolish things when I was only thirteen. On the other hand, five years on, I'm still doing some stupid, fucked-up things.

We turn into a narrow side street, where you can still see cobbles under patches of worn-out tarmac and we walk up to a very tall Victorian building that used to be a school. It looks creepy and a bit scary, like a scene from an old film about foggy London, and there's a security guard on the door. I feel a bit paranoid.

'We goin' in there?' I ask, doubtfully.

'Wait till you get inside, you'll be surprised,' Annie promises.

The security guard recognises them and tells me to sign in at the office. We go through the big old school doors and into a vestibule and I stop dead. It's like walking into a sunflower. The walls are a glowing yellow, there's orange and turquoise decorative features, and artwork on every space. 'Wow!' I say.

There's a small office to the left. The Academy receptionist Miriam asks if I want to register or just visit, and I say, 'Just visiting.'

'Welcome,' she says, 'let me know if you need anything.'

It's all very relaxed. We sign in and enter through the swinging doors into a large room that's like a scene from *The Arabian Nights*. The walls are tangerine, the floor and ceiling turquoise and salmon pink, there's

Persian arches and green and gold stars, plasterwork painted yellow and blue and pink, with blocks of colour in the alcoves decorated with paintings of huge tropical flowers and emerald-green palm trees, like it's Jamaica. People about my age are sitting at tables covered with oilcloth in zingy patterns and colours, chatting away. There's a long serving hatch at the back, where you can go up and be served good, nourishing food, like bean soup, pizza or pasta. It's got a real homely feel, nothing like I expected.

David and Annie give me a quick tour of the gym, an art room, a recording studio and a film studio. There's a massage room, a place to learn about beauty and nails, and lots of little therapy and private rooms, just to chat to advisors and keyworkers, packed into the old classrooms that have been divided. It's all humming, like an anthill.

I'm taking it all in. How come I never knew about it? Many kids like me are very screwed up, our lives a mess – living hand to mouth, on the street, abused, no one wants us. Only Kids does, Annie says. She tells me about some of the other support Kids Company offers, care packages like therapy, housing, financial aid and education. Kids Company itself, which is in Camberwell, is for the younger children who've fallen through the gaps and Urban Academy is for the older ones, many of whom have dropped out. I learn all this slowly – it's like an onion, the layers peeling, little by little. Nothing's forced on you.

Annie and David introduce me to Bella, who does all

the fashion courses – this is where they made the T-shirts that brought me here in the first place. I ask if I can make something, and I'm shown how to do silkscreen printing. After a while, as I mix the oils and prepare my design, I become aware of a woman who has come in quietly and is watching with a slight smile on her face. She's dressed in bright colours, a long, loose dress in emerald green, with a kind of floating overcoat in black and orange velvet and chiffon panels. The turban wrapped around her head has flowers with pink poppies, and her hoop earrings are gold. She's like nothing I've seen in this drab part of London, outside of Carnival. I catch her eye and she smiles directly at me. I feel like she looks into my soul. How's she doing that? This is Camila.

I should have walked up to her right away, asked her to help me sort out my head – but it simply never occurred to me. I've talked about my problems to so many people and they've helped as best they can – but it's never enough, or focused enough. I'm drawn to return to the Academy and this time I ask Miriam if I can sign up to a fashion and nails course and she says, 'Sure. Anything else?' I'm feeling pretty low and vulnerable that day, and almost before I know it, I'm blurting out, 'I need a care package.' To me, even saying those words is a big deal and I wonder what I'm letting myself in for. How many people do I really want prying into my life?

But Miriam nods and takes me seriously. 'We'll assign you a keyworker and take it from there. Leave it with me.'

For a while, Bella is my keyworker, and we get on well. She starts to help me resolve my issues, mostly by listening to me and being supportive, but she is busy running the fashion courses and, behind the scenes, Camila decides that I need someone who is exclusively hands-on as a keyworker.

One morning, Devon comes to the fashion studio and introduces herself as my new keyworker. She suggests we go and sit downstairs and chat during a lunch break. She wants to get to know me a little, so she can set up a proper meeting later where we can discuss things in private. I like the look of her. She's an attractive white girl with brown wavy hair and clear grey eyes. She seems laid-back and not bossy like some of the social workers I've been assigned down the years. I decide she's different.

We talk in the dining room with its relaxed atmosphere and I tell her a few things about me – how I've been in care and now live on my own. I tell her that I go to college, and we discuss my course. 'Do you want a career in care work?' she asks.

'To be honest, I'd rather do something in fashion. And I love the nails course.' I hold out my hands. My nails look really good, painted in green and pink stripes and dots. 'Unusual, hey?'

Devon says, 'It's really good.' Her hands are slender and strong-looking, and her nails nicely shaped and cut short and very clean, like she's a nurse. I can't imagine her with pink and green nails, and I smile to myself. I can see her riding a pony at the Pony Club and I'm really surprised when I learn she rides a motorbike. I really like her and agree that we can move on with the next step – which is for her to assess my needs.

'Will I meet Camila properly?' I ask.

'Oh, of course – Camila's always about and is very much involved with all our clients – that's kids like you.'

I've never been called a client before and it feels funny, like I can be in control and choose what's happening to me, instead of just being told what to do and how to do it. The next time I go, I'm one of those people in one of the small rooms off the downstairs corridor, talking one to one with my keyworker. I'm chatty, but guarded. I just let her write down the basic details I want her to know – like where I was born, my family structure, my age, and how I got to be in a home. I don't say too much about my mum, nor do I talk about the bad things I've done, or had done to me. I realise then that I'm in control of how much, or how little, help I want.

'I think you might find it helpful to talk to a counsellor,' Devon says. 'Would you like me to make you an appointment?'

'Where will I have to go?'

'Here,' she says. She looks around the brightly painted little room we're sitting in. 'It would be in a room just like this.'

'What will I have to do? Will I have to talk about myself? I might find that difficult.'

Devon smiles faintly. 'Most people like talking about themselves. It's up to you. Tell them anything you want. You'll get the hang of it,' she says encouragingly.

'OK.'

Very soon, I'm introduced to Elena, a lovely woman who I'm instantly at ease with. I sit on a sofa and she sits across from me, and my eyes wander around the room, looking at the paintings on the wall, and thinking a million things. I grow so dreamy, I almost fall asleep, while Elena sits patiently by.

'What are you thinking, Sugar?' she asks.

'Nothing,' I say.

'Nothing at all?'

'Yeah, about –' I stop. So many things crowd into my mind, I feel like it might explode. There are so many things just bursting to get out, I'm on overload. I'm so scared, I suck it all back in again quickly. It's like blowing a bubble with bubblegum. It bursts out of your mouth and grows big and round, until you suck it all quickly back in – and it's gone. 'I don't like talking about myself,' I say, lamely, not giving her any hint of how chaotic my mind is.

'That's all right. Don't talk about yourself. Would you like to talk about a memory, or someone you know – or somewhere you've been? What about your childhood – where did you grow up?'

So I start telling her about Constant Spring and Gully Bank. I describe the tar-paper shack and the aunties. I describe walking up the hill to school – the memories crowd in thick and fast, and soon I'm laughing as I act out the roles everyone played.

We go on like this for some weeks and I feel the pressures easing just a little – but it's as if there is always something big and black just sitting in my head, like a spider. Sometimes it's an electric thing, with crazy colours, cracking and sizzling, ready to blow me apart. I want to let it out, but can't. All this stuff is what happens in the therapy room with Elena. A soon as I leave, I'm in a parallel world, with my problems – like Mum and my brothers – still there, driving me mad, and problems I can't even begin to think about bugging me. I have a head full of black spiders and yellow wasps and every moment I'm smacking them down until I could scream.

Then Elena says she's going away to work in Switzerland, and I feel bereft. Even though I haven't touched on my deep issues, I valued our weekly sessions.

'You'll be assigned another therapist,' Elena says. 'You're doing very well and we feel Kirstie is the ideal person to take you to the next stage.' She explains that Kids Company takes any transition period from one keyworker or therapist to a new one very seriously and work hard to stop people from feeling stranded.

We arrange an appointment and I go in to meet Kristie. She has a kind face and I like her, but despite that, I had grown attached to Elena and I wonder if we'll connect in the same way. I turn and hug Elena.

'I'll miss you,' I say.

'And I'll miss you, Sugar. I wish you well.'

After Elena leaves, instead of looking on the Academy as a lifeline I've been thrown, I'm so confused that I don't keep appointments with Kirstie. Instead, I drift erratically for the next year or so. Sometimes I go several times a week to the various courses, and sometimes once a fortnight or month. I ignore the offer of more therapy. I am like a moth to the flame – flying into the circle, then fluttering away. But always, I feel that someone there is aware of my turmoil, watching from a distance, ready to help if and when I ask.

Chapter 15

Crystal Palace,

Early 2005

I haven't seen Mum for ages. We're like strangers now. Putting myself into care when I was fifteen opened a rift and caused such bitter resentment in her, I wonder if it will ever be healed. For a long time – maybe three years – I've kept in touch by phone and a couple of times have been down to Bristol for the weekend – mostly to see my brothers, who I miss – but it has always been difficult. Mum nags me to go, but when I do, she's always criticising, there's never any praise. Almost as soon as I arrive, I can't wait to get back to London and my friends, who feel more like family. Yet, with all those friends, I feel very alone. I'm always looking for someone who will love me, and keep throwing myself at boys, who only want to get into girls' knickers, not have a proper relationship. At the root of it all is my lack of confidence and self-hatred. Always ringing in my head are Mum's words – 'You're ugly, girl, jus' like your no-good, useless baby-father.'

One day, walking along the shopping centre in Brixton, I catch sight of this girl reflected in a big plate-glass window. She's so pretty – cute figure, jaunty walk. I smile in admiration and she smiles back. *It's me!* I want to hug her. She's beautiful.

A boy whistles, 'Hey babe!' and I strut my stuff, feeling good.

Men whistle all the time and try to pick me up, but the ugly me has never taken any notice. My mum says men will pick up any bitch because all they want is a quick jump – and I know she's right. But this boy is cute – real cute. I've seen him before, always hanging around on this corner. At the hairdresser's, I ask Millie if she knows the boy on the corner. She smiles slyly. 'Hmm-mm – you fancy him, girl?'

I giggle. 'He's a pretty boy, innit.'

'Oh, he pretty all right – but he a bad, bad boy. You be staying away from him. He called Hotride, innit.' She laughs. 'Hotride – uh-huh – you better believe it. He'll be landing you with twins, maybe triplets.' She laughs so hard, her fat wobbles.

I ask for a new style, some extra-long weaving, with maybe some blonde highlights. I don't realise it, but I'm setting out my lures to catch the pretty boy on the corner. Millie knows my mum. I know they call each other all the time for Mum to catch up on the gossip – and to discuss me. I can hear it in my head.

'You seen Sugar lately?' This is Mum.

'Yeah, she been in. She axed me for blonde highlights.

Thth-thth – she fancy this boy, Hotride. Thth-thth.' This
is Millie, the hairdresser.

'*Yeah? Hotride? She'll get burned.'* This is Mum,
being sarcastic.

Millie gets out the glue and the hot iron, Sizzle it
goes, smell of burned hair. *Thth-thth* go her teeth as
she clicks her tongue against them. 'You heard from
your mum recently?'

'No.' I never have much to say when she asks about
my mum. Hell, she talks to her more than I do, they're
like sisters.

'*Thth-thth.* She coming up London.'

I sit bolt upright. 'She coming to London – to see
me?'

'That's what she say.'

'When?'

'This afternoon.'

Must be urgent. Soon as my hair's done, instead of
showing off to Hotride like I intended, I fly home and
start to tidy up. The buzzer goes. Mum's there with her
boyfriend, Leo. I despise him. He's too glossy and uses
people. She pushes past me with a suitcase on wheels
and he lounges in behind her in his drape jacket and
baggy pants. So they're staying.

'Hello, Mum, Leo. Come on in.'

I go to kiss her. She seems preoccupied and skips the
kiss. She sits down on my nice black leather sofa, rubs
it to see if it's leather or plastic, and looks around.

'Nice place. You sharing it?'

'Like with who?'

'So it's just yours? Nobody else here?'

'It's my place and I don't share it with nobody.' I'm on the defensive again, wondering what she wants. 'You want a cup of coffee?'

I make coffee and sit on a chair across from them. 'How are you doing?'

'OK.'

'How are my brothers? Who's looking after them?'

My questions irritate her. She frowns and sips her coffee. 'They looking after theyselves. You criticising me, girl?'

I shake my head.

'Yeah, well don't tell me my business.' She cuts straight to the chase. 'So, this friend calls me, tells me you no good, you havin' a baby.'

I stare, eyes wide. 'What you sayin'?'

'So, it's true? You havin' a baby?'

'No!' I jump up, spill my coffee. 'Who's telling you this?'

'Never you mind. I come to see for myself.'

As I wipe up the mess, I think, no you haven't – you and your boyfriend want a free place to stay while you're doing your drug deals. I don't say it, of course. I'm angry and upset. For years she's shown no real interest in me – and now, all of a sudden, because someone has spread gossip about me, she comes all the way to London to tell me I'm no good.

'Mum, listen, I'm not pregnant – OK?'

'You sure?'

'I should know. Who told you I was?'

She looks vague, sips her coffee. 'So, life treating you OK? What you doing?'

'I'm going to college.'

'Yeah? What you learnin' about?'

'Health care.'

I don't mention my therapist and the classes I do at Urban Academy because I know she's not really interested in anything I do – so what does she want? I soon find out. Apart from needing a place to stay for a couple of days, she wants me to return with her to Bristol for a while. Instantly, I wonder why – she has to be up to something. I haven't been going to Kids Company long enough to start to analyse myself or to look too deeply into how the motives of other people affect me – I only know that my mum has never done anything spontaneous, out of affection.

'Why do you want me to go back to Bristol with you?' I ask suspiciously.

'Your brothers been axing after you. Where's Sugar, we never see her no more.'

I know she's not telling the truth. Probably she's going away and wants a baby-sitter, I think. Going back with her will disrupt Urban Academy and college, but despite my cynicism, suddenly I want to go. She has never asked me to do anything before and, even if she does have an underhand motive for asking me, I can't help wanting to please her. Then I'm angry at how easy it is for her to push my buttons. I whisper inside, '*Mum, I wish you loved me more – it's not a lot to ask, is it?*'

I've always done my best, I'm respectful towards her, yet she seems so cold and hostile whenever she looks at me.

I don't see much of her for the next few days. Most of the time she's out, seeing friends, selling drugs. I worry that she'll be arrested. She's on the run – doesn't it worry her that she's putting herself at risk? When she's in she's tired and edgy and Leo's always there, so we don't have time for a proper chat. I really want to get to know her better and be a proper daughter to her. The hollow years in children's homes and struggling to survive on my own since have been very painful. I loved the family life we had in Jamaica. For all its bad points, my childhood in Jamaica was happy, and I long to recapture it. So, although I fight it, my mum still has power over me. I know I'll drop everything and go to Bristol like she wants. I think, I can take time off college and my rent is paid by Social Services because I'm a student – it won't hurt for a few days. I don't bother to call Devon or my course tutor at college.

When they have taken care of all their business and got rid of all the drugs, we head to Victoria Coach Station. Leo has a tight grip on a bag stuffed full of money. It reminds me of the old days, when I was Milton's little drug runner. Now Mum is Leo's slave. I wonder what role my brothers play – Mum is bound to use them, one way or another. They have seats together upfront in the coach and I'm down the back, so we don't chat. When we arrive, Leo goes off to his own house and family, while Mum and I catch the bus to her house. She says she's rented out the spare room upstairs, so I'll have to sleep in the living room.

My brothers are still in bed when we arrive in the middle of the afternoon. They get up moaning that they're hungry, they want something to eat. They rummage about in the kitchen, saying there's nothing, and Mum says, 'I left you plenty of food – what have you done, fed the five thousand?'

After a while, Paul and Wayan come slouching in. They act cool, but I can tell they're pleased to see me. They're rude to Mum, though, for leaving them on their own. I can see that she's got no control over them. When I go upstairs to the bathroom, I glance around and there's no lodger – just rows of weed in the spare room, like there was last time I was here. It's high-quality skunk, enough to stone the entire street. It wouldn't surprise me if they could smell it across the Bristol Channel in Wales. My brothers openly smoke it and when their friends drop in they all roll fat joints and turn up the music top volume.

Mum says, 'Turn that down, me and Sugar are talking,' but Paul turns it up louder. They demand food, demand drinks, make a mess. They help themselves to money from her bag without asking.

When they've gone out with their little gang, I say, 'Mum, they rude and disrespectful to you. Why you letting them? They run this house like you're their servant.'

Her eyes flicker uncertainly for a moment, then she's angry. 'Boys will be boys. Who's been here to help me with them all these years? Not you.'

'Yeah, Mum, I know – but I've had to look after myself.'

It leads to an argument, as I knew it would. I try not to talk back – I know how wild it makes her. It's hard to defend myself without talking back, but she's very unreasonable. I want to cry, remembering the lonely years in the children's homes, the cold hostility of my temporary foster mother. I've struggled, done things I regret, just to survive. Why can't she see how hard it has been for me? All she does is tell me how hard her life is and how much she's done for me and how ungrateful I am and how I won't help her with my brothers when it's my duty. She insists that's what girls are for – to help their mothers with chores and to take care of their siblings. We fall out, and after a few days I return to London.

Some months later, I'm sleeping when the phone wakes me. It's Mum. She's crying. I'm shocked, she never cries. I sit up and try to snap out of sleep and focus. 'Mum? It's the middle of the night. What's up?'

She sobs, 'I don't know what to do –'

'What's happened, Mum – are you all right?'

She sounds terrified. 'It's Paul. He's been arrested, the police have an e-fit on him. He was called up on a gang rape – it happened in my house,' she wails. 'Right here. Jesus Lord – I'll be deported.'

'A girl was raped in your house?' I repeat while I try to gather my thoughts. 'Were you there?'

'No, of course not. I was out. Think I'd let it happen if I was home?'

'So it did happen? They got proof?'

'Little slut says it happened. What was she doing here with all them boys? What was she thinking of?'

It's always the same – it's the girl's fault. I think back to what happened to me, and her reaction – when she beat *me* for being raped at the age of eight. She calms down and says she can't cope. Paul's growing weed in the house, there's a huge electric bill, she can't pay it, she doesn't know what to do. Forensics will come round, they'll find the weed –

'Mum, get rid of it,' I interrupt. 'Make Paul throw it all out. Do it now.'

'He can't – he'll get cut up or killed. He growing it for Dr Snip. He's the big man round here.'

'Mum!' I'm frustrated, unable to get through to her.

'It's a bad atmosphere down here – they both going wild. I gotta get them away or they'll end up in prison or dead, like their dad. That Dr Snip, he'll cut up Wayan as well, you don't know what it like. You can have them for a change. They both beyond control. It's 'bout time you helped out.' She's hysterical, while I'm trying to get a word in sideways.

Her words are so unfair, but I know I have to help. If I do nothing and Paul goes to jail or both of them get killed by this Dr Snip, I'll be blamed. Mum says she's going to put my brothers on the coach up to town right away.

'But Mum, you just said Paul's been arrested.'

'Leo's solicitor got him released on police bail. They can't lock him up, he just a kid, innit?'

I go to Victoria Coach Station to collect them, wondering what I'm letting myself in for. They look dozy and bleary-eyed, like they've been on weed all the way up from Bristol. Trainer laces untied and trailing in the dirt, they shamble along behind me on the tube to Brixton. 'Come on, hurry,' I keep chivvying them along as we walk to the bus stop.

I spot Hotride on the corner, selling baggies. He grins at me, and his eyes flick over my brothers. I've never spoken to him before, but now I say, 'Hi.'

'How you doin', Sugar?' he says, looking at me, full of admiration, like I'm gorgeous or something.

I'm astonished that he knows my name, and I start to preen a little, puff out my chest – until I remember the trouble my brothers are in. Quickly I say, 'See ya – got to get my brothers home.'

'Sure.' His admiring look is burning a hole in my back. I turn and risk a quick glance. He grins and winks and I get all hot.

Back at my flat in Crystal Palace, I show my brothers around. I say they can share my bed and I'll sleep on the sofa. It's OK to start with, but they're soon bored and fed up. They don't have any friends locally, don't know their way about, don't have any money. It's all moan, moan, moan. Paul doesn't seem at all worried that he's skipped bail, or is wanted for a rape. It's all water off a duck's back to him – someone else will take care of the mess. They hang out in the park all day, messing about. They can't return to their old school in Peckham and I'm scared of registering them in another one in case the police have them on a list. Technically, they're hiding out. When they complain they're bored, I say, 'OK, pack your things, you're going home. Paul will end up in jail, what do I care? Suit yourself.' It shuts them up, but not for long. It's like nothing is their responsibility.

I'm at college most of the week and I run out the door early in the morning. I leave a bit of food for them – sometimes, it's just bread and beans, but it's the best I can do. I can't afford to give them any spending money, so they can't go to the cinema or buy a burger. They want to buy weed and I won't let them. I remind them, 'Hey guys, it's weed that got you into trouble.' I also want to fit in time at Kids Company, so sometimes I'm gone a long time and I dread going home.

Money is always a problem. I keep calling Mum. 'You said you'd send money for the boys. I can't afford to keep them.' At first, she promises that she'll send some, but after a while, she just sounds annoyed when I call, and says she's broke. 'But Mum, if they were there with you, you'd have to feed them,' I say.

'Fuck off,' she says. Click.

One day I rush into Kids Company and I'm starving. I haven't eaten all day, and I'm grateful for the free food, the big bowl of steaming chilli and beans. But all the time I'm eating, I feel guilty. There's days to go before my next benefit cheque and there's no money left to feed the boys or feed the electric. If the electric runs out, they won't have even the TV to watch, or music to listen to. They'll drive themselves and me bonkers. My mobile phone has run out of credit, so after class, I ask a friend if I can use her landline and call Mum again. It's the same old story. She has no money, she can't help. It never occurs to me to ask Devon. The boys have become my problem, not hers. I wish I'd known better, because it would have saved me a big headache.

I decide to go down Brixton, hoping I might bump into somebody who might have some cash I can borrow. The first person I see is Hotride.

'Hey, Sugar – what's up?'

I can't believe it when I start to tell him my problems, like he's an old friend. 'Yeah, well, remember my brothers?' He nods. 'They eatin' me out of the house and my mum ain't sent no money yet. How am I supposed to feed two big boys like that on no money?' I can't believe I'm telling him this – I don't even know him, he's just another boy on the street.

Without hesitating, he pulls out a small wad and peels off some notes. I stare. Fifty pounds. 'There you go –' he says.

'Yeah, thanks. I can't take it.'

'Sure you can. Look, I got all this.' He waves the rest under my nose. 'Pay me back some day.'

I take the money, put it in my purse, and hang around talking some, just to be polite. I really fancy him and know if it wasn't for my circumstances, and having my brothers to sort out, we would get it on. 'Thanks for the money, see ya –'

Then I'm off like a whirlwind, shopping in the market

for food, ten pounds on gas, twenty pounds on electricity, run home, cook a big dinner. It's great! You feel better with a full belly, the outlook is better. While we eat, I suddenly remember that in Bristol my brothers are registered at school under different names – maybe I can use those IDs.

But the next day when I go along, my advisor tells me she can't help, our mum has to register them, they need birth certificates and passports. I think they have fake ones in Bristol, but getting Mum to send them to me would be like getting blood out of a stone.

Chapter 16

Crystal Palace,

Mid-2005

Hotride is my boyfriend now. On the one hand, I'm so happy I could skip about all day; on the other hand, I've got big problems, in the shape of my brothers. They're there, like heavy clouds, but they won't fit in, won't adjust, won't help. Just sitting, waiting for me to sort out their lives, feed them, clothe them, get them into school, make it all work. Man – I can just about make my own life work without this.

I can't tell Hotride about my mum and all that. He's got problems of his own. His mum ran away from his dad when he was a baby. She died when he was about six, so he was left living hand to mouth in the ghetto in Jamaica, like those street kids who end up washed in on the morning tide. His dad had gone to England and didn't know any of this. Then Hotride got in with gangs and his enemies were out to get him. By then his dad, Harold, was a big man, with influence. Somehow, he heard his son's life was in danger. He brought him over to England on a visitor's visa, and Hotride overran his time, and stayed illegally. But his dad had a girlfriend and a new family in London and there was no room for a wild young kid under their roof. Hotride was dumped again when he reached eighteen and told to get on with it.

When I meet him he's living nowhere and everywhere. He's got baby-mothers he stays with – but they were before me. I tell him, 'The past is done, you can't change it.' I believe in starting with a clean slate.

He talks about getting off the street, having a fresh start. 'I'd like a job,' he says, when we're sitting in McDonald's in Brixton.

'Yeah? What kind of job?'

'When I came from Jamaica, my dad got me this job working in a garage as a mechanic. I liked that. But I don't have no papers, no visa or work permit and the bastard don't want to pay me. He gave me sixty pounds for working seven days a week. Eighty hours. That's seventy-five pence an hour, innit.'

'So you left?'

'Yeah, slavery's illegal.'

I ask what else he can do. He hasn't got much going for him. He can't read or write and can barely count.

I say, 'No school?'

He shakes head, says he was abandoned on the street at six years old – who was gonna pay for him to go to school?

'I'll help you. I'll teach you,' I say eagerly, wanting to reach out to him.

'Yeah, OK.' He dismisses it, casually. Maybe other

people have offered to help and not followed through. I know it's hard for him to admit that he's illiterate. But he's quick – his card-sharping, the cons and scams he pulls – all quick, quick, quick, man, I say, giggling. He's like a living pack of cards, shuffling fast, fooling the eye. The boy's got brains, plenty of potential. It's all been wasted, I think. I remember how my mum worked hard in Jamaica to pay for me and my brothers to go to school. She knew what it took to have a good start. I'm grateful to her for that, even if things went wrong later. I'm trying to understand her more, but I need more time, more knowledge of myself before I can work her out.

He starts to drop by my flat. My brothers are always there, so we can't get it on – but I'm not ready, anyway. I've gone from being a girl who doesn't value her body to one who puts a high value on it. It's strange, that – how I've gone from sleeping with gangsters and scum to not sleeping with the boy I'm falling in love with. It's some other little mystery about myself to figure out. But even without having sex, he trusts me enough to leave his stash of money in a vase on my shelf. One day, some of it is missing. He stands there counting it, then glares at me with a tight face and mean eyes. 'You've taken it,' he accuses.

Shame sweeps over me. I don't want him to know it's not me but my brothers. I take the blame. I hang my head and whisper, 'I needed to do some shopping. I'll pay you back.'

'Yeah, bitch,' he says. 'Last time I trust you – you just a tief.'

My heart is breaking as he storms off. When my brothers come in, giggling, heads full of weed, that foolish druggy look in their eyes, I shout, 'You stole from Hotride. He's been good to us – why you do that?'

They giggle some more and deny it. In the garden, they recline like lords in the sun, smoking strong skunk, stinking out the neighbourhood. I could kill them.

I call Mum and tell her they're thieves. She's not interested. 'Kids will be kids,' she says. As far as she's concerned, the money was probably stolen by Hotride in the first place.

'How come you never said "kids will be kids" to me when I was growing up?' I ask. 'You beat me for everything. You gave me no leeway.'

'They boys. Boys will be boys,' is her answer, as if I'm stupid for not seeing it.

I beg her to come and stay to help with my brothers. She says she had to raise her brother since the age of seven, she's done her share of child-raising. What if she were dead – who'd take care of them then?

'But you're not dead, Mum,' I protest. 'You're alive and just fine – and I got them here, trying to keep them on no money. I'm dropping behind in college. I'm struggling.'

'Work it out,' she says, and hangs up.

I go to college, but when I return home and walk through the door, I reel. The place stinks. One of the boys has messed up the bathroom big time because there's no loo paper left. There's a big cut on the arm

249

of my black leather sofa, all my stuff is smashed up where they've been fighting. Each brother blames the other one. *He done it – no, he did – it was him.* They bat the blame back and forth like a hot potato until I blow my cool.

I scream, 'It's my stuff! I paid for it!'

They stare at me, sulky. 'Fuck off. I want some weed. I want my money,' Paul sneers.

'You ain't got no money,' I snap.

'Yeah, we have – Mum said she'd send you some.'

'Yeah, you holding out on us,' Wayan adds.

Angrily, I say, 'She didn't send nothing.' I punch in Mum's number on my mobile. 'You got to come and help me. They impossible.'

'It's your turn,' she says. 'I done it all for years – now it's up to you.'

'They your kids.'

'They your brothers,' she counters.

'Mum, if you don't help, I'm leaving them down the Social,' I say, wanting to shout at her, rattle some sense into her head. I glance at the boys – they're giggling, punching each other, not taking me seriously.

She sighs. 'Yeah, OK. Let me talk to Paul.'

I hand him the phone. Her voice is so loud, I can hear her baby-talking him. She lets him off the hook. She promises she will send them some money. He smirks when he hands back the phone. I say nothing. I buy some black electrical tape, tape up the sofa.

I won't inflict these boys on Kids Company, I decide, not realising that's exactly what I should do. Camila has worked hard, setting up Kids to help lost kids like me and my brothers. Instead, next morning, first thing, I go down the Social and talk to my new advisor. I tell him he's got to do something. He says they can't offer any help or support. Then he pauses, looks at me like he's thinking hard. 'The only option is foster care,' he says, like it's a death sentence.

I feel cold. I've been there and it made me feel crazy. It's like being dumped in a bath of ice. It leaves you cold and dead inside. I shake my head. 'No, I won't do that. It was horrible.'

'It doesn't have to be like that,' he says piously. 'We have some really good foster parents, like angels.' I wonder if he believes this crap.

'Yeah, well let me think about it,' I say.

I go outside and walk up and down, on the phone to Mum, telling her that I'm at Social Services and they want to take my brothers into foster care.

'What that you saying? Are you out of your head?' she protests.

'I need some space, Mum. I can't keep on – you don't even send the money you promised – you don't care.'

'Hold on, I need time to think. I'll let you know in a week.'

'I don't have a week. I'm going crazy right now.' My voice rises. I control myself – she's too good at hanging up. 'Please, Mum, you got to help.'

'I'll call you back.' *Click.*

I stare at the phone. She's some unnatural mother. She says she adores her sons – but she has a fine way of showing it. She knows I can't put my brothers into care unless she agrees – she has me over a barrel.

I cash my two-weekly allowance and spend half of it on groceries. When I walk into my flat, it's like a smoke-house, and full of boys. I could get high on the smoke. I'm tired and pissed off. I yell at my brothers. They were supposed to meet me to help carry the shopping. What am I, an ass or maybe a donkey to lug it all on my own? I dump the shopping in the kitchen and storm back to the living room. I'm not feeding this crowd, no way.

'Who are they?' I shout.

Sulkily, Paul says, 'They our friends.'

'Yeah? Where have you got all these friends from?'

I chase the friends out, come back in and start on the attack, about how my brothers are useless sacks of shit. They need to straighten up, or they're going into foster care. They don't believe me – it's just Sugar ranting, as usual.

They say, 'Mum never asked us to help at home. You supposed to do – you're the girl.'

'More fool her,' I say. It's all Mum's fault – she has ruined them, like all Jamaican women ruin their sons. No wonder so many families are going to rack and ruin.

I call Mum. 'Next week, they go into foster care,' I say firmly. She knows I'm bluffing so, glibly, she just says she's coming up on Saturday. I stay in all day, waiting for her to show, but she never comes and I get on the phone again, feeling like a nag. 'Listen, Mum, I'm gonna dump them outside the police station.'

She panics. 'I'll be there next Saturday.'

I ask, 'So what's wrong with tomorrow?' She comes out with some crap about needing money for a ticket and having to do some work. I've heard it all before. 'One week,' I say. 'I'll wait one more week – then that's it.'

Hotride asks me for help in finding him a flat. He's got the money for the deposit and he wants a nice place of his own. He smiles, giving me a special sexy look, 'I want a place for us, you and me, honey, where your brothers aren't hanging out all the time,' he says. I think it proves that he's getting serious about me. It's been impossible to have time on our own, my brothers are always there, and the place is always a mess, always noisy.

We find one room with a shared kitchen and bathroom. It's bright and clean and I can make it nice. We stand in the room and kiss. 'Mm-mm – you all sugar and honey,' he says, like he wants to drink me.

Mum comes up next Saturday. She's in a mood, but I don't care. I can't wait for her to settle in before I make ready to leave. 'Where the hell you going?' she asks.

'Gonna spend the weekend with my friends,' I say.

'You can't leave me on my own with the boys.'

'Yeah, I can. You their mother –'

'You their sister.'

We pout our lips at each other. It's the same old same old crap. I say, 'I'm going, Mum. Flat's too small for four of us. Call me on my mobile if there's a problem.'

I switch off my phone as soon as I've closed my front

door behind me. Me and Hotride, we spend the weekend in bed, don't go anywhere, don't see nobody. We're wrapped in a cocoon of love.

I don't switch my phone back on until Monday morning, before I'm properly awake. As soon as I do, the phone rings. It's Mum, enraged. 'Where the hell you been? Get your ass round here. I'm going home.'

I say, 'I've looked after them for six months. I'm with my boyfriend.'

'Yeah, well, he don't mean nothing to me.'

'Yeah, where do you think I got the money to feed them?'

Mum said, 'You a whore?'

I counter, 'Are you?' I click off and go to college. In the afternoon, I return to Hotride's place. I fix something to eat and we go to bed again. We can't keep our hands off each other. But Mum has the last laugh. She just packs her bag and goes back to Bristol. Two, three days pass, then the boys call me, complaining, 'We got nothing to eat.'

'Ask your mum,' I say.

'She gone.'

I sigh and head home with Hotride. Where I am is where he wants to sleep, he says. He gives up his flat – it was just a dream, a few days' respite. The boys have my bed. Hotride and me, we squeeze on the sofa. Maybe with a man in the house, the boys will straighten up. But Hotride smokes dope, so he's not much of a good example. I join them, just like I did at the children's home – if you can't beat 'em, join 'em.

still snoring their heads off in my
coffee, drink it slowly, have a bath
ff the moment.

sed and catch the bus to Social Ser-
isor that I want a Jamaican couple,
e, and he shows me a list of possible
others. I go with him to interview a
f the list and settle on two, Mr and
ey're an elderly Jamaican couple with
values. Their house is immaculate.
hoolteacher, kindly, like a real mum,
njoy taking the boys to football, cricket
es. You have to give boys plenty to do
nework, they say. All that energy needs

hool? I ask. Yes, school is important,
owed. Firm but fair rules. We discuss
ooling and I tell them how much they've
ys are years behind. But Mrs McIntyre
or them and that they will be registered
hool. Fortunately, Mum has sent me the
rth certificates and their passports (from
t came from Jamaica), so I know they
enrol at school. I visualise all those years
d well-behaved kids Mrs McIntyre has
ordered classroom and know I'm doing
ng. I should have done it months ago.
ell my advisor, but I want to keep my eye
says, no problem. My brothers will still
ers, they'll just be brought up by people

The boys take advantage of Hotride's good nature
and nick his CDs and leave the cases so he doesn't know
they're empty until he comes to use them. They're rude
to him, says he ain't their dad when he scolds them.
I'm in the middle and it's getting me down. I am
desperate to get my brothers into care – but it seems
the ultimate betrayal, and I just can't bring myself to
do it. What makes it worse is they know all my threats
are empty ones, and they use this against me. I'm being
manipulated and allow it because I'm their big sister
and Mum has brainwashed me into believing it's my
duty to take care of them.

I stopped going to Kids Company long ago and I'm
scared I'll also drop out of college and end up with
nothing. I'm tired of it. Hotride and me, we should be
in our idyllic season, making love, being as one, but we
are just caretakers to two spoiled brats who think they're
little gods.

Six months after they came from Bristol to live with
me, Paul turns fifteen. The 'rape' case seems to have
vanished and I never ask about it. We throw a little
party for him, invite friends, get some bottles in, I fix
food, fire up the barbecue. I warn the neighbours, and
they're cool. The party goes on all night. In the morning,
words are exchanged between Paul and Hotride. Hotride
tells Paul he's done something wrong and Paul gets in
his face, disrespecting him, really rude, says he has no
right to talk to him like that.

I telephone Mum and ask her to talk to Paul. 'He

doesn't listen to anyone because he's angry all the time. My boyfriend tries to talk to him, but he ignores him. You've got to come – you didn't even come for his birthday.'

'You don't listen to my boyfriend, so why should your brother listen to your boyfriend?' Mum says.

I'm crying, there's a row raging behind me, with my brothers and Hotride shouting at each other. They sound so loud and aggressive, I'm scared. 'Mum, these boys are getting too big and too disrespectful for me to control any more. They won't listen to nobody. It's not my job to bring them up.'

Her voice flat and nasty, she says, 'Run off, then, tail between your legs. Consult with Social Services. Have them put in care if you can't be bothered. I've done my share.' *Click.*

My brothers run off to hang out round some street corner doing their drugs. 'Let them go,' Hotride says. 'Maybe they'll get picked up by the police. Serve them right if they are.' I'm angry with him and nothing he says consoles me.

It has been a while since I've been to Urban Academy but, in the end, I call Devon and she says to meet her in the office. I feel my life is hopeless when I go there that afternoon. As I walk through the front door, I'm crying. I see Camila in the vestibule, talking to a small group of kids. She's wearing one of her amazing outfits, of purple velvet with red silk floaty panels, and beads that chime as she moves. Her winding chiffon turban is of blue and pink flowers, and she has long earrings.

She's
walk

'Hel
me. I'n
knows
ders an
'Let's so

We go
and I sit
me about

I let it al
years of tr
almost inco
eyes and do
fast, I'm dro
be a proper r
and pressures
intent and ver
why. I'm shoc

Talking to C
not to trouble h
it myself. First
Social Services a
offer: I want my
after them any m
do my best.

'I want to choo
soon as the words
filled with guilt an
floods of tears, Hotr

money, the boys are
bed. I make some
and soak, putting
Finally, I get dres
vices. I tell my adv
good, decent peop
matches for my br
few I've chosen of
Mrs McIntyre. Th
good hearts and
She's a retired sc
and he says he'll e
and other activiti
and a proper frar
channelling.

What about s
no truanting all
my brothers' sch
missed. The bo
says she can tu
with a local sc
boys' proper b
when they firs
will be able to
of earnest an
taught in her
the right thi
They'll do, I
on them. He
be my broth

who are able to do it properly. I have to get a police check because the boys will be spending weekends at my house. When they say that Mum has to have a police check too, because the boys might be going there for holidays, my courage falters a bit. I know her response. I call her to tell her and, predictably, she explodes.

'Why have you put them into care?' she raves. 'Why can't you look after them like I told you? I've looked after you kids for years. All it involves is a little food and a few clothes now and then.'

'Mum, we've been through this over and over. It's not just the money. I can't control them. They're wild and heading to be locked up. And you know I can't afford to keep two big boys. They eat like horses, they want nice clothes like their friends, sneakers costing a hundred pounds a pair. They want to go out, buy CDs, go cinema.'

'If you can't afford it, you should get a job,' she says. 'Get out on street like I do. What's so sacred about your body? Young girl like you could make a ton. Hell, you can send me some. Think I like to walk streets, deal drugs? It's about time you kept *me*!'

Amazing. Is she crazy? What kind of a mother tells her daughter to be a prostitute? I say calmly, 'They your kids, not mine. I have no kids, so why am I going through this stress?'

'It's your duty!' she yells, so loudly my ear vibrates. I put the phone down on the table and, from a distance, I hear her voice ranting. After a while, when the vibration stops and I know she's gone, I turn the phone off and change the number. I should have done it years ago. I tell Social Services that I don't know where our mother is. It means that they can't check her out – and this means that the boys must not see her again until she *is* checked out.

Even though I've done my best to make a bad situation better, I'm in pain. We shouldn't be like this – we should be a family, united, helping each other. We're fractured like a broken dish. Hotride cradles me in his arms. 'Don't cry, babe – she ain't worth it. I'll take care of you. We'll start a new family, a new dynasty.'

His extravagant words make me smile. 'Yeah, you be king and I'll be queen. One for all and all for one, united.' I wonder what he sees in a girl like me – a girl whose own mother calls ugly. He's a pretty boy, narrow hips, wide shoulders, long, silky hair. He seems to read my mind. 'With your genes and my genes, we'd make a nice baby,' he whispers in my ear. I feel myself melting, then common sense kicks in.

I've got too much to do to be tied down by a kid. I joke, 'Hey – we just got rid of two, remember?'

'Yeah, but they not ours,' he says, kissing me.

But, weak though I am, and as much as I long for a family of my own, someone to love me, a little warning voice inside stops me from letting him make me pregnant. It's nothing to him – just another feather in his cap, proving he's a man. He's got other baby-mothers. He's not ready to support me and a baby. I don't want to repeat my mum's life. I'll wait until I'm ready.

Chapter 17

London, Summer 2005
to Spring 2006

The experiment of having them fostered seems to be working and I wish I'd done it sooner. My brothers have been going to school regularly and their education has improved. Paul has missed so much school over so many years, he's never learned to read or write. He has extra tuition and surges ahead – faster even than Hotride. I hope it will change his life. But my little brother Wayan is a star. His memory is amazing. He becomes fluent in French and wins lots of awards. It would never have happened without the foster carers. Mrs McIntyre really pushes him hard, but in a way that makes him blossom. My brothers realise they can learn – it's not a mystery. To start with, they tell me, they worked hard to get away from Mrs McIntyre's nagging, but after a few months it's all fallen into place and becomes easy.

But they're cunning, and they play Mr and Mrs McIntyre off against me. In the summer, Mrs McIntyre telephones and suggests it would be nice if they have a short holiday with me. Perhaps I can take them on day trips outside London – proper outings, she says, not just hanging around my estate. I ask for suggestions and she says, 'Chessington Zoo is nice. It's a big place in the country, like a safari park and they'll love it. Then they might like going to Brighton, or Southend. Have they ever paddled in the sea?'

'Yes, in Jamaica,' I say, remembering the good times we had with Frankie.

'Ah yes, of course. You know, honey, I miss all that. It's so cold here. Keep the receipts and I'll reimburse you,' she adds, before hanging up.

But as soon as the boys come to my flat, they start to nag and wheedle. They moan they don't want to go to the boring seaside, or Chessington Zoo, where they've been to with their school. They miss Mum and want to go see her. They say Mrs McIntyre won't let them go, she's a spiteful witch.

I say, 'You know you can't go to stay with Mum because she hasn't been checked out.'

'We can go for the day. Nobody will know,' Wayan wheedles.

In the end, I give in and take them to Bristol. I say we can make it a day trip and they agree. I don't realise that they have already secretly called Mum and fixed it up to stay there for the summer. When I get to Mum's and realise the trap I've walked into, I'm worried sick, too scared to call Mrs McIntyre. But maybe she needn't find out. I can pretend the boys and I went off on day trips. For five days I try to get the boys back to London, but they won't budge. They love it with Mum – they can hang out, smoke weed, do nothing and let her spoil them. But Mum has grown used to not having them around, to not having to keep them or lift a finger for two big, lazy boys. By now, Wayan has grown. At eleven he's massive, far bigger than Paul, who's four years older. He towers over us all, and Mum's boyfriend Leo is a bit scared of him. Leo tells Mum he wants them gone, but she says they can stay. They keep arguing.

I want to return to London, but I'm annoyed with Leo being so bossy. It's Mum's flat and she pays for it and works for him, doing his illegal deals. He contributes nothing. Mum only has one bedroom now, which we all share. There's barely space for a double bed and a cupboard. Mum and I have the bed and the boys share a mattress on the floor, squeezed in between the bed and the wall – you have to walk over the mattress to get out of the door. When Leo comes, he wants to have sex with Mum and we have to sit waiting in the other room, until they've finished heaving and moaning, every sound travelling through the linking door, until we can put the mattress down to sleep. My brothers veer between giggling and embarrassment. It's just not decent, and I turn the television up real loud to drown it out.

After the boys fall asleep, I hear a big argument between Mum and Leo. He complains that we're always around, they've got no privacy. Mum shouts back that we're a nuisance – but what's she supposed to do?

'Get rid of them. It's them or me. I'm not coming back until they gone,' Leo says, and storms out, almost stepping on me.

The next morning, Mum wakes me at 6 a.m. 'Get your brothers up,' she says. 'You've got to go.'

At the coach station my brothers are sulky and angry with me. They want to stay with Mum, they moan, why are we leaving? They say I just want to get back to London and my boyfriend.

What am I supposed to do? I can't tell them that their own mum doesn't want them, that her boyfriend is more important to her. I just say we have to go, the holiday is over. They hate me and are rude and aggressive on the coach. I'm so angry, I refuse to talk to them. At Victoria, I give them the keys to my flat, buy them Burger King and send them home.

'Get out of my sight,' I say. I go to Brixton, where I find Hotride in the street. I hug him and start crying.

'What's up, babe?' he asks, patting me on the back, soothingly.

It all pours out – how our own mum threw us out and how my brothers are always lying to me and how they now blame me for their mother's actions. 'So, where's your brothers now?' he asks.

'At my house. I am so fed up with them. Why am I lumbered with them?'

'Look, you better go on home, make sure they all right, yeah? I'll come as soon as I can. I gotta work.'

I give him another hug and go home to my little flat

at Crystal Palace, dreading what I might find there. It should be my sanctuary, but it's not.

As soon as I walk in the door, my brothers gang up on me, demanding money for weed. *Nag nag nag.*

'Shuddup!' I yell. 'Leave me alone. I'm sick of you.'

Paul says he's going to his foster carers to get his pocket money. I say, 'I won't let you use it for weed. Grow up.'

They shoot off back to their foster parents to tell them a load of bull about me and how they didn't have a proper holiday. Of course, they won't admit that we went to Bristol, because they know they'll get into trouble. I know this is what happens, because later that day there's a buzz at my door and it's Mrs McIntyre. 'Can I come in?' she says. I open the door wide, invite her to sit down, offer her a cold drink. She says the boys are unhappy because I didn't take them on holiday like I said. They didn't even have a day out at Chessington Zoo. They'd been trapped in my flat for days in the heatwave.

'They such liars –' I start to say, then bite my tongue.

'Do you have receipts?' she ask. 'I must refund their expenses.'

I know she wants to prove to me that I'm a liar, and I'm stuck because I don't have receipts for Chessington fucking Zoo, and I can't show her receipts for the bus to Bristol because I'm not allowed to take the boys there. I hang my head and in a small voice I say I lost the receipts.

She shakes her head and gets up to go. 'Sugar, I'm disappointed in you,' she says.

I want to cry. I call Mum and tell her what has happened, and what little shits my brothers are. I know it's pointless telling her, but there's no one else to tell and I'm hoping she'll sympathise. She says, 'It's your fault. You should have given them five pounds for weed, then none of this would have happened.'

I'm speechless. I try to patch things up, but my relationship with Mr and Mrs McIntyre starts to break down. I can't tell them the truth and they think I'm a bad influence. It's all my brothers' fault. When I see them again, I take my house keys away from them and say, 'You've got to straighten up, or you'll end up in prison. You can't go through life doing what you want and telling lies.'

They're angry and jealous that Hotride has keys when I've taken theirs. Wayan shouts, 'Why has he got keys?'

There's almost nothing I can say that scares them, and I've run out of threats and options. Some weeks later, at the end of the long summer holidays, when they visit me again, Paul slouches in acting the cool dude, and I soon find out why. He's brought a friend with him who has a gun. He's flashing it about in my living room, very cool, aiming it out the French windows like he's taking pot shots at targets.

'Hey, what do you think you're up to?' I say. 'I don't want no guns in my house.' I tell them to go. Paul is sulky and says I've shown him up in front of his friend. I don't care. 'Guns are for idiots,' I say. 'Guns are for little guys.'

It's just the tip of the iceberg, a sign of worse to come.

In the streets, there's a war going on that very few ordinary people living their lives in that district even see or have any idea of. Maybe the police know what's happening, though I don't see too many of them around. The south London Jamaican boys are rushing up to the Midlands, to Birmingham and Wolverhampton, to fight the Asian gangs up there. Asian gangs come down the motorways from the Midlands to wage war on the south London gangs. Jamaicans against Africans, against Turks, all fighting each other. It's crazy, all happening under the surface. I don't see it on the news, it's not in the newspapers – it's like a parallel world. They make lightning strikes on each other's turf. There are ambushes and bullets flying, vicious knife fights in the estates with machetes and Japanese swords. It's like scenes from hell. Sometimes, someone calls the police – the police race up in cars, sirens screaming – and everyone splits.

I open the door one day and see an armed mob run by – and my blood runs cold. They're after Paul. He dashes around the side of my house, over the fence, and gets away. I stand on the pavement, yelling at them that I'm calling the police. Next time I see Paul he tells me he's ashamed, I made him look small in front of his friends.

'They were going to kill you,' I say.

'No,' he says, 'it was all cool. They were chasing the Asian boys, gonna kill them.'

'You idiot,' I say. 'One day my phone will be ringing and I'll be called down the morgue to identify you.' He just rolls his eyes like I'm crazy, fussing over nothing. I get the story out of Wayan – they want Paul because

267

somebody stole £13,000-worth of weed he was holding for someone else. I'm horrified. How did he get hold of so much stuff, how did he get involved? I know if they don't get who they want, they come after the family.

Paul gets on the phone, calls Mum, tells her lies about me. She calls up to scold me – I say, 'Hold on, Mum, he's a liar.' I don't tell her he's walking around with boys with guns, or about the thirteen grand. She doesn't believe me, because her precious little prince, who she doesn't want living with her, never lies. Just me, I'm the liar. I can't stand it. All this crap going on when I just want to be left alone to get on with my life. I've got a lot to think about, lots of decisions to make.

Ever since I got together with Hotride, he's been pressuring me to get pregnant. 'Man, I'm only nineteen. I'm not ready yet, I don't even know what I want to do with my life,' I say.

All he does is kiss me and nuzzle my neck and say, 'I want you to have my baby. I'll take care of both of you. Yo made to have babies, innit?'

I feel I'm weakening. 'Yeah, I'd like your baby – but maybe in a year's time. I just ain't ready yet, honey.'

'A year's time!' he explodes. 'Nah, that no good – you'll find another man, he'll do it to you, you'll have his baby, not mine, innit? If you're carrying my baby, you can't have his, innit?' He's agitated and angry. 'You don' love me!'

'Yeah, I do.'

'If you loved me you'd have my baby.'

The arguments go in circles, but I'm weakening more each day. Whatever I say about being too young, or having too much shit going on in my life, what with my brothers and my mum, he just says none of it matters. All that matters is him and me, and me having his baby. At times, I get the sneaky feeling that I don't really count – he just wants to show that he's a man. I think, why doesn't he just want *me*? We've got plenty of time ahead to settle down. Then I dream of what it would be like to have our own little family unit. I could make a better job of it than my mum has.

In the end, I give in. 'Yeah,' I say. 'Yeah, let's do it.'

In thirty seconds flat we're in bed, and he's doing it. Man, the sex is good when I know I'm gonna get pregnant as a result. Afterwards, I lie there, feeling good, but worried. This is for real – this is my body. I'll never be the same again.

Hotride starts to take a special interest in my menstrual cycle. 'Have you missed your period?' he asks me every other day. I tell him it's not time yet, give me a chance. But he's counting. Soon he says, 'Yeah, it's been too long, you missed it.' I've always been regular, so I know he's right. 'Yo pregnant!' he shouts, jumping up and down. He's so happy, I laugh, but it doesn't feel real, it's like it's happening to someone else. I guess I won't believe it until I've done a test and I make an appointment with the doctor.

But before I go, I bleed out. I get on the phone to him, crying my heart out because I feel I've let him down. 'Honey, I just had a miscarriage.'

'Oh no! You sure?' Hotride asks.

I clutch my stomach. 'Yeah, I'm sure.'

'I'm coming round,' he says. 'You sure?'

'Yeah. Don't come, I don't feel well.'

As soon as I'm clear, we try again. Again he keeps asking me, 'You pregnant yet?' and I keep saying, 'No.' Then I miss another period and we go through the same cycle, with him getting excited and me bleeding out. In the end I don't think I can get pregnant, and he's blaming me. 'You've got a shallow womb. Go see the doctor, have tests.'

I'm miserable, thinking after all this time of insisting on condoms I might as well not have bothered – I'm just not able to have kids. I know he'll leave me and each time I have a miscarriage, I walk around clutching my stomach and crying. I get another late period and he says, 'Yeah, this time I scored bull's-eye. Let's go to doctor, have a test.'

I shake my head. 'Let's wait.' I'm sure I'll just lose it, like I've lost all the others. But time passes, and I miss again. It's March 2006 when he insists I go down to the doctor's without an appointment. We sit there waiting until my name is called, and he goes in with me. The doctor looks surprised. 'This my partner,' I say. 'Doctor, I want a pregnancy test.'

She nods. 'How many periods have you missed?'

'Two. I should be having one now, but it hasn't come.'

She asks if there are any other signs, like sore breasts, or morning sickness, and I say not really, though I want to pee a lot. I take a pregnancy test and it comes up positive – but I don't believe it. 'It must be wrong!' I insist. 'I've missed so many times, it's gotta be wrong. Can you do it again?'

She says, 'Pregnancy tests are very accurate.'

But I'm agitated, and in the end she does another test, and she shows me the results. 'My dear, you are definitely pregnant.'

Hotride is over the moon, punching the air and laughing.

The doctor looks at me. 'Well, Sugar, what do you want to do?'

Before I can answer, Hotride's erupted. He jumps up from his chair and is in the doctor's face, 'What do you mean? What do you *mean*? People like you kill kids!'

'Please sit down,' she says quietly. He's walking in a circle shouting, 'She ain't having no abortion!' Then he sits down on the edge of his chair, agitated, drumming with his fingers on the arms of his chair.

The doctor looks at me. 'Sugar, what do you want to do?'

'I want to have my baby,' I say.

She glances at Hotride, who's still drumming his fingers, then back at me. 'Do you want to talk to me privately?'

'No, it's OK, doctor. We going to have this baby, yeah?'

'Yes, of course.' Then she's brisk, and books me into the antenatal clinic and gives me some literature. I flick through the booklets, and there's one that says smoking, drugs and alcohol are bad for the developing baby. I have been smoking weed for years, ever since the children's home, and I've partied with crack and cocaine – but I guess it's time to straighten up and quit.

The doctor is showing us to her office door. 'Come and see me if you have any problems,' she says to me.

'Thank you, doctor,' Hotride says. He shakes the doctor's hand, like he's the patient.

We leave. In the street outside the surgery Hotride's on his phone, calling his dad, walking up and down, excited. 'Yo, Dad, Sugar's pregnant, she having my baby.' He talks to him a bit more, then he's calling everyone, 'Yeah, she pregnant, she having my kid . . .' He's like a big kid himself. As I walk along beside him, I'm thinking, 'How am I gonna tell my mum?'

When we get back to my flat, I beg him to call my mum. 'You tell her,' I say, dreading it. 'She's gonna cane my ear.'

So Hotride punches in the numbers and, when my mum answers, he says, 'Yo, gran'ma!' I wince – she's 42 but thinks she's a spring chicken. 'Yeah, it's me, Hotride. Sugar's pregnant, you gonna be a granny.'

My mouth drops open when Hotride chuckles, 'Yeah, yeah, thanks, she's jus' fine. Glad yo' happy!' It's the last thing I expect. I was sure she would be ranting and abusing me – but instead, she and Hotride are having a good old natter, like they're best friends.

When he hangs up, he says, 'She pleased. Said to take care of you – I said, yeah, she carrying my baby, I goin' take real good care of her.'

Chapter 18

Crystal Palace, Spring
to Autumn 2006

I'm pregnant. I can't think about it yet. I need space.
But at the same time, I feel kind of frantic. It's all
rushing up on me – my life, my mum, my brothers,
Hotride, the baby. I call Devon and we meet up at
Urban Academy. We sit chatting about this and that at
one of the tables in the dining room, having tea and a
sandwich, and then she takes me into one of the little
rooms for a heart-to-heart private talk. I'm suddenly shy
about telling her I'm pregnant. For some reason I feel I'm
letting her down after all the hard work Kids Company
has already done on sorting out my head and helping me
to calm down. Ever since I found out that I'm pregnant,
I've been feeling up one moment, down the next.

'What do you want to discuss?' she asks.

'I'm pregnant –' I blurt out. There, I've said it.

She looks thoughtful. 'What will you do – are you
OK with it?'

I know what she means. Everyone acts like I want to

get rid of it. I say, 'I'm fine. Abortion doesn't come into the picture. God never gives you more than you can bear.'

She nods as if she understands what I mean. 'You know I'm not pressurising you in any way. It has to be up to you – it's your choice. I'm here to support you, whatever you decide.'

'Yeah, I know. But to me, it's better to not have sex than have sex and have a child and kill it.'

Devon says, 'It's up to the individual to do what they believe and what's best for them.' We discuss it some more, and she says that it might be better for me to switch from the Urban Academy, which has a tougher environment, to Kids Company in Camberwell, which is more mother- and child-oriented. She says that they run care packages and programmes there that offer special support to mums. It sounds strange, calling me a mum. It just doesn't seem real.

'But I don't want to lose you – and I'd still like to come here, to the fashion course,' I say. 'I really enjoy it.'

'Sure. You can do both, and I'll still be your keyworker,' Devon agrees. She suggests that we go along at once to check out Kids Company at Camberwell and when I agree, we jump on a bus.

In Camberwell, we get off the bus on the main road near the big hospital that has played such a major part in my life, go down a side street and a little alley, walking towards a big set of metal gates. An old primary school is set a little way back, surrounded by tall flats and Victorian houses. The former school playground is filled with huts that Devon points out – 'Those are for therapy and keyworkers. There's a job hut where you go to ask about work opportunities and we have a GP.'

'A doctor?'

'Sure. Our mums and kids find it very helpful to have a doctor on site.'

We walk in past the security guard at the gate – who knows Devon well – and then into the main building. 'It's just like the Academy!' I exclaim. The large room – the old school hall – is painted Moroccan-style, in warm, strong colours and all around the walls are pictures and blown-up photographs of children. Bookshelves and big old comfortable sofas are all down one side, so keyworkers and mothers might read to children. Children are running about, playing with toys, watched by nannies – one of whom, Jewel, will later be assigned to help me. At the back is a long counter, serving food from the kitchen. Mothers and children can sit at the long tables and have lunch and dinner, a big plate of one dish only each time, consisting of a vegetarian or meat option. Devon introduces me to the cook, a friendly woman, who asks if I'm hungry.

I love the warm atmosphere and instant acceptance, and I know I'll enjoy coming here. Devon shows me the art room, the snooker room and a room where Julia does nails and teaches – at the same time doing what she calls 'chat therapy', in an informal, non-technical way, so mums can feel relaxed enough to open up. I understand that. Before I started going to London Bridge, I bottled it all up inside, pushing it all deep down until it was destroying me.

'What do you think?' Devon asks.

'I think it's great. I want to come here!' I say.

I've barely got home, my head is still full of everything I've seen and talked about, when my door buzzes. It's Flintman, an older man, the local drug dealer, who's standing there, asking me where his little soldiers are. I stare at him, puzzled, keeping the edge of the door between us. 'What little soldiers?'

'Yeah, your bros, innit. They my soldiers.'

'Crap,' I say. 'Fuck off, Flintman, go play with people your own age – don't screw up my little brothers.'

He scowls and I slam the door, put the chain on. Someone's at my door, banging hard. I yell, 'Fuck off!' and it's Hotride, shouting back, asking to be let in. I take the chain off and he comes in, demanding, 'Why you lock me out?'

'I didn't. I had that piece of crap, Flintman, round, looking for my brothers.'

'What he want them for?'

'How do I know? But they'd better keep away from him – he's trouble.'

I'm making a point because I know Hotride used to buy from him before they fell out – but Hotride's protected, because of his dad, who's like a boss, the big man. A few minutes later, my phone rings and it's Flintman. He says in a real nasty voice that he'll be back and I'll be sorry. I say, 'Why? What have I done to you, dickhead?'

He says I'm a bitch and he'll be there in three minutes.

I scream 'Fuck off!' at him, and Hotride grabs my phone. 'What you saying to my girl?'

I snatch my phone back and switch it off. 'Stay out of it, honey,' I tell Hotride.

He says, 'I'm goin' round his place – gonna kill him.'

I grab hold of him. 'No, don't go, you'll get hurt.'

'Yo think I'm scared?' And he's running down the road with me rushing after him. We get to Flintman's place, Flintman comes running down the stairs from his front door and they face up in the street, screaming abuse, then they're fighting, kicking, punching – holy shit! I've got to stop it, but I can't call the police. I see my brothers hiding in the house, peering out and I run up the steps, bang on the windows and yell, 'Come out of there, you little sneaks, do something!'

I'm on the phone to Harold and I scream at Hotride that his dad's coming. Flintman runs back into his house, slams the door.

Hotride says, 'Why did you stop us? I was going to kill him.'

'That's why I stopped you,' I say. 'Do you want to spend the rest of your life in jail?' I'm crying as we walk back to my place. My brothers are going to be gangsters, my boyfriend's going to be killed. *I'm pregnant.* The thought keeps surfacing and I keep pushing it down, not because it really scares me, but because I'm just not used to it. It's like it's happening to someone else. My stomach's as flat as a pancake, there's nothing to see yet.

When I get in, I telephone Mrs McIntyre. 'You got

to do something about these boys. They're dealing drugs, running in a gang, smoking weed.'

'What did you say?'

I repeat what I said and she says, 'Are you telling the truth, Sugar?

'Of course I am!'

'How long have you known this?'

'All the time – they're no good. But now they're going to get killed if they don't stop. They're mixing with bad people.'

She calls Paul on his mobile and tells him they've got to go home at once. Paul shouts down the phone, reverting to patois, which she doesn't allow them to use at home. 'She a liar! She always causing trouble.' He goes on that they're with nice friends, been to the Science Museum like she told them – usual lies, usual crap.

She calls me back, sighs. 'What are you doing, Sugar, telling these stories?' She says I have no right to cause trouble, what's the point? She asks me why I am so angry with my brothers.

I blurt out, 'Listen to me. I'm telling you the truth. I can't keep putting up with their lies, trying to keep them out of trouble, always defending them when they've done wrong. I'm pregnant. I've got to think of myself.'

Long silence. Long sigh. 'Oh dear. This is a great pity. It's a tragedy. What were you thinking of?' Another long sigh. 'Sugar, I'm so disappointed in you. You could have made something of your life. What about finishing college, getting your diploma like you've planned?'

'I am making something of my life. I'm living,' I say,

and click off. She's so education-oriented, that's all she thinks of. I make the decision that I'll have Wayan to stay weekends, but not Paul. Paul needs a sharp lesson, but there's nobody he listens to. Not me, not our mum, not his foster carers.

A couple of weeks later, I'm walking with Hotride to the bus to go to the hospital for my first scan, when we see Paul with Flintman waiting at the same stop. I ignore Flintman, and look at my brother. 'Why aren't you in school?' Paul smirks and reminds me that he's sixteen now.

'What you doing with him?' I nod my head towards Flintman. He and Hotride are watching each other warily, like a pair of dogs. I don't need a fight at the bus stop. I pray for the bus to come quickly. Answering my prayers, I see a police car cruise into view, then it slows. Maybe they're watching Flintman. So now my brother's marked. Maybe they're watching Hotride. Maybe they're watching all three. Jesus, I'm with a den of thieves and gangsters. I ask myself, do I need to bring an innocent child into this environment?

Paul scowls. 'So, why you let Wayan stay wit you and not me?'

I say, 'I don't need you around. You're a fool, headin' for jail.'

The bus to the hospital comes and Hotride and I hop on. Paul and Flintman are waiting for the next one to go down Brixton. The day has been ruined. I'd started out excited about seeing the scan, but now I'm dreading it because it makes the baby real, and I'm not mentally ready. I'm also worried in case the scan shows up something bad.

In the hospital, I watch the grey images on the scanner. It's just a blob. 'Is it OK?' I ask, anxiously. The technician says it's too soon to tell, though they do routine screening.

'Is it a boy or a girl?' Hotride asks, staring hard at the blob. The technician says it's also too soon to tell this. 'We'll be able to tell on the next scan,' she says. 'Are you sure you want to know?'

'Yeah, I want to know,' I say. I look at Hotride, suddenly full of love for him. I'm so happy that he's come with me – that he hasn't made me pregnant and then done a runner, like lots of boys do. He looks proud because he's a man and can make babies. But I know that he also thinks that once men make babies, it becomes women's work. Only JETs provide a home and work at regular jobs to support their kids. Boys like Hotride just want to cruise through life. I need a JET to take care of me – but JETs are boring. I take my pretty boy's hand. I can't believe we're here, looking at the baby we made, like a regular couple.

But there's a dark shadow over me, saying, 'How are you going to cope?' Some of my friends say I could get an abortion, there's time. They make me angry. Surely they know I'd never do that, I don't even want to consider it? This is my baby and I'm having it. I know it will love me, and whatever it is – boy or girl – I'll love it. But the future is unclear. The doctor at the antenatal clinic has offered me a blood test for sickle-cell anaemia and thalassaemia, which is carried by West Indians and Africans, so we go along and have it done as well. There seems so much to be done – almost every few weeks there's an appointment for something.

Everything's going smoothly when Hotride phones. 'Your brother's gonna get himself killed. There's a fight round Flintman's place. I'm going round to sort them out.'

I shout, 'Oh my God, what's going on?' But he's gone.

I dash around there and see cars screaming up. Car doors fly open, young men – some of whom I know – dive into boots, grab machetes, axes, swords. I'm on the phone, bawling for the police.

'Help! A riot!' I shriek.

The gang rushes up the steps to Flintman's. He runs out his front door, his gang behind him, armed to the teeth. The whole crowd turns like a shoal of fish and rushes back into the street where there's space to hack each other to bits. I'm watching at a distance, hands to mouth, my feet rooted to the ground in horror.

It's like *Braveheart* – axes swinging, blood, body parts flying off. Flintman's dead. A good kid I used to know, at school with Paul, is lying in the gutter, blood spurting – he's dead, for sure. Every week there's news of another boy I once knew, stabbed or shot. One kid was machine-gunned in his own bed in Peckham – *machine-gunned*! It turned out he was the wrong boy. The gang who killed him meant to kill another boy – they climbed in the wrong window. It seems like half the boys in Paul's class at his old school are dead. It's crazy, what's going on?

Paul's not there. I don't see Hotride. Where are they – are they safe? I throw away my phone in case the police trace that call I made, and run. I wait for the cops to come find me, to ask what I saw, but they don't. It's like a nightmare, something I dreamed. I can't get the scene out of my mind, though. All I can see is blood and cut flesh.

Hotride strolls in a couple of hours later and I fall on his neck, sobbing hysterically. 'Where you been? Why didn't you call me?'

'Yeah, I did – but your phone's switched off.'

'I threw it away.' I feel like a fool and start laughing wildly. 'Where's Paul?'

'I grabbed him and took him out of it. He gone home on bus, lying low.'

I'm so relieved, I start sobbing. 'I can't live like this. I've got to get away.'

Hotride wants to show he's serious about taking care of me and arranges for me to go on holiday to Jamaica to meet his family. I'm pleased, but surprised. First, where does he get the money from? Second, I didn't know he had a family. How come he lived on the streets as a kid? Turns out it's his dad's family. They live in the country outside Kingston. I ask him why I have to go on my own. 'Why can't you come too?' I ask, kissing him seductively and trying to get him to imagine the fun we could have on the beach.

'I can't go, babe,' he says. 'I've got my enemies there – and you know I'm illegal. Suppose I can't get back into England? You going to come live with me in Jamaica?'

'Yeah,' I say, 'I'd follow you to the ends of the earth, like it says in the Bible, in the story of Ruth.'

Thanks to my Social Services advisor, I've got a temporary visa and permission to stay in the UK – and I tell Hotride that he should apply, get his status sorted out, but he acts vague and I wonder if there's more in it than meets the eye. Has he done something he's wanted for, like my mum? I don't ask him, though – it's something else that's not my business. It strikes me that our lives are pretty complicated and fucked up.

I don't bother to tell anyone that I'm going to be away for six weeks – I just take off. I fly to Kingston and take a taxi from the airport out to Hotride's family home, which is in a small town fifty miles outside Kingston. I'm amazed to see that it's as big as a mansion, surrounded by lawns and trees. It looks like it's been added onto over the years, with several wings and porches stuck on randomly. It's so big inside, I get lost in the corridors and never know which room lies behind which door. They seem pleased to see me and make me welcome. Momo is Hotride's stepmother. He didn't grow up with her and barely knows her. It doesn't surprise me that he's arranged for me to come to stay with people he doesn't know well. Jamaicans are very hospitable and families are fluid. Every member is accepted and called a brother, a sister, an uncle, aunt or cousin.

They arrange a few fun things for me to do, like going swimming. We go to the races, the beach, play team games – but I'd forgotten how hot it is. I swelter during the heat of the day and stay indoors in the shade. The sun sets at six o'clock in the evening and it grows cooler. We come out into the courtyard as night breezes blow in from the sea and sit on the veranda with cool drinks rattling with ice, and chat, constantly swatting mosquitoes.

I grow bored. I miss Hotride, and my flat – I even miss London. Momo tries to be kind to me, but she has a big, fancy clothes shop and she's out working all day, making pots of money. There's Hotride's half-brother, but he's lazy and hangs out all day, doing nothing. The women pander to him, treat him like a lord. They work hard, clean the house, cook and shop. He eats, sleeps, eats again. Get a life, I think. I beg them to take me to visit my aunties at Constant Spring, but they won't.

'It's a bad place,' Momo says, sipping a cold drink. 'Stay here where you're safe, honey.'

'Yeah, it dangerous, I wouldn't go,' Old Auntie says, fanning herself.

I think they're scared because it's out of their gangster territory. I was so young when I left, I'd forgotten how it was, with all the murders. I have flashbacks and remember how Dadda B died in a hail of bullets and blood. I see the blood soaking into the dirt road and his eyes going from bright and alive to dead, like a fish.

Without telling them, I figure out how I can get to

Constant Spring. I take a bus into Kingston and then change. But it's not that easy and I get lost. Finally, I get there when it's getting dark, and I can't find anyone. The landmarks look unfamiliar and I'm followed by hungry dogs, looking for food and affection. Maybe they've got rabies. One slinks up, belly to ground, licks my hand. She so skinny, big liquid eyes and sharp little baby teeth. My heart melts with pain. I sit in the stinky gutter, being bitten by mosquitoes, and wonder why I bothered to come.

When I was five or six, I was grounded for being naughty – I don't remember what for now – and I bugged Nathan with questions. Why is the sky blue, what are the stars? He grew tired and told me he was writing a song and to leave him in peace. 'Find something to do,' he said. I sat on the floor beneath the windows behind the old sofa and with a big pair of scissors, I cut out squares of fabric from the red curtains to make clothes for my dolly. The curtains hung down to the ground behind the sofa where nobody could see them, and I didn't think it mattered. I could sew big stitches, so I cut the squares into dress shapes. Slowly and carefully, my big scissors snipped away and I was totally preoccupied. I never heard Nathan approaching to see what I was up to.

'Holy mackerel! Look what you done, girl, your mum's going to freak.'

I stared up and then down at my little outfits. I thought they were really nice. My dolly was going to love them. My eyes wandered to the curtains and I froze. The bottoms looked like an old woman's mouth when most of her teeth had fallen out. As soon as he saw what I'd done, Uncle beat me. I shrieked – *Owch! Ooooh!* My little dressmaking session had seemed so harmless at the time, but Mum had saved up for those new red curtains.

Mum came home and asked, 'Why you beating Sugar?'

''Cause she done wrong. See what she done to your new curtains?'

'Holy mackerel!' Mum stared – and then she got vexed and beat me. I ran into the yard, hollering, holding my sore bum. When I turned around, Mum and Nathan were laughing.

Sitting in the gutter on the Boulevard, I remember all the bad times and all the good times, and think how strange it is that even though I'm living in London now, very little has changed. My brothers are still fighting and vexing our mother. I'm still getting into trouble.

I'm lonely and homesick, and miss Hotride. Everything about this holiday is going wrong. I have to find a phone in a bar and ask Momo how to get back to her house.

She shouts at me, 'Where you gone? What you playing at? We responsible for you.'

When I get back to the house, they lecture me. I told you so, they all say, what you trying to prove? I know it's because they're worried about me – and they're right. Constant Spring is not safe. In the middle of their lecture, I get a telephone call from Mum. Paul's been arrested for trying to use my bankcard. I'd left it behind because Hotride gave me some spending money and I didn't need it.

'You've got to get back here, see if he's OK,' Mum wails.

We argue. I can't afford to change my ticket, he's got his foster carers and social workers – it's not my job. When I hang up, I'm even more depressed. There's always something. I'm too ashamed to tell Momo, but I know she listened in and heard.

When I finally get home to London, I'm so tired and stressed that Hotride and I have a massive argument. It escalates into our first physical fight. Paul's angry that he was kept in jail overnight and blames me – for stealing *my* bankcard! He and Mum have been on the phone all the time to Hotride telling him bad shit about me. Mum said I was evil, she was going to go to the witchdoctor to get me cleansed, and Paul said I was seeing other men.

When Hotride says I'm a liar, I say, 'Fuck you, we're done,' and I throw him out.

Not even a week passes before we make up and he comes back. Within three weeks we're fighting again. These fights aren't about us, but about other people. His other girlfriend, a bitch named Patricia, tells him I'm going to give my baby away. I'm in the bathroom cleaning my teeth and we're yelling back and forth at each other.

'Who you going to give my baby to?' he asks.

'No one.'

'You a liar. You been to see Social Services, they taking it into care, soon as it born.'

I'm outraged. 'Who said that?'

'Patricia tell me,' he says, coming into the bathroom, crowding me. 'It's true, innit?'

I'm furious that he's brought her name to me, right into my house. Evil spirits can ride in on the back of her bad name. 'How dare you bring her name in here!' I scream, stabbing him in the eye with my toothbrush.

He explodes – we're rolling around in bathroom punching, scratching, whacking each other. I hit my head on the basin, he crashes back against the wall. We making such a noise that the neighbours hear us and call out, 'We getting the police.' I scream at him that we're through, I never want to see him again. He runs off, I'm sobbing with pain and rage, feeling like my heart is breaking. What happened to our love, what happened to my dreams of a happy relationship of my own? I've got nobody.

I call Devon, as I always seem to do when my need is greatest, and tell her what's been happening. She says when things get bad, don't let them escalate into a fight. If you can't calm it down, leave, she says.

'What if we're fighting in my house?'

'It doesn't matter. Just leave. Put some space between you, take time out to diffuse the situation.'

I promise her I will. I add, using the kind of language that I learned from my lovely Elena, 'And I really need to sort out my deep issues if I'm going to be a mother.'

Devon reminds me that I had largely ignored Kirstie,

the counsellor I had been assigned to replace Elena, repeatedly breaking appointments.

'Would you like to start over again with her?' she asks.

I say yes.

'Ok, I'll make an appointment for you.' But it doesn't matter anyway, because Hotride and me, we've split up. I don't want him back.

Through all this, I'm aware that Camila is keeping an eye on me, which makes me feel safe. When there's a problem, somehow, she's always there, ready to sort it out in an amazing way. It's like she's a wizard, looking into a crystal ball. I hear her name mentioned all the time. People in the office are always saying, 'We'll have to ask Camila,' whenever there's something that needs resolving.

I'm walking through the main hall at London Bridge on my way to Kirstie's room for my first session with her, when I bump into Camila. I feel as if she knows I'll be there. She stops and takes me by the hand and looks into my eyes. 'How are you?' she asks.

'OK.'

'Are you?'

'No, I'm not. I've got issues,' I burst out. I want to talk about my entire life. There's so much, it hurts.

'Do you want to talk?' she asks.

'There's too much,' I say. 'Right from the start, when I was a happy little girl –' I break off, wondering if I was really happy – or was I just unaware?

'You could write it all down,' Camila says, sowing

the seeds for me to write this book. She says it almost casually, but I feel that nothing she says is ever casual. She still has my hand in hers. 'I'm here for you, day and night. A phonecall to Devon will reach me. Whatever you want to do will be your decision.' She doesn't say about what, but it's not important. I think she means about anything at all. 'I think Kirstie's waiting. Why don't you go in?'

I knock on the door and open it. Kirstie greets me. She's young and Scottish, with short, dark, curly hair and blue eyes. She says, 'Would you like to sit down?' There's a table and chairs there, but she points to an armchair and sofa. She sits in the chair, and I sit on the deep, cushioned sofa. It's so comfortable, I could fall asleep.

She asks me a little about myself, like where I came from today, and what the journey is like, when my baby is due – that kind of thing. 'How do you feel about talking about yourself?' she asks.

I reply, 'I find talking about myself alienating.'

'Ah yes. That's an interesting word. Does anyone you know use it?'

'My last therapist, Elena, did. I told her I couldn't talk about my mum and she said I must find it alienating.'

'Do you?'

'Yes.'

She nods. Instead, we chat about all kinds of things, just like friends who have met for tea. She's warm, caring, understanding and patient – all those fuzzy words I need her to be. She doesn't rush me. When I stop for long periods and gaze into space, reliving something, she says quietly, 'It's OK – in your own time.' I start to feel totally at ease with her.

She points out a big sandbox on the table. 'You know, sometimes people like to play in that.'

I'm curious and jump up and stand at the table. It's a shallow, square box, filled with clean white sand. I put out a hand and smooth the surface. It feels cool and pleasant. 'What do you do?'

'You might like to run your hands through it – just play. Perhaps make patterns, draw things, make heaps. It doesn't matter. It's very relaxing, like a Buddhist's beads – you know?'

By now, I'm running my hands through the sand, lifting up small amounts and letting them trickle through my fingers, like an hourglass. It's very soothing. I pull up a chair at the table. With my back to Kirstie, suddenly I'm talking about my mother, saying things I've never told anyone.

When I stop for a moment, Kirstie says, 'I wonder why your mother did that?'

I've never wondered about why my mum's done something or other – I've just railed about the results. I let the sand trickle and start to think about why my mother did something to hurt me. Or something damaging to me and my brothers. My mind works overtime, and before I realise, I'm in her shoes, seeing things through her eyes. For the first time, I see that often she has drifted into things, like I have – and she has ended up without choices. In Jamaica, for example, I tell Kirstie, a girl often has few choices. She has to do things just to survive, and one thing leads to another and before she knows it, she's in the shit up to her neck.

I glance down at the sandbox and see I have made a circle, like a whirlpool in the middle. 'That's my mum's life,' I say, pointing. 'A whirlpool that sucks her to the bottom and there's no escape.'

'What about you?'

I'm reflective. It's strange how a quiet moment thinking can lead me into a state of turmoil. From out of the blue, I say, 'On one hand I'm pregnant – and on the other, I see the result of lawlessness.'

'That's a lot to think about. It's quite a conjunction.'

'I know – it's like this –' I draw a slash across the sandbox with the flat of my hand, and want to turn it over, but I get up and walk away. I fling myself down on the sofa. 'I hate myself!' I burst out.

'Do you?'

Little by little, things I'm stuck on get fixed. I always know what's fixed after – never before. At some stage, I tell Kirstie that our sessions are making me think more about my own worth and self-respect. 'At fifteen, all I was interested in was blocking out things. I couldn't sleep, so I went raving, got into drugs, got around guns and knives, mixed with bad men, no-good useless people who lived like rats in sewers. It was like that film, *Gangs of New York*, all meat cleavers, machetes, axes and violence.'

'You hate it, don't you?'

'It's no way to live. It's not what I want. When I got

pregnant, I wanted to change. I've spent hours thinking about things – where I am going, how I'll cope with this responsibility. I don't want my baby to go through the crap I went through. I want to be a good mother – the kind of mother I wish my mum had been to me.'

Having them – Camila, Devon and Kirstie – just a phonecall away saves my sanity and my life, because as things progress between me and Hotride, they turn real nasty.

After a couple of quiet, though lonely, months, Hotride comes round again, acting nonchalant, as if it's all OK and we've never split up. We start to argue. I want to kill him. He refuses to leave, thinks he can sweet-talk me round. So I go into my bedroom and start to pack up.

He follows me in. 'What you doing?' he demands, angry.

'I'm leaving.' I say it calmly and throw more clothes into my suitcase.

He's confused. 'Where you going?'

'Anywhere.'

'You going to stay with your boyfriend,' he shouts in my face.

'You dumbass,' I say.

'Yo bitch! Yo ain't going nowhere!' He grabs my house keys and runs around, locking the security catches on my windows. Then he slams out the front door and locks me into my own house from the outside. I need a key to escape – and I'm trapped. My immediate urge is to call someone, but I count slowly to ten like Devon suggested, and calm down. I don't want to take our fight to everyone else, it's not their business – and it shames me to always be fighting like this. I say to myself, 'Sugar, you got food, electricity and credit on your phone. Hole up and chill out.'

I switch off my phone and relax. I watch TV, play music, sleep, give myself some beauty therapy. After three days, I call Harold. 'Can you ask your son to let me out of my house?'

Harold says, 'Why don't you ask him yourself?'

I say, 'If I see him, I'm going to attack him. I've got a sword and a machete – I even have a kitchen drawer full of sharp knives.'

Harold gets Hotride around his house in double-fast time and demands my keys, then Harold comes round and lets me out. 'What's going on, Sugar?'

'Hotride and me, we're not boyfriend and girlfriend no more.'

Harold sits me down, makes me a cup of tea, and says, 'You still baby-mother and baby-father together. You made this life. You've got to get on, for sake of the baby.'

'It's Hotride's fault,' I say, still angry with him. 'He hit me.'

Harold shook his head. 'That's not right, I'll talk to him.'

Harold is a strong father figure who Hotride fears. Harold won't let Hotride smoke dope and would kill him if he knew he was on crack – so I can't tell him that part of the problem is drugs. They get Hotride going, make him act crazy.

Harold gets on the phone and calls Hotride. 'How dare you touch a pregnant girl? How would it look if another man hit your sister? She someone else's daughter – what you thinking of, man?'

He hangs up and says I should go away for a while, before Hotride and me end up killing each other – and I've got the baby to think of. So I pack my bag again and go to stay with a friend in Croydon.

All the time, Hotride is calling me non-stop. 'Where have you gone with my baby? You stolen it.'

I say, 'It's still in my belly – anywhere I go, it has to go too.'

'Get your ass back here where you belong!' he shouts.

'Bollocks,' I say.

Then he says, quieter, 'Your mum made me think the baby not mine.'

'What you doing calling my mum and my brother and badmouthing me?'

'So, bitch, who's the father?' he presses in a mean voice.

'You say that one more time and you'll never see us again.'

I can hear he's going crazy, yelling one minute, calm the next. He pleads, 'Babe, I can't help it – when your own mum says shit like that, what am I supposed to think? It's my baby – I want to see your belly growing. I put her in there – she's mine.'

'What makes you think it's a girl?'

'I know it – she's a beautiful little girl.'

My heart melts again for him. I miss him a lot. He's really a good boy, but very confused, because his whole life has been fucked up. He doesn't trust anyone because they've all let him down. I try to see things from his perspective.

'Aw, honey, come on home. I'll be waiting for you,' he says.

'No, we need to talk in neutral territory.' That's another lesson I've learned from Kids Company. I agree to meet him in Croydon. Make the rules, stick to them. 'I want you to take me out to a film and a nice meal, we need to talk like proper grown-ups,' I say.

We meet outside the cinema and he touches my belly. 'How's my baby?' he asks.

'We're fine,' I say. I kiss him briefly on the cheek. Let him sweat. In the cinema, he holds my hand and I let him. He puts an arm around my shoulders and I snuggle in.

'Wanna go bed?' he whispers.

I sit up. 'I'm not ready. We need to talk.'

After the film, we have a meal in a nice Chinese restaurant with pink cloths on the tables and red lanterns. It's very romantic.

'So are you coming home with me?' he asks.

'Yeah, I guess so. But you got to learn to treat me right. I don't want you listening to my mum or my brother telling lies about me. They got their own agendas. And I don't want you bringing no bitch ho' baby-mother's name into my house.'

We go home together, very lovey-dovey. I pretend everything is fine and I give up going to Kids Company. Half of me is ashamed that, after their help, I'm back where I started with Hotride – on a rocky road. I don't want to confront it through their eyes – because I know how it must seem, even to the most non-judgmental person.

When I'm eight months pregnant we have a major fight. Hotride punches me in the mouth and splits my lip. Blood gushes everywhere and my face is a mess. I'm screaming down the phone to Devon, 'Help me! I'm being murdered!'

Although we haven't spoken for a while, she is instantly alert. She says, 'Hang on, I'm calling the police.' As soon as he hears that, Hotride runs off. When Devon and the police show up, foolishly I won't press charges, and Devon takes me to hospital to be stitched up.

Devon says I can't stay at home, it's too risky. I'm scared and don't want to stay. I think Hotride is getting crazier – I'm sure next time he'll kill me. After I'm stitched up, we go to Kids Company and talk to the domestic violence unit. They put me in a hotel, but it's too expensive long term. The only option is a domestic violence hostel, and I hate it. It's worse than being back in the children's home – it's like I'm going backwards, and because the state won't pay for me to live in two places, I'm worried I'll lose my flat.

'Are you sure going home is a wise thing to do?' Devon asks me. 'Your baby's life could be at risk.'

I want to be positive. 'Yeah, I think Hotride learned a lesson. Next time, I'll press charges, he'll go to jail. That'll scare him.'

Devon looks concerned. She spells it out. 'You're an abused woman – it's not a good place to be. Men who batter women don't find it easy to change. Battered women can end up dead.'

But I'm confident – and I know Hotride loves me. He might be violent, but he will stop short of really hurting me. 'He really loves me,' I say, not realising that all battered women sing this song. I guess I haven't been through the pain and fear barrier yet.

I return home, and within hours, Hotride is back and we're snuggled up in bed, a nice little family unit.

But we're not a full-time family. Hotride is like many baby-fathers – he comes and goes, sleeps here, there and everywhere. He promises me he's not sleeping with other girls, but says I can't tie him down, or ask him questions. 'I got to make a living,' he says. 'Sometimes, I got to stay up all night, do a little dealing, play cards – you know how it is. You want me give you money for baby, help out with bills, where it's going come, eh?'

I don't remind him that while he is generous, it's only now and then. There's no regular sum I can depend on – but I'm grateful for the money he does give me, and grateful that he spends several nights a week with me. It could be worse.

Chapter 19

Crystal Palace,

Winter 2006–2007

I'm nine months gone and baby-sitting a little cousin when at about nine-thirty at night I start going into labour. The first pains take me completely by surprise. Oh hell, I think, I can't have the baby here – what about the kid I'm baby-sitting, what on earth will I do with her? Just then, the kid's mum phones to see if everything is all right, and I practically scream, 'I'm having my baby!'

'Where your boyfriend?'

'At the hairdresser's,' I groan as another big pain hits me.

'Hang on, I'll send my boyfriend round,' she shouts. Darren comes around at once, looking panicky. 'You OK, Sugar? Now don't do anyting until I get you to hospital, OK?'

I clutch my swollen belly. 'Wait, I can't talk,' I gasp.

He's an experienced dad and says, 'How often are the pains?'

'Oooh-ow!' I yelp. 'I ain't been counting, have I?'

He gets someone to look after the little cousin I've been watching, and when I can walk, he drives me home to pick up my hospital bag, which contains all the things they've said I'd need. But when we reach my house, in my confusion I've left my keys behind where I was baby-sitting. I get another wave of pain and lean against the front door, waiting for it to pass. He tries to kick the door down, but it's too strong. A neighbour comes to see what the noise is all about.

'Hey, I thought it was burglars,' he says.

'No, it's Sugar about to give birth,' Darren says.

Oh, man! The neighbour runs and returns with a jemmy. He forces open my door, and I don't care that it's all splintered to bits and thieves could get in. I just want to get the hell to that hospital. I grab my bag and waddle out to the car and Darren jumps in quick. 'Let's go, doll!' he says. 'Hold on!'

It's almost Guy Fawkes night, and from the heights of my flat in Crystal Palace, I see the skies filled with exploding fireworks, which adds to the madness of the drive through waves of pain and light-headedness. He's driving fast, swerving round corners, jumping lights. Fortunately, the hospital isn't far away, or I'd be sick, he's going so fast. It's 10 p.m. when we arrive and he rushes in, leaving me in the car outside, engine running, lights on. He gets a wheelchair and puts me in it. He careers to reception, like I'm in a shopping trolley. 'She's in labour,' he calls out. 'Clear the way!'

A nurse takes over and wheels me to a cubicle. Darren

says he has to go, almost runs away. The nurse smiles. 'Your boyfriend?' she asks.

'No, he's my cousin's boyfriend. My boyfriend's at the hairdresser, having his hair braided.'

'Men!' she says, rolling her eyes. She puts on gloves and jelly and checks to see how dilated I am. *Owch!* I yelp. 'You're only one centimetre,' she says. 'You can go home until you're three centimetres dilated.'

I sit up. 'I ain't going home! I'm having labour pains. I'm in pain!'

The nurse laughs. 'Yes, but you're nowhere near ready to give birth, trust me.'

'I can't go home. My lift's gone – and I'll be on my own at home. Can't I stay? I'm sure I'm almost ready.'

'Well, we can't have you being on your own,' the nurse says, and she gives me a reassuring pat. 'OK, honey, let's put you in the mums' waiting room.'

I waddle like a duck with her to the anteroom, where half a dozen pregnant women are in different stages of labour. I'm in pain, but it's not excruciating – they're all screaming and squawking like they're about to die. Two are on the floor, rolling about in agony. 'You OK?' I ask one of the women on the floor. 'Nurse! She needs you!'

'Leave me alone,' the woman gasps. 'I want to die.' I stare at her, thinking that nothing could be that bad, short of having your leg amputated without anaesthetic – then another pain hits me and I hold my stomach and climb onto a couch. *Ooow-ow!* I scream, joining in. It's crazy. Nothing has prepared me for this.

Hotride shows up towards midnight and they put me in a cubicle so I can be with him. 'You OK?' he asks, rubbing my back.

'I didn't think it would hurt this bad.'

The nurse checks. 'You're three centimetres dilated.'

'Can I have some gas and air?' I say.

'No, let's wait until you're four centimetres.'

'But, nurse, you said three –'

She smiles. 'Did I?' then she whisks out.

A couple more hours pass and I'm tired of the pain and nothing happening. My supportive boyfriend has found a birthing mat and he's lying on the floor next to my bed, asleep. Suddenly a big one hits, and I get off the bed and boot him in the back.

'Ouch! Why do that?' he says, sitting up, bleary-eyed.

'I'm in pain! Why are you sleeping?'

Nobody's told us we can't have a mobile phone in hospital, so when Mum phones from Bristol, see how I'm doing, I grab the phone off Hotride, and tell her I'm going to die. She's telling me I'll be all right.

I ask for a hot bath, but it doesn't help. I have gas and air and feel giddy – it's just going on too long. If Hotride wasn't here, I wouldn't be able to stand it, but he keeps rubbing my back, saying, 'You'll be OK, hang in, you doing just fine.'

Towards 6 a.m. the waves are coming faster and I call for the nurse. The midwife comes. She finds me lying there, pushing. 'Don't push!' she says.

'I want this baby out,' I say, bearing down again.

Hotride gets my mum on the speakerphone towards

quarter to seven in the morning, and it's all speeding up. 'Push!' Mum's shouting, talking me through it.

'No – don't push until you're ten centimetres. You'll tear yourself,' the midwife says and Mum is shouting, 'Yes! Push! Push!'

While we're arguing – *push* – *don't push* – I hear a pop. 'Ooh! My water's broken!'

'Where?' says the midwife, and she looks, her head colliding with Hotride's – who's down there, having a look himself. My waters haven't broken and I wonder what the pop was. Suddenly, I feel the waters flood and the head comes out at the same time. Hotride's right down there, his face between my legs, watching the whole shebang – while the midwife tries to sort me out around his head.

'Wait, don't push – slow down – you're doing this too fast –'

I'm saying, 'She wants to come – I can't stop her –'

Then she's born and crawling up my belly to my breast and starts sucking. The midwife says, 'She's a quick learner!' And meanwhile, I'm still in pain – far worse pain and shouting, 'No! – No! – No!' The midwife says, 'It's the placenta – let it come.' I've got the weight of the baby on my chest, and feeling like I'm about to give birth to an elephant. *So much pain.* I'm screaming and Hotride's hanging onto baby in case she slips off me. The afterbirth plops out – huge and heavy. Blissful – the relief. Hotride snips the cord and misses. He cuts again and the baby is separated from the afterbirth. The midwife takes over and ties the cord off and cleans her up. Me, I'm tired, just want to sleep.

The midwife leaves us, and Hotride says, 'I'm taking her home with me.'

My eyes fly open. 'What?'

'Yeah, I want her with me – she my kid.'

I think he's joking, and say, 'She's gotta stay here with me – how you gonna feed her?'

In the end, he lies down on the birthing mat, saying he's going to move in with me until I leave. The nurse and doctor come to check on me and they boot him out. Suddenly I'm full of energy and can't lie still. I get up and go walkabout, looking at the other women who were in the waiting room with me, cooing over their babies. When Hotride returns later with flowers, he's running up and down, looking for me. His family comes – all talking, laughing, happy to see the baby. 'What you going call her?'

'Aimee.'

After the first feed, she refuses to take more. After two days, I'm concerned. Her little stomach looks swollen – the nurses say she's fine, but I know she's not. My mum always told me that if a baby is sick, you lie it on its side. I try this, lying her on her side on my bed, and I'm amazed to see all this water gushing out. I'm scared and run and fetch the nurse.

She looks at her, and says, 'She's fine. She swallowed a lot of amniotic fluid. It's quite normal.'

As she changes the sheet, I think, if it's so normal, how come you didn't get it out of her, and leave her hungry for two days? Soon as I picked her up and put her to my breast, she starts feeding like she's starving. The doctors come and check us out, and I'm allowed home in a cab with Hotride. It feels really strange, going home with my baby. I glance down at her sleeping and think, she's got the sweetest face. Good thing she looks like her dad. Hotride next to me keeps looking at her like he's never seen a baby before. I never guessed he could be soft as butter like this.

Soon as we get in, he changes her and tells me that it's his job, he wants to do it. I'm tired and go to lie down, glad that he's here to help out. But after her next feed, when she cries, I go to change her – and he's racing me to it. Within a few days, we're almost arguing over whose turn it is. 'She my baby too,' I find myself saying.

That first week, Devon comes to see me at home, a big smile on her face as she breezes in.

'How you doing, Sugar? What a drama!'

'I'm just fine.' Proudly, I hold out little Aimee and Devon's taken her in her arms and is making cooing sounds, like everyone does with new babies. 'Oh, she's beautiful! So sweet!' Devon looks up, 'Are you managing well?'

Yes, I say, I got a lot of advice from Kids Company and the antenatal clinic the doctor sent me to, so I know how to do this and that – and I helped my mum with my brothers, and with other kids. But I know what she means. She's really asking, *Will Hotride be there for you?* She needs have no fears on that score, I tell her. He's just popped out to the shops, but he washes and changes her all the time, he won't let me do a thing. I say, 'To be honest, I was annoyed – I wanted to change her, but he said he'd do it, he's taking real good care of her.'

Devon is pleased and tells me that if I want anything, call her at once. I'm on my own – but feel quite exhilarated. Me and Hotride and Aimee – we're a proper little family unit. I think the future is looking good.

I wish I could say that things stay rosy, but they don't. After a few weeks he stops helping as much and I'm nagging him – why won't you do this or that? We start bickering and it gets so bad, I say, 'Honey, we can't do this. Let's make a plan.'

'What kind of plan?' he asks, not really listening, watching TV, his legs sprawled on the arm of the armchair.

'Like a schedule, whose turn it is to look after Aimee,' I explain. 'I don't mind doing it all day, if you'll help in the evening, or weekends. Maybe at night, when I'm tired.'

'Yeah, OK,' he agrees.

Next thing, we're kissing and cuddling and he wants to make another baby. I push him off and say, 'I've only just had this one, my body's not ready yet. Let's wait.'

But, apart from a few skirmishes, when we push and shove each other, we're as happy as any couple can be with never enough money and an uncertain future.

When Aimee is about a month old, I go to spend the weekend with a girlfriend. When I return I find a pair of knickers near my bed that I know for sure aren't mine. They're size twelve, and I'm a ten. I ask Hotride what the fuck's been going on – and he says it's my brother – Paul must have brought a girl back.

'It can't be Paul, he doesn't have any keys to my house,' I say. He keeps denying it, and I scream, 'You brought a slut back and fucked her in my bed. What the hell you playing at? This is my house – it's where me and Aimee live. You think I want my daughter sleeping in a bed where her dad's been fucking a slut?'

The fight escalates and he shoves me around. I shout that I'm leaving and taking Aimee, and he says, really nastily, 'Why are you taking my daughter away from me?'

Things get heated and I run into the bedroom, crying. I think, I can't be doing this – one day Aimee will get hurt. I pack a few things and call the police to escort me to the railway station, so I can leave him and go to Bristol. I know if the police aren't there he'll never let me take Aimee. Then I call Devon and tell her what's happening.

'I'll be there in twenty minutes' she says. 'Lock yourself in your bedroom and sit tight. Whatever you do, don't get into a screaming match with him, OK?' Devon also calls the police, to make sure that they're coming. When she gets there, I'm still talking to the police and Hotride is arguing with them.

'Let's go,' Devon says, and I pick up Aimee and we leave. At Paddington, Devon gives me a hug. 'Take all the time you need to think things through and let me know, OK?'

I hug her back, glad that she's such a strong, supportive friend, and I get on the train.

Mum is surprised to see me. 'Why didn't you call?' she asks.

'Because I don't want Hotride to know where I am. If he calls, tell him you not seen me – OK? We having our problems.' I feel I can't tell her too much. I just say that Hotride and me, we had a fight.

Mum says, 'People always fighting – it don't mean much. He's a nice boy.'

'I come to see you, Mum. Anyway, it's time you saw Aimee.'

Mum loves her and kisses and rocks her like she's a little princess. She gets her some pretty clothes and we dress her up in them, and although it's cold, it's a sunny, bright day and we take her for a walk. It's the first time I get on with my mum and we sit and play with the baby and talk like friends. Friends drop in with little gifts and we have a nice dinner. Mum's boyfriend is away in Jamaica, so it's just the two of us. It's the best visit ever, but after a week, I'm missing Hotride like crazy, and I return to London hoping we can work things out.

But within a couple of weeks I wake up to a medical problem that needs attending and go to the STD clinic. 'You've got chlamydia,' the doctor says.

I'm mortified and furious, and can't wait to get home to launch my attack. Hotride's still in bed sleeping, one arm around Aimee, who I fed before I went out. My brothers are lounging around on the sofa, bored, watching TV. I change the baby in silence and put her in her crib, then turn my attention to Hotride, who's just woken up. He smirks and pats the bed. 'You coming back to bed, honey?'

I get down in his face and snarl. 'Screw you. You can fuck your dirty girl, but don't bring her disease to me. All this time you telling me I'm the one fooling around, and you are out there, spreading venereal shit.'

'What you on about?' he whines. He tries to hug me in bed but I push him away and, enraged, he yells I probably screwed someone when I was away.

'Fuck you!' I scream back, and he punches me in the face with all his force, like a boxer. My neck snaps back and it feels like stars are shooting out of the base of my skull. I see Jupiter and Mars and black spots before my eyes. When I lean over the edge of the bed to stop choking, there's blood flowing into great gobs on the rug.

I jump up and look in the mirror. When I see the mess he's made of my face, I run to the kitchen for the machete. He locks himself in the bedroom and pushes the bed behind the door. I've got the strength of six women and fling myself at the door, chop chop chopping at the wooden panels. My brothers yell and jump up and down, too scared to stop me. When I begin to tire, I run round the side and look in through the window. Hotride's pushing against the door, wondering why it's gone quiet.

Like kung fu I hurl myself through the double glazing, not caring if I cut my head off with shards of glass.

'Keep away from me, you fuckin' lunatic!' he yells, and drags the bed away, shooting through the broken door.

I grab the two-pronged Japanese martial arts sword we keep for protection and tear after him. My brothers open the front door and help him escape. They stand back out of my reach, laughing, 'Go, go, go!'

Maybe they don't like him, or think I'm playing. But me, I'm deadly serious. This useless boy ain't going to live to see another day.

He's half-naked, in his boxers, running like a rabbit through the estate. I was a champion runner at school – I could move like the wind and I've got demented rage on my side. 'I'm gonna get you, you bastard,' I scream. 'You're dead meat!'

I corner him down an alley near the bins like the rat he is. I scream, 'I hate you!' and I stab him in the buttock with the heavy sword. 'Bastard! Die!'

Blood flowers over his boxers, spreading like red ink on wet paper. He screams and takes off, rocket-propelled, and I hear sirens coming closer. Holy shit – what have I done?

I run the opposite way and throw the sword into some bushes as I pass. There's the police, a fire truck, an ambulance, the cops jump out and come running. I face them, my lip and nose split wide open, my face masked with blood. They think I'm the victim and I'm strapped into a stretcher and taken to hospital. My face is stitched up with only local anaesthetic (the doctor says they have to be careful using anaesthetic with a head injury) and they have to scrape me off the ceiling. I want to kill him all over again.

Next morning, he comes to see me in hospital. He's holding onto the wall, barely able to walk. We're hugging each other and crying. I look at his buttock and see this huge hole, like a cannonball wound, full of blood. You better show the nurse, I say, get it stitched up.

It's the last time he lays a hand on me, but he's gone from being my knight in shining armour to my victimiser. I wonder why he treats me like that – if you want someone, you cherish them. I stop caring about the way I look, throw any old clothes on, raggy, torn, hair sticking up like a bush. Friends notice and comment, 'What's up, Sugar, you ill?'

Yeah, I'm ill – sick of the way I'm living, sick of him. I say, 'Let's split up.'

He loses his temper, balls his fist, snarls, 'No man is growing my child.'

I say, 'It's got nothing to do with another man. You don't love me, you treat me like dirt.'

He explodes and I run out of my house, down the street. I'm frantic, punching in automatic calling to get Devon on my phone and trying to get out of his way at the same time. I'm scared of him, I tell Devon as I run.

He yells, 'Yo bitch, get back here, I won't touch you.'

I go back and he says if he attacks me, Devon will have him arrested.

'Yeah, you better believe it,' I say.

Devon comes and tries to broker the peace. She asks

me, 'Do you feel safe? Do you want to go to a woman's hostel?'

'Nah, I'll be all right,' I say.

Turns out *he's* scared of me. He can't sleep, watching to see what I might do, while I can only see the destructive things in him. Our relationship changes from positive to negative. He's paranoid, convinced that I've found another man. He thinks all those hours away from me he's spending with his dirty sluts must be time I'm spending with other men. Things get so bad between us that, just before Christmas, I throw him out and tell him to stay away.

Chapter 20

Bristol, Winter

to Summer 2007

After another big argument just after Christmas, when Aimee is two months old, Hotride grabs Aimee and holds her hostage in a friend's flat. I'm petrified. I'm crying down the phone to Devon, 'You've got to help me, he's taken my baby. Please come.'

Devon calls the police, then she gets through to Hotride and calms him down, trying to convince him that this is a really bad mistake. She can't get his back up, she has to be reasonable – while I'm so hysterical that if I got on the phone to him, I'd threaten to kill him. At the end of it all, to my amazement, she's talked him into going to anger-management classes. Instead of hitting me, he'll be able to say, 'Time out.' But that will take time and, meanwhile, I need some space. She gets my baby back safely, and I drop charges, but I won't let him stay in my house. We can't even look at each other now without acting like we're in a boxing ring.

When he's gone and I've calmed down, Devon says,

'What do you want to do? You've got to be safe.'

I say, 'I won't go into a hostel for battered women – and I want to keep my flat. It's my sanctuary.'

We discuss it and decide that Hotride won't think of looking for me in Bristol with my mum, because she kept her word and never did tell him I'd been there before. After so many years on my own, I want some comfort and help. It could be a fresh start, maybe now I'm older I can build on the new relationship with my mum we'd started a few months earlier, last time I ran away.

Now that I've got a child of my own, I want to know what makes my mum tick. She was a brilliant mum to us when we were little – she worked all hours at some really hard jobs just to feed us and the neighbourhood kids and to send me to school. She didn't have to, but she did it. She beat us hard – but everyone beat the kids, it was in our culture. The Bible says, spare the rod and spoil the child, and from way back, our people acted on that. It was only later that she lost the plot and lost interest in me. Maybe I'll finally find out why, what happened to make her change. I know we can do it, I tell myself, thinking of how sweet she was with Aimee.

Camila agrees that Kids Company will support me with rent, food, clothes – everything I need until I get on my feet, however long it takes. I'm all set and within a day, we're heading for Bristol. It's a warm, sunny day early in the New Year and I'm up, full of new resolutions.

Mum's smiling when we come and shows Devon round her small flat, like she want to make a good impression on her. She's dressed nicely in jeans and a low-cut top that shows off her figure. She's still a beautiful woman, very exotic. I wonder how come she's got such a loser like Leo for her boyfriend. He's got property, a wife, a family – how come, with her looks and vibrant personality, she's not a wife to some rich man with a couple of houses? How come other women are always the wives – never my mum?

'What do you think of your first grandchild?' Devon says.

'She's lovely, but I want Sugar to have a better life than I did. Children are a hindrance.'

I feel embarrassed. Mum's always showing me up in front of people. I think, I've got a lovely baby – why spoil it with criticism?

My mum's only got two rooms, a living room with a bedroom off it in a tall, squalid house, with filthy stairs and landings. But her two rooms are clean and neat. Aimee and me, we'll share her bed.

'Aimee should sleep in her crib,' Devon says. I don't argue, though she usually sleeps with me at home. Mum says how much rent she wants and it's all arranged. When Devon leaves, I feel sad, like I'm saying goodbye to a friend.

'Call me any time,' she says. 'And remember, I'll come down whenever you need me. If you suspect Hotride is around, call me at once, or call the police. At the moment, it's not a good idea for you to be around each other.'

I wave Devon goodbye and feel desolate. I miss

Hotride, even though I'm still angry with him. I go back upstairs to Mum's flat. She doesn't have a lot of furniture, even after so many years down in Bristol. She's moved around a lot, gone from a big house with four bedrooms to this shabby bedsit.

Devon has found me a small job, making and designing lingerie, and I enjoy it, as well as earning some money. Mum mocks me. 'You just a wage slave,' she says. 'You'd make more in drugs.'

I say, 'Yeah, but I don't want to live like that.' I want to hold up my head, make something of myself. I'm learning a lot. I want to work in fashion, do my own things – and I'm learning cutting out and sewing.

Everything's fine the first week. We get on and start to talk. But Mum's very deep, and if I pry too much about her and me and our relationship like I want to, she clams her mouth shut. I have a ton of questions, like why did she do this and that, but she's not prepared to dwell on such things too much. She's happy to talk about our old life in Jamaica and the aunties. We have a laugh, remembering how she beat the boys against a papaya tree to make their dicks long.

'It a good thing you didn't have no boy,' she winks. 'There's no papaya trees in England.' We discuss traditional medicines, like soursop to stop you wetting the bed, and Mum tells me how in the country after a birth, women bury the placenta and umbilical cord and plant a little tree over it, like a coconut. It's called the baby tree. 'Did you do this for me?' I ask and she shakes her head, no.

'I miss ackee,' she says. 'Remember our big old ackee tree in yard? Ackee and salt cod and bammy for supper, mmm-mmm!' She sucks her teeth as if still tasting it.

'And lobster on the beach with Frankie. Wonder what he's doing now?' I giggle. 'I wonder if he still has all them goats in back of pick-up truck?'

It all comes flooding back and we have fun as we reminisce. I tell her I'm glad I grew up in Jamaica. She nods, 'The old ways are best, for sure.'

She wants to hold Aimee all the time. 'You so pretty,' she coos. 'My baby doll.' When Leo comes, my mum runs around after him, offers him tea, coffee, a bottle of beer. I can see they've got something on their mind.

He looks Aimee over carefully and says, 'Hmm, hmm, she got fine bones, she got a nice-shaped head,' like she's at Crufts dog show. 'You axed her?' he says to my mum.

She shakes her head. 'Uh-uh – not yet.'

'Axed me what?' I say.

His words make me drop through the floor with shock. 'I want a baby with yo' mum, but she's too old. You got good genes, make nice babies – we axing you to carry a baby for us.'

I jump up. 'What you saying! You crazy.'

He looks at me like I'm simple-minded. 'It just a baby – no big deal. You just had one, so what's the problem? Pop out one, pop out two, it's all the same.'

'No way!' I almost snatch back Aimee and glare at him. 'I ain't having your baby, end of story.'

I take Aimee for a walk to get her out of the house.

317

It's freezing cold and not a very nice area, unsafe after dark, but I don't want to return to Mum's place. There's always something to bring me down. When I get in, they both nag me, like it's my duty to have their baby, like I'm a baby machine. Mum says, 'After all I done for you,' and Leo says, 'Yeah, after all your mum done for you, bringing you into the world, paying for you to come to England when she could have left you in Jamaica.'

I want to say to my mum, 'Why are you doing this to me? Why you want a child with this man, who has a wife and daughters, who comes here just to sleep with you, who gives you nothing, who uses you and abuses you. Have you got no self-respect at all?'

I have to be strong because the pressure increases. My mum and Leo nag me endlessly. One night he comes over, and they have a few drinks, sit around. It gets late and I feed Aimee and get ready for bed. When I go into the bedroom, Leo's in the bed, lounging there like a slob.

I say, 'Are you staying here tonight?'

'Yeah,' he says, sort of insolently, like what am I gonna do about it?

I say, 'So where's me and Aimee gonna sleep?'

He smirks. 'You can get yo' ass into this bed, yeah?'

'Fuck you. I ain't sleeping with you.'

Mum comes in, and when she says, 'Well, fuck you, you can sleep in the street,' I feel betrayed.

I spend the night on the sofa, holding Aimee. I'm crying, wondering why I thought my mum would be a safe haven. I'd rather take my chances with Hotride. In the morning, I call Devon. 'I'm coming back to London.' I don't tell her what's going down with this surrogate crap. How can I tell her what my mum is really like, how depraved her boyfriend is?

'What's wrong?' Devon says.

'Mum's flat's too crowded, we don't get any sleep,' I say.

'Try to hang on for a bit longer, give yourself a chance,' Devon says. She can say this because she doesn't know the full picture. She's just dealing with what I tell her, not the truth. I try not to show how upset I am, but I'm under pressure from Leo and my mum. Mum knows I want her to love me – and she thinks I'll do anything to win her love.

I call Devon again and tell her I need help. She hears the desperation in my voice and comes at once. I can't tell her about what Mum and Leo have asked me to do, so she probably thinks I'm making a fuss.

'It's not working out with my mum and Leo,' I say. 'They want their privacy. I can make a go of it in Bristol, but I want my own place.'

There's a room downstairs in Mum's house, and Devon rents this for me. It's small, but there's a lock on the door. Devon takes me out and we buy furniture. A bed, a cot for Aimee, a small wardrobe, chairs and a table. A television, and refrigerator. I have to share the kitchen and bathroom. Everyone in the house lives like pigs. They won't clean up, won't scrub the bath. I'm terrified Aimee will catch some disease, and when

I'm not working, I'm scrub, scrub, scrubbing like I'm obsessed. My hands get sore and my knees are sore from always being on the floor scrubbing.

Devon arranges for me to continue with my fashion course, long distance, and I am overwhelmed when Bella comes to my house to work with me every couple of weeks, travelling down from London on the train. On the one hand, all these strangers are giving me a lot of support – while on the other, my own family and family connections are giving me a hard time and demanding more than I can give.

Leo adds a new pressure. He wants me to be a mule, carrying Class A drugs from Jamaica. He thinks if my mum is in the courier business, I should be, too. He says he'll buy me a ticket, like he's Father Christmas, handing out gifts.

I look at my mum and say, 'Just because you want to live in a gangster ghetto, I don't have to.'

'How else am I supposed to live?' Mum asks. 'I don't have no social security number and I'm still wanted by the police.'

I say the way she lives is like being in a war zone. I don't want a part of it. 'You're willing to sacrifice me,' I say. 'When my brothers were growing all that pot in your house when they lived down here, you told them off. You said they'd get into trouble. Yet I'm disposable.'

Leo shouts, 'It will be OK. You'll get away with it – your face isn't known. Just do it.'

Mum keeps nagging. She's got no moral compass.

'What will happen to my daughter if I'm locked up for years?' I say, feeling angry and frustrated. 'She'll get taken into care, maybe adopted. I don't want her growing up in a children's home like me.'

Leo says, 'Oh, we'll take care of Aimee if you get caught. We'll send her to Jamaica. She can live with the family if you get sent down.'

I'm so horrified that I start sobbing, 'You're my mum. You should not do this to me. You're willing to compromise me, but not my brothers? Why don't you love me? I have always tried to be good, to please you.'

'You don't try to please me,' she sneers. 'You fight against me, like I'm your enemy. Why won't you help us?'

In the end, I give way, though I refuse to touch Class A. Leo wants to give me weed to look after for him, in case he's raided. He says if he's arrested, he'll go to prison – while for me it would be a first offence and they'd take that and my age into consideration. I tell him, 'Give it to your daughter to look after.' But I give in under the pressure. I do it because it's only cannabis and it's for a short while – but it makes me angry. It's like I'm worthless and could be thrown away if it doesn't work out.

The next day, he carries all this pot into my room, tightly packed in black bin bags, and I stack it in the bottom of the wardrobe that Devon got me. 'Good girl,' he says, counting out £40 into my hands. He thinks that's OK, that I'll be happy with earning 'so much' for doing nothing – when he knows damn well

I'm risking my safety and freedom and even losing my daughter.

Devon arranges for a childminder and, even though we're arguing, Mum says she'll help out a bit looking after Aimee, and I get a bar job and work as a cleaner rather than get sucked up in that shit, looking after Leo's drugs. From five until seven in the evening, I clean toilets, then work in a bar from nine at night until two in the morning. Mum watches me and sneers, 'What you doing? Get your ass in the street, sell drugs like I do. You think you're above all that?'

No guts, no glory – that's her attitude when she's trying to get me to do something bad. She has no respect for me. I'm not the kind of person she wants me to be – but I don't want to be a street person, dealing drugs, selling my body and soul like she has done all her life. Where has it got her?

The small room is OK for a few months, but as Aimee gets older and starts to crawl at about seven or eight months, she's into everything. I leave her with my mum one day and, when I return, I find her crawling along the passage towards the stairs. She's filthy! Her white clothes are black as soot. I snatch her up. 'Look at the state of the floor!' I yell.

'You're always moaning,' my mum says. 'A little bit of dirt never hurt you, it protects against germs.'

I can't stand living like this, always struggling to make it work. Most of all, I've been missing Hotride like an ache in my heart. He was bad, but not as bad as my mum, and definitely not evil like Leo. I've gone from the frying pan into the fire, and the frying pan feels like a better place to be. I miss my friends, I miss my brothers. Annoying as Paul is, he's still my brother. I throw some clothes into a bag for Aimee and me and catch the bus back to London in time for my twenty-first birthday at the end of June. I feel like I'm going home.

Chapter 21

London, Summer
to Winter 2007

I call Hotride as soon as I'm in London, and he comes to my flat to meet me. We've missed each other so much – and he's missed Aimee. He hugs and kisses her like she's his little lost treasure.

'She remembers me!' he says.

'Of course she does. She's your little girl.'

She laughs and gurgles and smiles up at him like she remembers his face and voice.

'Yes, you're daddy's little girl,' he tells her.

He spends so much time with her that I feel a bit neglected. I know we've had some hard times – but I really want a fresh start, and on the phone he assured me he was going to work hard to control his temper and get some training or something. It's the 'something' that worries me, because it's so vague – but I push those thoughts to the back of my mind, because I'm so happy to be back with him. I feel like I'm falling in love with him all over again. I feel guilty that I took Aimee away.

I forget the pain and hurt he put me through, his wild, uncontrollable rages.

After a while, he puts Aimee down to sleep and finally gives me his full attention. It's not long before we're back in bed and going for it. I guess part of missing him was my raging hormones and, when he says he wants to make another baby, I don't argue.

For a while, I ignore Devon. Mostly, it's because I feel that I've let her down by going back with Hotride – yet she would never put that kind of pressure on me. She might offer her opinion, but she doesn't try to live my life for me. When I see her number come up on my mobile, I switch it off. In the end, I throw my phone away and get a new number. Besides, Hotride's doing well. He's been taking anger-management classes. He tells me that whenever he sees red he counts up to five to control his rage.

We have a lot to talk about and for a while we're happy. But he's still a boy making a living on the street, and it bothers me. I suspect I'm pregnant again, so he'll soon have two children to support and he can't even support one. He gives me money and buys presents for Aimee, but it's erratic.

I've tried to teach him to read and write, but it hasn't worked out. We talk about him having proper literacy classes. 'What about going to the Urban Academy?' I suggest, but he's dismissive. I tell him if he gets some training, maybe I can set up a small business and he can help me run it. But talk like this irritates him. He says I'm trying to control his life.

I think I can see that we're heading down the same path of niggling arguments again, and I go in to Kids Company and catch up with Devon. I don't mention that I'm back with Hotride, or that I think I'm pregnant again. I pin a smile on my face and act very up.

'Are you back in London permanently now?' Devon asks.

'Yeah, it got too claustrophobic at my mum's,' I say.

'You know we've been paying your rent down there, don't you? What about all your things – did you bring it all back?'

'No, I just came on the coach.'

We talk it through and Devon says we'd better go and get it all. There's the new furniture and refrigerator Kids Company bought me, and a lot else, including a sewing machine. She gets one of the workers to drive us down in a van – but when we reach Mum's house, my room is absolutely empty. There's not a stick of furniture or bed linen and even my new rug and all my clothes have gone. When I confront Mum, she just shrugs. 'Leo took it all. We didn't think you were coming back.'

'But, Mum, Kids paid my rent up to date – it was my room. He had no right to go in there. I bought a lot of new clothes for me and Aimee.'

'Don't bother me,' is all she says.

I call Leo and he's dismissive. 'You abandoned it, girl.'

'No, I didn't! We were always coming back to get it.'

He drops the bombshell that he's packed it all up in huge shipping barrels and sent it to Jamaica through Bristol Docks for his daughters. I'm furious. I knew he sent a lot of stuff over there, because he was building a house on some land his mother had given him, but the idea of shipping my clothes out of reach and giving them to his greedy daughters is too much. 'I want it back!' He laughs at me and hangs up.

'See?' Mum says. 'You might as well just forget it. All your stuff will be there for me to use when we go live Jamaica.'

I laugh at her faith. I know she has been giving Leo all her savings and helping to pay for the new house. But sure as eggs is eggs, I think, she won't be living there. She's told me his family don't like her. Despondently, I get back in the van and we return to London empty-handed.

The stress gives me stomach cramps and I go to see my GP. The test shows I'm pregnant, as I knew it would. There's no euphoria but, equally, I want to keep this new baby. I call Mum to tell her and I'm really upset when she sneers, 'You breeding like a duck?' I don't get her meaning, until I remember that in our culture we say that ducks have ducklings every ten months.

'Mum, I'm pleased. I want Aimee to have someone close to her age to play with.'

'Girl, if you want to ruin your life like I did, just go ahead and have it. Kids are nothing but trouble. I think you should have an abortion. What you going to do with yourself? I thought you wanted a career.'

'I'll do just fine. I'm living – just living. It's enough for now.'

*　　*　　*

Shortly after that, divine retribution lands on my mum's head in a big and very unexpected way. One morning, I get the devastating news that she's been arrested.

She calls me from the police station, crying down the phone, asking me to get her a lawyer. I say, 'Mum, you know I have no money.'

'Can't that Devon get one? They helped you – can't they help me?'

'Mum, Kids Company is for kids. Anyway I can't ask her. What happened?'

She tells me that Leo's barrels are what's got them into trouble. Some of the things he has been shipping to Jamaica are hairdressing supplies for his family's business, including big bottles of hydrogen peroxide and other chemicals. I think Mum's lost her mind, going on about hydrogen peroxide – but she's shouting about it in the police station to make a point. 'They said we running a bomb factory. They said we terrorists.'

It's like a movie. Mum was asleep when sixty armed members of the anti-terrorist squad rammed into her house and charged up the stairs. There was a helicopter flying overhead and the streets had been blocked off. They didn't find any evidence of terrorism, but they found a big stash of weed and when they took my mum in, they discovered that she had absconded while on bail for 'alleged' Class A drug offences.

Oh my God, I thought when I heard this. They'll lock her up and throw away the keys. I tell her she must get legal aid because I can't help her, and although she's hysterical, she knows I'm right.

I need Kids Company like never before, and I return on a regular basis. Devon asks me what's been happening, but in a concerned way, without judgement. She arranges for me to have a childminder that Kids Company pays for, so I can have Aimee taken care of while I return to my fashion course and also do an entrepreneur's course so I can apply to the Prince's Trust for funds if I set up a business. Thanks to Kids, I know that I should channel my energy and ambition into something positive that might give me a living. It's all making sense and coming together – so my shock when Harold calls me a few weeks later is extreme.

'Hotride's been arrested. He's in Brixton police station,' he says.

'What for – what's he done?'

'He caused an affray. I'm going down to see if I can see him. He wasn't allowed a phonecall and he's been processed.'

'Processed? What does that mean?'

'They moving it along quickly. We've got him a lawyer. He's in big trouble.'

An affray doesn't sound too serious and I ask, 'Can I see him?'

'Maybe after the lawyer's been. He's applying for bail.'

I can't believe that both my mother and boyfriend have been arrested in quick succession. After Harold rings off, I break down in tears. It's like everything's unwinding. I'm on edge, waiting to get another call from Harold – but instead, he comes round to my house. When he walks in, I know at once that it's bad news.

Hotride was in the betting shop opposite Brixton Market – not betting of course, but just chatting to a friend, Harold says – when he heard some yelling outside and went to have a look. He saw a friend of his being beaten up by the police. Instead of minding his own business, Hotride started taking pictures with his mobile phone, and was dancing around, mocking the police and saying they were thugs. Next thing, they're trying to take his phone off him, there's a tussle, and Hotride got an elbow in his mouth. He saw red and started fighting. It took six coppers to hold him down and he was arrested and carted off to the police station along the road.

I'm indignant. 'Well, he should sue them for assault.'

Harold looks at me cynically. 'Maybe. So far, we've only got his side of things. My son should know better – you just don't go around fighting with the police. But he's got a problem anyway – they've found he's illegal and his lawyer says they want to deport him.'

I go cold. 'Can they do it?'

'Lawyer seems to think they can. They refused him bail.'

We talk it through. 'The fact that he has a baby daughter will help, won't it?' I ask. I tell Harold that I'm expecting again, and he doesn't look very impressed. 'Another baby? That boy!' is all he says.

I'm upset by his words, but I understand why he said them when, early one morning, Hotride's bitch, Patricia, telephones.

'Yo, Sugar, is that you?'

'Who's this?'

'It's Patricia, and before you hang up' – which I was on the brink of doing – she says, 'I got some news for you.'

'Yeah?'

'Yeah. Me and Hotride, we expecting another baby. Next April.'

I almost choke. 'Fuck you!' I say and snap my phone off.

My baby is due in March – this means Hotride's been screwing around after we got back together. I'm so furious that I call Harold and tell him it's the end of the road for Hotride and me – we're through.

It's Christmas morning 2007, and I lie in bed, hugging Aimee, too depressed to get up. I'm twenty-one years old, six months pregnant (again), on my own and I've run out of money. My room is dark and I've got no electricity. I don't even have any credit on my phone, so I can't call anyone.

After lying there for a while feeling sorry for myself, I look down at Aimee and whisper to her, 'Happy Christmas, my angel.' She's almost fourteen months old and it's her second Christmas. Her dad and grandma are in jail and she's only got me. I have to do something to make the day special for her.

There's hot water because my gas is still on. I get up and wash and dress myself and Aimee. I put her in her buggy and close my door behind us. It's bright and sunny, almost balmy, and I start walking.

On Christmas Day, Kids Company throws a big

Christmas party in Camberwell, and we've spent time decorating. There's a huge tree, and tinsel everywhere. Some of the older kids have made a rustic little Mother Santa hut inside the big hall, near the towering Christmas tree and Camila's inside the hut, handing out presents to everyone. I don't know if there'll be a present for me because I'm not a child, but when I ask, one of the volunteers says, 'Of course there is! There's a present for everyone.' I line up with Aimee, and eventually it's our turn. Camila is dressed in a patchwork of fabrics and colours, like a quilt, and a scarlet turban is wound around her head. She looks perfectly at ease, surrounded by a huge stack of gifts, and gives us a beaming smile.

'Happy Christmas, Sugar.' I'm still amazed anew each time she remembers my name when there must be over eight hundred kids of all ages – from toddler to teen – mobbing around in the big room. They're making so much noise I want to run out and tell them to be quiet – but Camila is quite serene. Nothing seems to faze her. 'Oh, and look at Aimee – how she's grown!' she exclaims. 'Can I hold her?'

I put her into Camila's arms. Camila smiles down her. She looks as if she has spent a lifetime nursing children. Aimee is mesmerised by Camila's gold earrings and reaches up to touch one. After a cuddle, Camila returns Aimee to me, and considers the great heap of parcels completely surrounding her. 'Now, let me see. Ah yes –' she selects a gift for Aimee, and then one for me.

'Happy Christmas, my darlings,' she says once again.
I take the parcels and want to hug Camila. I don't

tell her that these will be our only gifts. I haven't even had any cards, although I've decorated my flat a bit. I don't have much money for food either, so the traditional hot turkey dinner and Christmas pudding feast we're being served will be a treat – not just for me, but for all the other kids of all ages and their mums who have come here on Christmas Day, rather than stay in bleak homes.

When I leave the hut, I put Aimee into her buggy and tuck her present safely away underneath, for later. Mine is bigger, so I lay it on the top. I'm chatting when someone steals my present. I'm so upset, I'm running about, shouting, making a big fuss, trying to see who's taken it. I'm telling the kids to shut up and stop making so much noise, and almost losing it. All the pressures of the past months seem to come together in a great ball of passion and anger and I'm hitting out hysterically. I'm feeling so crappy, I start to howl and can't stop.

Then Camila's there, putting her arms around me, holding me close and soothing me. 'It's OK, sweetheart,' she says. 'Of course you feel upset. Let's go to a quiet place and talk.'

In a quiet therapy room, Camila says, 'Tell me about it.' I want to, but I hold a lot back. The theft of my Christmas present somehow represents my miserable life. I don't tell Camila that Hotride's in jail and I've run out of money for essentials because I spent most of my last allowance taking Aimee to see him. I gave him some cash as well, so he could make phonecalls, and bought him some toiletries. But just talking to Camila calms me. I know she has a great deal to do, and many people demand her attention, but she seems relaxed and content to stay with me for as long as I want.

Soon, the tears and anger go. 'I'm all right now,' I say.

'Well, I have something for you,' she says and from somewhere she produces some vouchers from Boots. 'They have some lovely things – get yourself something personal,' she says with a twinkle.

After dinner, I trudge home to find my flat is flooded. To my utter despair, I realise I didn't fully turn off the bath tap or pull the bath plug out when I left home earlier in the day. I paddle through the water to turn the tap off, but I'm too exhausted and disheartened to clean it all up. My flat is on the ground floor, so it will run away through my French doors to the garden. I'll deal with it all tomorrow. I get into bed where it's warm and fall asleep, waiting for the next morning to come around. I don't want to intrude on Harold's family's Christmas Day, but he won't mind if I go there for a few days from tomorrow, until I get my next benefit payment.

Chapter 22

London, Spring 2008

Hotride has been found guilty and sentenced to a year in jail. He's in Canterbury prison in Kent, which is where all illegal aliens are sent to serve their time before being deported. When he phones to tell me this, reality hits home. 'They sending you back to Jamaica?' I ask.

'Yeah. Though I might ask to go to America. I got family in New York.'

'Will they let you into the US with a record?' I ask naïvely, and he's annoyed.

'Trust you to bring me down,' he snaps. 'I was going to send you a visitor's order, but I don't know if I will. You a bitch.'

'Yeah, well what about your bitch? I don't appreciate it when someone calls me and says she's pregnant, having your baby,' I shout.

'Who you mean?'

'You know who I mean – that whore you fucked after we got back together again –'

We're screaming and yelling and he hangs up. I'm

crying with rage and frustration and want to kill him. If he was there, we'd have another huge fight and one of us might end up dead. I am so angry that he betrayed me and then got himself locked up where I can't get my hands on him. Why did I choose him as the father of my children? I'm tied to a no-good loser, I tell myself. It takes days before I calm down and try to come to terms with what is.

I go to see Kirstie and she asks me how I feel about it. 'I hate him,' I say. 'He's no good for me.' But by the time I've talked through my pain and anger, I end up saying, 'What is, is. I've got to deal with that, yeah?'

Kirstie says, 'Can you?'

'I guess. Maybe I've got to understand him better. He's had a tough life, too – it makes him take chances and make stupid choices.'

At the end of February, Harold comes round and says Hotride has sent us both VOs – do I want to ride down with him in his car? I guess he's sent one to his dad as well, to make the visit easier. With Harold there, he thinks I won't lose it and beat up on him.

I spend all day Saturday and all my money having long, golden-brown hair extensions like J-Lo's put in. I look a real glamourpuss and preen in front of the mirror as I apply tons of mascara. The hairdresser shows me fake lashes made of mohair that you glue into place, one at a time, but someone tells me they can cause eye infections, and they know someone who has glued their eye shut, so I settle for mascara.

'Hot dog! Yo sure are gorgeous, Miss Sugar!' I say,

looking at myself in the mirror on Sunday morning as I wait for Harold. I smile down at Aimee. 'Do you think your mum is beautiful?'

Her smiles give me the answer I want. But when we walk in to the visitors' hall at the prison, Hotride barely looks at me. After he greets his dad, his attention is all on Aimee. He cuddles her, but she wriggles free and shrieks. When he puts her down, she's running all over the place and the staff tell me to control her. I have to keep following her because she won't sit still in her buggy and won't be held. I think she's confused by all the people, the bright overhead lights and the prison warders in the dark uniforms who are around the walls, watching. Hotride talks to his father, moaning about his treatment and how he's been in some fights. He's lost privileges and has lost time off.

Finally, he glances at me. 'Yo, Sugar – what's wrong with you?'

'What do you mean?'

'You look rough,' he says. 'Couldn't you make yourself look better?'

The wind is taken right out of my sails. I subside back into my seat and feel waves of shame. I had spent hours getting ready and spent all my money – money I needed to live on – on making myself look good for him. I want to shout in his face, 'What you expect? I'm almost nine months pregnant! I'm tired.' But I sit there, crying, the mascara running down my cheeks. Harold hands me a tissue and goes off to get me a drink from the machine.

In retaliation, I ask Hotride why he slept with Patricia – what was he thinking of? He snarls, 'She's not a nag – that's why.' The whole visit unravels and Harold suggests we leave. When we return to London, I ask Harold if he can keep Aimee for a while – I need time to think. He understands and agrees. She loves going round to his house. Sondra, Hotride's stepmum, has got a child Aimee's age and they love to play together.

I'm very low and stay in my flat for days, not going anywhere or answering my phone to anyone, thinking about many things. Mothering Sunday is approaching and I lie in bed, thinking about my mother. I wonder why she abused me when I needed her, why she put higher demands on me, yet is easy on my brothers. She lets them be rude to her, insult her, even hit her – yet she would never let me get away with it.

Slowly, I get around to thinking deeply and honestly about Hotride, something I've been avoiding, but which my therapy has taught me is important. I know for sure he's no good for me. Why can't I admit it and let go? Love is such a painful thing – it is beautiful, but also destructive. I have had the highs, now I'm paying the price. Finally I surface from my long meditation time, convinced that I will move on without my mum and without Hotride. I have a new family now – that's where my future lies.

My new baby takes a long time to be born. He's overdue and towards the end of March, I go to hospital on a Monday to be induced. But after an examination, they decide that I'm not ready and send me home. By Friday, I'm feeling pains, but my phone's out of credit and I have no money to top it up, so I just switch it off. Hotride calls from prison to talk to me and when he can't get through, he calls Sondra and asks her to check on me. She comes round and I open the door, groaning.

'Mercy!' she says. 'Is it your time?'

I wait for the wave to pass, and invite her in. Aimee is running around and grins at her, impishly. 'Do you want me to call a taxi?' Sondra asks.

I shake my head. 'The pains are too far apart. Can you call Annie and ask her to come round? I can't take care of Aimee on my own.'

Sondra stays until Annie arrives. When she comes, I explain some of my symptoms and she's jumping up and down in a panic, shouting, 'Baby's coming!'

I say, 'No it's not,' but she's not listening. She's on the phone, calling everyone. I know she's made a mistake and I tell her to slow down. We have a bit of a giggle over her panic and settle down to watch TV. Later that night, Annie has to go and she tells me to call her if I need to.

'I can't,' I say, 'I've got no credit on my phone.'

'Oh, yeah, I forgot. Well, I'll check with you tomorrow.'

I thank her, and switch my phone back on to get incoming calls. I'm on my own and go to bed and rest. All the next day, there are blocks of pain, then nothing for an hour or more. I wish I could call someone – or that someone would call me. This is the worst of times to be on my own and out of touch. The following day, Sunday, I have such a big pain I can't move. I lie in bed in agony, wishing I could just die. I pray for God to do something. Out of the blue, my phone rings. I snatch it up. It's Devon! Thank God! She has been ill with flu at her parents' home in the country, and she says she suddenly felt I was in trouble.

I almost weep with relief. 'Oh, Devon, help me!' I beg. She talks me through the wave of pain, then says, 'I'm going to hang up and sort some stuff out, then I'll get back to you. Hang in there, sweetheart.'

Devon calls for an ambulance, for my childminder to come and get Aimee, and calls my mum and Hotride in prison. Mum calls me back, and I drop the phone. *Pain!* Then the doorbell is buzzing and I'm on the bed, knees up, in pain, screaming my head off. Aimee is running around nearly naked. She's taken her wet nappy off and there are puddles on the floor. The buzzer keeps going, and I get up when I can and let my childminder in – just as the ambulance turns up. For a moment, there's chaos. The ambulance men ask me for the address – and I keep yelling, 'Pain! Pain!'

'Where are you going, love?' one of them says patiently. He must be used to crazy women in labour. 'Which hospital?'

'Pain! Pain!' I scream. They give me gas and air to calm me, and, finally, I tell them the name of the hospital. I go in at 10 a.m., without my knickers and hardly any clothes – I even forget my hospital bag. In the labour room, I lose it totally. I keep begging for more gas and air, but the midwife says I've come in too late. I'm screaming over and over, 'The Lord is my *shep–*' ending on a high shriek. I think she gets the message, because she gives me some gas and air to shut me up. As soon as she does, I feel better. '*Thank you, Lord!*' I gasp inside the mask.

After a few moments, the midwife tries to take the mask away. 'You've had enough, let it go –' I hang on to it for dear life. 'No! I need it.' We almost tussle for the mask, but I win. It keeps me out of it and I'm relaxed, floating on the pain instead of fighting it. This time, it's far more painful than I remember with Aimee.

During my antenatal visits, I'd arranged to use the birthing pool, and I ask for it. For some reason, they won't fill it. I say, 'I'm already five centimetres, it's almost time.' I keep demanding it and finally, she fills it. I try to get in, but she says I have to wait until it's full or I could damage baby. I'm begging for some relief, so she gives me a big ball to roll on. I'm on all fours over the ball, one hand holding my belly, when I feel a big pop and then a weight on my legs. I've no idea what it is. Silence. The pain leaves.

The midwife is behind me and she's saying baby's half out, now push! I go on gas and air and I push. I roll around to see what's happening, and she catches the baby as it comes out. She cuts the cord while I'm still on my hands and knees and then helps me onto a bed. I'm worried. He's not crying. 'Nurse?' I call. 'Nurse!'

Suddenly, there's a huge roar. Yeah! I almost cheer.

Then I call Harold, and to my astonishment, he's

there immediately, like he's flown in a rocket. 'How did you get here so fast?' I gasp.

'My girlfriend's in the next ward,' he says, grinning. She's pregnant too, and is ill with pre-eclampsia – a kind of high blood pressure – so they've taken her in to watch her. We're laughing about my reaction to his amazingly fast arrival by my bed, when the phone rings. It's Hotride, finally calling from a payphone in the prison. 'How are you doing, babe?' he asks.

'I've just had the baby, a little boy,' I say, feeling depressed and angry because he's not been there for me, after he insisted on making this child. I want to say to him, 'It's easy making babies – but someone has to be there for them.'

'What time was he born?' he asks.

'I got here at ten this morning, and he was born at eleven forty-five. He took just one-and-a-half hours to pop out.'

'Oh.' He sighs. 'I wanted to be there. I'm sorry I wasn't there for you, honey.' Right in the middle of him apologising, he runs out of money and we're cut off. I stare at my mobile and feel flat. I wanted to tell him about how I'd been in labour for three days, so he could share what I'd been through, like he was there every step of the way for Aimee – but what's the point? Thanks to his stupidity, he's not here for me. I've given birth alone – and I've got two little kids to bring up on my own until his life is sorted out. But after those days I'd spent alone in my flat weighing up the options, I think, 'No it will never be sorted out. You're just a baby yourself, Hotride, you're never gonna grow up. You're just a bum.'

Hotride's sister turns up and we sit chatting. At least his side of the family is there for me. The doctor checks me out and gives me the all-clear. I think they want my bed because I'm told I can leave. Harold's still in the hospital and he drops me home at about four o'clock that same afternoon. My baby-sitter is shocked to see me when I walk in through the door.

'They let you out already?' she says.

'Yeah – I feel fine.' Even so, I'm ready to lie down in my bed with the new baby. I've decided to call him Romeo, and I whisper his name as he nuzzles up to me. 'Welcome home, Romeo, you my little sweetie.'

I smile at Aimee. She looks enormous! 'Come and meet your baby brother,' I say. Aimee runs over and stares. She gives him a tentative poke, but doesn't speak. I'm suddenly tired and just want to sleep. My baby-sitter arranges to keep Aimee each night for that first week. She brings her over during the day, and collects her each evening.

During this period, Aimee gets used to the baby and accepts him quickly. But I can't get used to being on my own, having to do everything. I really want Hotride there, because he did so much when Aimee was born. I start to feel bad because I'm robbing her of the time we spend together. Now, she has to share it, and it doesn't seem fair on her. She's such a little girl – and she needs my attention. After a while, she starts attacking her baby brother and I have to be alert.

I remember how Wayan was quite a tyrant, spoiled by Mum because of his poor start in life. She wouldn't allow anyone to beat him, treating him like a fragile eggshell. Able to get away with murder, he'd run around with a big metal spoon and really whack you with it – it hurt! When anyone complained, she said he had carte blanche to do as he wanted until he was four – then it would stop. The day he was four, me and Paul got him, and he howled the place down in anger and shock. Then Mum beat him, too, over something, and that was an even worse shock. After that, he never picked up that metal spoon again. I remember how Uncle Nathan tried to stop us fighting. 'Grow up,' he said. 'You're always going to be brothers and sister. Get on with each other.'

I wonder if Aimee is going to try bullying her new little brother in the same way. There are so many issues I have to resolve on my own, it makes me depressed and I start sobbing.

Next day, Wayan comes to see me. Mum has telephoned him from prison. 'She wants to know if she can come and stay with you when they release her,' he says.

'But I thought she's going to be deported,' I say, surprised. The UK has a new policy of deporting all illegals who have got a criminal record.

'She said to tell you that if you agree to let her stay with you, they might let her out on probation.'

It doesn't make sense to me and I ask around. It seems that if she has grounds to appeal her deportation when she is released from prison, she might be allowed to stay if she has a place to go to – only I know that she has no grounds to appeal, any more than Hotride has. In her case, Class A drugs are a very serious offence, and on top of that she skipped bail for several years. But I still think about it and it makes my head hurt. I get angry – why has she put this on me? I can't have her living in my house. She'll take over and bully and abuse me, just like she always has done. All my life, whenever I argue with her, she doesn't discuss it, but instantly offers to have a fight – and by that, I mean a physical fight, with fists, biting, clawing.

I tell Wayan that she can't come. He's outraged. 'She's our mum! You're unnatural.'

'Maybe,' I say, 'but I have to think of my own little family. I don't have any room.'

After that, he and Paul put pressure on me, nagging me and calling me names. Then Mum calls me and screams at me abusively. I can't stand it any more, and, once again, I throw away my phone and get a new one so she can't call me.

Hot on the heels of that, a probation officer telephones me. She says. 'Your partner has put down your address as a place to be released to.'

'What's that? He's getting probation?' I say.

'Not necessarily. But he's appealing – and one of the conditions is that he has a place to live. Do you agree to an inspection?' I'm told I'll have to have a police check done. I've had one already, I say, for when my brothers came to stay with me.

I'm confused, yet in despair. I want Hotride to be with me – but I'm angry with him. I wonder why I, with two small babies to care for on my own, and very little money and not a clue what I want to do with my life, have the burden of having my mum and my boyfriend suddenly dependent on me for their freedom. It overwhelms me, and I climb into bed and retreat for days on end. Finally, I hear that his appeal has failed and, while I've been expecting it, I'm gutted.

When things can't seem any worse, there's always a ray of light at the end of the tunnel. When Devon contacts me to say I have been selected by Camila to meet Prince Charles and give a small speech at a special awards dinner, I'm thrilled. I can't believe it. This little girl from the ghetto meeting the future King of England is an amazing thing.

I see Camila and we go through everything. 'You can do it, Sugar,' she says, and I bask in her approval. I would do anything in the world for her because she does so much for people like me. Each time I talk to her, I feel as if she is unwinding the mess I've become and exposing that pure, clean little star shining inside.

They make a small film with me in it, talking about Kids Company and the work they do. Everyone seems to like it and the star shines a little more.

Then comes the night of the gala. I dress up to the nines and wear an evening dress. The pavilions in Battersea Park are lit up like a fairytale palace. They seem to float in the mist from the river, the white awnings like snowy mountain peaks. There's a red carpet and people clapping, and inside, banks and banks of flowers and lanterns. People are sitting at round tables being served with food and wine. I sit at a table with Devon, who looks lovely. She has really worked hard to pull this evening together. Camila, in a robe of tulips and sunflowers and a yellow and blue turban, is up there with Prince Charles. After my speech to the Prince, he bends forward and whispers, 'Well done, Sugar!'

Later, after dinner, when people are still chatting at the tables, I think he looks a little lonely and I ask Devon, 'Do you think it would be all right if I went and talked to him?'

'I don't see why not,' she agrees.

I approach and curtsey. 'Your Royal Highness, I thought I'd have a little chat. How are you?'

If he's surprised by this bold approach, he doesn't show it. We have a real chat about real things and I think, 'Mmm, he's sensible and really does know a lot.' Then I curtsey again, because I don't want to overstay my welcome, and as I turn to run back to my table, Camila catches my eye. It's the closest she's ever come to a wink, and I blossom. It's one of the best days of my life.

Chapter 23

Dover, Summer 2008

Right from the time he went to jail, I knew Hotride would be deported after he served his time – but, even though I've been expecting it for months, it's still a shock when he telephones in early June to say he's been moved to Dover in the next step in the deportation process. I ask, 'How long have you got?'

'Just a couple of weeks I think,' he says. 'Soon as they have flights arranged, I'll be held at Heathrow Airport.'

I think we're spelling it out to stop thinking about it too much. I can tell from his voice that he is close to panic and I feel like I've been kicked in the stomach. I veer between loving and loathing him. He's done this to himself and I might have more sympathy if it wasn't for all the other mistakes – like two-timing me with Patricia.

He tells me that even though he's served his time, he's still in custody until they ship him out – but he has been allowed a mobile phone. I can call him now whenever I want, he says, and he can call me. His dad has given him a phone with plenty of credit on it.

'I want to see my son,' Hotride says.